Leadership for Inclu

MW01106745

CRITICAL ISSUES IN THE FUTURE OF LEARNING AND TEACHING

Volume 3

Series Editors:

Michael Kompf - *Brock University, Canada*
Pamela M Denicolo - *University of Reading, UK*

Scope:

This series represents a forum for important issues that do and will affect how learning and teaching are thought about and practised. All educational venues and situations are undergoing change because of information and communications technology, globalization and paradigmatic shifts in determining what knowledge is valued. Our scope includes matters in primary, secondary and tertiary education as well as community-based informal circumstances. Important and significant differences between information and knowledge represent a departure from traditional educational offerings heightening the need for further and deeper understanding of the implications such opportunities have for influencing what happens in schools, colleges and universities around the globe. An inclusive approach helps attend to important current and future issues related to learners, teachers and the variety of cultures and venues in which educational efforts occur. We invite forward-looking contributions that reflect an international comparative perspective illustrating similarities and differences in situations, problems, solutions and outcomes.

Leadership for Inclusion

A Practical Guide

Alan L. Edmunds
Robert B. Macmillan

The University of Western Ontario

SENSE PUBLISHERS
ROTTERDAM/BOSTON/TAIPEI

A C.I.P. record for this book is available from the Library of Congress.

ISBN 978-94-6091-135-4 (paperback)
ISBN 978-94-6091-136-1 (hardback)
ISBN 978-94-6091-137-8 (e-book)

Published by: Sense Publishers,
P.O. Box 21858,
3001 AW Rotterdam,
The Netherlands
http://www.sensepublishers.com

Printed on acid-free paper

DEDICATION

This book is dedicated to all educational leaders who are invariably involved in the education of students with exceptionalities; their patience and effort makes the difference in the lives of the children for whom they are responsible.

ACKNOWLEDGEMENTS

This book would not have been possible without the cooperation and skillful efforts of each of the contributors. Their willingness to step outside the box and consider both leadership and inclusion from slightly different perspectives has resulted in an important collection of ideas. We hope this work will be a catalyst for many other future endeavors between the two disciplines.

EDITOR BIOGRAPHIES

Alan L. Edmunds is Associate Professor of Educational Psychology and Special Education in the Faculty of Education at the University of Western Ontario in London, Ontario, Canada. His primary teaching and research interests focus on inclusion, profound giftedness and precocity, and school-wide approaches to behavior and classroom management. He can be reached at aedmunds@uwo.ca.

Robert B. Macmillan is Associate Dean of Graduate Programs and Research at the Faculty of Education at the University of Western Ontario, London, Ontario, Canada. His areas of teaching and research are in leadership and leadership succession and the creation of school cultures that lead to the improvement of student achievement. He can be reached at rmacmil@uwo.ca.

TABLE OF CONTENTS

PREFACE

In the last three decades, no other aspect of educational practice has undergone as much change or has received as much critical attention as inclusion. Inclusion is a philosophical position that advocates for the regular classroom as the first-choice educational placement for students with exceptionalities. Thus, all practicing teachers, not just specialists, are now responsible for educating many more students with special educational needs. However, while the instructional responsibility for inclusion certainly lies with classroom teachers, its leadership responsibility ultimately rests with principals. "Leaders are called upon to support student learning in many ways ... to address critical problems of practice ... [and] to improve their knowledge about constructive educational leadership" (Firestone & Riehl, 2005, p. x–xi). In fact, in the vast majority of educational jurisdictions, principals are legally accountable for the educational progress outlined in the IEP of each student with an exceptionality. Nonetheless, despite such ultimate accountability and responsibility, the only truly meaningful influence that principals can exert on inclusion occurs *indirectly*. Aside from endorsing a school board's or school district's philosophy of inclusion and making sure extant policies are properly implemented, the predominant direct educational influence that principals exert on inclusion is to facilitate the actions of teachers. Considering the abundant evidence regarding the significant difficulties that teachers constantly face as they navigate inclusion, and considering the high positive impact that principals can have on teachers' instructional effectiveness, it is time that educational leaders' roles in the lives of the teachers who enact inclusion is clearly examined and delineated. It is only by such careful delineation that educational leaders, primarily principals, can proactively facilitate inclusion.

Leadership for inclusion means seeking out an understanding of the fundamental tenets of inclusion and constructing an administrative approach that complements the execution of those tenets by teachers. Without the aforementioned understandings and an active and carefully directed administrative approach, the facilitation of inclusion will occur more by happenstance than by professional design. Unfortunately, very little has been published to address the seemingly evident connections between educational leaders, teachers, and the enactment of inclusion. Moreover, equally little has been produced that specifically addresses the professional development needs of educational leaders regarding inclusion. Until now, educational leaders have been without the proper tools to carry out the vital role they play in the important educational enterprise called inclusion. This book is an attempt to remedy that problem.

Despite the fact that this collection of writings emanates from a predominantly North American perspective, the issues pertaining to inclusion that are examined, discussed and referenced herein have universal relevance for educators around the world. Readers will also find that the results and mindful suggestions that stem from the issues explored in each chapter hold important implications for all jurisdictions interested in leadership for inclusion within school systems.

There is near universal agreement that including children with exceptionalities in regular classrooms is laudable and should be the ideal that all schools and educators strive towards. The Organization for Economic Cooperation and Development (OECD; 2000; 1995), in a review of more than 23 jurisdictions worldwide, acknowledged that special education/inclusion is a complex and idiosyncratic organic system wherein almost every nation and school jurisdiction interested in supporting students with exceptionalities demonstrates common best practices as well as common concerns and dilemmas. For example, the research framing the various discourses about inclusion included in this volume presents a global, international perspective drawn from empirical studies undertaken throughout the world. In addition to adhering to a common overarching philosophy of inclusion, there is also universal agreement upon, and worldwide use of, the more applied aspects of inclusion such as preferences for early identification, expert assessment, individualized educational programs, and suitably differentiated curricula, instruction, and student assessment and evaluation. The shared ultimate objective of such educational practices and systems is to provide the very best opportunities for students with exceptionalities to maximize their educational potential.

As such, these perspectives inherently mesh with our pervasive and global views about children with exceptionalities and their education. De Jong's (2005) systematic review of student behavior provided a perspective common in many countries; "positive relationships, particularly between student and teacher, are critical for maximizing appropriate behaviour and achieving learning outcomes" (p. 358). Studies from around the globe also reveal that the inclusion of children with special needs has been thoughtfully investigated and that children's and adolescents' acceptance of children with special needs and programs that facilitate inclusion are of international interest. It is also evident that the world-wide movement of assessment reform has increased pressure on educational leaders to incorporate the principles of assessment and accountability in inclusive education with a view towards enhancing assessment literacy in inclusive environments.

Despite the uniformity of opinion concerning the merits of inclusion, educators still appear to struggle to understand the philosophy of inclusion and the policies that govern its implementation, although it is widely viewed that these struggles primarily stem from the evident disconnect between the educational needs of students with exceptionalities and the abilities of educators to meet them. This particular problem, for example, caused the National Union of Teachers of Great Britain to recently call for an end to the policy of inclusion stating that inclusion had failed many children and had demonstrated very clearly the failures in policy and practice in their education system and schools (Halpin, 2006). By the same token, it is also widely agreed that improved teacher education and more university and school partnerships are seen as the strongest potential solutions to this dilemma. To this end, this book provides a discussion of school climate and classroom ethos and how educators' professional development can empower them to make schools more inclusive.

Finally, the universality of the topics and issues presented by the wide array of contributors to this volume is an accurate reflection of the themes of numerous international conferences that foster inclusion. Each of the chapters would be well-reviewed and well-attended sessions at any of these conferences regardless of the country or city that hosted the gathering. This is a testament to the worldwide applicability of the common ideas, efforts, and strategies that create and support teachers and students in inclusive environments.

The concept for this book was prompted by two somewhat related bodies of knowledge. The first to come to our attention was the reverberating demand in recent educational administration literature for enhanced research in leadership that served to strengthen the field's ability to build knowledge that informed practice.

> research will be more effective if it consistently focuses on how leadership contributes to student learning. We recognize that leaders are called upon to support student learning in many ways, some more direct than others, and we think it is important to understand how all of them can be improved ... to address critical problems of practice (Firestone & Riehl, 2005, p. x–xi).

Based on this literature, there appeared to be several aspects of leadership that could make unique and important contributions to how inclusion functions in schools. These facets of leadership were: exemplary leadership practice; administrative trust and team-building; and the particular problems faced by educational leaders (Fullan, 2001; Leithwood & Riehl, 2005). The second came to our attention whilst we were conducting a small but important study that investigated principals' perspectives on the inclusiveness of their schools (detailed in Chapter 13). The study was based on the foundational elements extensively reported as the underpinnings of inclusion which had been previously documented in studies examining teachers' perceptions of inclusion. Those foundational elements were: philosophy; policies; instruction; assessment; behaviour and discipline; community connections; attitudes and perceptions; student evaluation; professional development; and field-based evidence (Edmunds, 2003a; 2003b; 1999; Edmunds & Edmunds, 2008; Edmunds, Macmillan, Nowicki, Specht, & Edmunds, in press; IDEA, 1997; 2004; King & Edmunds, 2001). The results of that study revealed a broader need for the specific understandings and actions that educational leaders required to better facilitate inclusion for teachers. Combined, the issues surrounding these two bodies of knowledge coalesced into an excellent opportunity to improve our knowledge about constructive leadership and to articulate how links can be made between learning, leadership, inclusion, and educational equity. To this end, topical experts with unique research perspectives and expertise were sought from both disciplines (several of whom have experience in both domains) to provide comprehensive portrayals of each respective underpinning of inclusion and to provide explicit recommendations for those in educational leadership.

As well as providing careful analyses of the pertinent issues and thoughtful, practicable recommendations, the book introduces educational leaders to global and practical understandings of the subtle nuances of inclusion heretofore only understood by teachers, and rarely appreciated or provided for by principals. In doing so, the chapters richly contextualizes inclusion for principals highlighting how their leadership is crucial to the overall process, yet also making them aware of the day-to-day dilemmas that teachers face. These explicit elements of the book will allow leaders to proactively support teachers in their schools as never before. As of this writing, there is nothing for educational leaders that compares to the work contained in this volume.

The overarching thrust of this collection of writings from a group of respected multi-national experts in special education and educational administration/leadership, is that leaders enhance school effectiveness by influencing the capacities and motivations of teachers. Each of the contributions, most of which are multi-authored, has gone to great lengths to make administrative and pedagogical suggestions for principals that will have practical and meaningful impacts on teachers lives. The intended results of this manuscript are to heighten the awareness of inclusion for educational leaders so that they can explicitly facilitate inclusion for teachers and, by extension, improve the educational and social outcomes of students with special needs. This book does not address inclusive pedagogy *per se*, however, some of the chapters address actions that leaders can take to further enhance teachers' specialized methods and programs where appropriate.

There is no question that the advent of inclusion has dramatically changed the way schooling is currently practiced - it has changed the lives of the teachers who enact it and the lives of the students who receive it. Thus, educational leaders have to support teachers by demonstrating that the problems they encounter while changing inclusive practices will be taken seriously and that administrative help and support will be provided (Louis, Toole, & Hargreaves, 1999).

REFERENCES

De Jong, T. (2005). A framework of principles and best practice for managing student behaviour in the Australian education context. *School Psychology International, 26*, 353–370.

Edmunds, A. L. (2003a). The inclusive classroom: Can teachers keep up? A comparison of Nova Scotia and Newfoundland & Labrador perspectives. *Exceptionality Education Canada, 13*(1), 29–48.

Edmunds, A. L. (2003b). Preparing Canadian teachers for inclusion. *Exceptionality Education Canada, 13*(1), 5–7.

Edmunds, A. L. (1999). Classroom teachers are not prepared for the inclusive classroom. *Exceptionality Education Canada, 8*(2), 27–40.

Edmunds, A. L., & Edmunds, G. A. (2008). *Special education in Canada.* Toronto, ON: McGraw-Hill Ryerson.

Edmunds, A. L., Macmillan, R. B., Nowicki, E., Specht, J., & Edmunds, G. A. (in press). Principals and inclusive schools: Insight into practice. *The Journal of Educational Administration and Foundations.*

Firestone, W. A., & Riehl, C. (Eds.). (2005). *A new agenda for research in educational leadership.* New York: Teachers College Press.

Fullan, M. (2001). *The new meaning of educational change* (3rd ed.). New York: Teachers College Press.

Halpin, T. (2006, May 17). Mainstream schools can't manage special needs pupils, say teachers. *The Times* [retrieved from http://www.timesonline.co.uk/printFriendly/0,,1-2-2184133-2,00.html]

King, W., & Edmunds, A. L. (2001). Teachers' perceived needs for more effective inclusive practice: A single school study. *Exceptionality Education Canada, 10*(3), 3–23.

Leithwood, K. A., & Riehl, C. (2005). What do we already know about educational leadership? In W. A. Firestone & C. Riehl, (Eds.), *A new agenda for research in educational leadership* (pp. 12–27). New York: Teachers College Press.

Louis, K. S., Toole, J., & Hargreaves, A. (1999). Rethinking school improvement. In J. Murphy & K. S. Louis (Eds.), *Handbook of research on educational administration*, (2nd ed., pp. 251–276). San Francisco: Jossey Bass.

Organization for Economic Co-operation and Development. (2000). *Education at a glance: OECD indicators*. Paris: Organization for Economic Co-operation and Development.

Organization for Economic Co-operation and Development. (1995). *Integrating students with special needs into mainstream schools*. Paris: Organization for Economic Co-operation and Development.

ROBERT B. MACMILLAN AND ALAN L. EDMUNDS

1. LEADERSHIP FOR INCLUSION: QUESTIONS & DILEMMAS

INTRODUCTION

Over the previous century, we have seen significant changes in the education of students with exceptionalities. Initially, the common practice was to place these students in institutions designed to address their specific educational needs based on fairly incomplete beliefs about the nature of each exceptionality. In most cases, these students were not equipped to later integrate easily into their communities and to meaningfully participate in wider society. As we gained better techniques for identification and diagnoses, our understanding of the spectrum and characteristics of each exceptionality improved as did our conceptualizations of meeting their educational needs. With this increasing understanding, we began to shift away from institutional care towards developing programs delivered in separate classrooms within schools that provided specialized instruction and which allowed students to experience a somewhat "normal" school environment outside of their classroom. While good intentioned, these initial steps still forced students with special needs to be segregated and excluded. Eventually, programming in separate classrooms was replaced by "pull-out" programs, some of which remain today, and later by attempts to include fully students with exceptionalities in all aspects of school life and, by extension, in all aspects of life out of school.

In the last three decades, the right of children with exceptionalities to be included in the "regular" classroom has become accepted, at least philosophically if not practically (Bunch, Lupart & Brown, 1997), but we are still struggling with how to include these children while delivering appropriate programs designed to meet the individual needs of each child. There is scant but significant evidence that the success of such inclusive programs is largely attributable to the leadership of the principal and the ability of that administrator to create an inclusive school environment (Baker, 2007; Reyes & Wagstaff, 2006; Ryan, 2006). This book has been designed to help school leaders to first think about, and then address, the issues involved in leading for inclusion.

Educational Change

Two predominant factors led to changes in the types of education provided for students with special needs. The first has been an increasingly better understanding of the range and nuances of exceptionalities. Advances in this area have helped

A. L. Edmunds and R. B. Macmillan (eds.), Leadership for Inclusion: A Practical Guide, 01–06.

to inform educators who design specialized educational programs that incorporate our current understanding of the roots and characteristics of each exceptionality. When these programs enable students to accomplish what had been previously believed not possible or not feasible, we have seen changes in community and societal beliefs about what these students can and cannot do. This has often followed by commensurate shifts in attitudes about what comprises an appropriate education for such students. The second factor has been changes to the laws concerning students with special needs. Some laws have set the framework for the educational rights of all children, and especially for children with special needs. The courts, through decisions on specific cases, have been instrumental in clarifying and defining the implementation of the laws, particularly those governing the issues of equity and equality, and the responsibilities of schools to students with exceptionalities (Williams & Macmillan, 2001; 2003; 2005). Unfortunately, some decisions have left schools and school systems struggling to understand all implications emerging from such decisions and attempting to translate the essence of those decisions into practice. This has resulted in teachers attempting to do what is best for children within the spirit of the law, but having to do so without a definitive framework. Without a clear framework, teachers have experienced a great deal of professional discomfort due their uncertainty about the appropriateness of their decisions (Macmillan & Meyer, 2006). For principals, this task is especially troublesome because they are responsible for supporting teachers and for creating an inclusive environment (Ryan, 2006), but without a clear, legal direction about how this is to be done. Moreover, because principals mostly play an indirect role in the enactment of inclusion, they also have not had a clear set of practical directions about how to help their teachers working on the front lines of inclusion day-to-day.

The overriding problem for educators is: how can schools who must adapt to a broad spectrum of abilities and needs in their students address all their inherent specific and personal abilities and needs, especially given current resources? This book is an attempt to help administrators examine these complex issues, to analyze and reframe them in a way that may provide insights, and to provide possible indications about how to proceed. The purpose of this first chapter is to lay the groundwork for the subsequent chapters. The authors of each chapter identify areas that we, as educators and particularly administrators, need to consider in order to properly engage in the work of creating inclusive schools. We acknowledge that some of the suggested approaches are reasonably straightforward and may indicate rudimentary and easy paths to follow. However, we also recognize that not all of these complex issues are easily resolved and will remain dilemmas to varying degrees because no clear path to a solution exists. For this reason, the insights, suggestions and recommendations provided here are meant for the reader to consider, to analyze, and to use in ways that are appropriate to his or her administrative context. We hope that in the process, we have provided assistance to those charged with the difficult, but essential, task of envisioning, creating, leading, and sustaining inclusive schools.

A Leadership Framework

One of the key foci of recent research on school leadership has been: what practices do successful leaders use? Over the past twenty years, we have gained better insights into these skills and practices. Leithwood's chapter examines this body of research and groups leaders' practices into four broad categories: setting directions; developing people; redesigning the organization; and managing the instructional program. These broad categories are evident in the chapters by the other contributors to this volume.

Setting Direction

To be inclusive, schools must establish inclusion as an overarching goal that permeates throughout everything they do, with principals leading the effort to specifically define and redefine the direction to be taken. This direction must be clear, contextualized, and framed within the philosophy and policies behind inclusion. In an attempt to provide leaders with the appropriate background, D. Young's chapter outlines the philosophy and policies of inclusive practice. However, the gap between knowing what must be done and putting it into practice is often quite large. For this reason, principals need to take an active role in helping teachers create an inclusive environment, but they may not be able to achieve this goal unless they have the trust of the staff; trust between a principal and teachers is an essential component of inclusive leadership. Some insights into how a principal can develop trust with teachers and build collaborative teams are provided by Macmillan's chapter, which focuses on the development of a positive relationship between principals and teachers if the school is to work together.

Developing People

Once the school's direction has been set, the next task is to help the staff understand the implications that inclusion may have for their instructional practice and for potential changes that may affect their beliefs about the way children with exceptionalities learn and don't learn. Toward this end, Nowicki and Samuels examine how principals can help teachers build better understandings about ways to encourage and develop among all children positive perceptions of their peers' abilities. Through an increase in teachers' knowledge, shifts in attitudes and beliefs can lead to better understandings of the experiences of all children by all children.

A key factor in charting the progressing academic abilities and needs of students is appropriate and accurate school subject assessment methods. Clear and precise assessment methods are also a key element in reporting students' school performances and progress to all stakeholders, especially parents. Renihan and Noonan provide an overview of what principals need to know about current assessment practices designed to support student learning, given recent changes in assessment for inclusion. Using these practices, principals can properly support teachers as they modify, where necessary, their specific instructional and grading approaches to suit the specific abilities and needs of each child.

A model for implementing and sustaining a shift in instruction is the development of a community of practice. Before people can develop a community of practice built on the concepts foundational to inclusion, they have to understand what it is and what it is not. Pudlas' chapter adroitly suggests that professional development is the primary means by which this can be achieved. His notions about the types of professional development required to accomplish this are those that not only focus on inclusive practice, but also focus on models that involve teachers in examining the fundamentals concepts *behind* inclusive practice. By fostering such deep appreciations about and for inclusion, principals will enhance teachers' everyday practices.

In addition to professional development initiatives designed to foster community, Specht and Young make specific suggestions which principals may consider in order to foster inclusive communities of practice. They also suggest that shifting the focus from individual teacher effort to community effort is more effective in the creation of inclusive schools.

Redesigning the Organization

Setting directions and developing people are insufficient, however, if the broader objective is to sustain an inclusive environment; in this instance, the fundamentals of the organization, including the beliefs, values, actions, and expectations have to change as well. In some cases, the redesign of a school will require a serious questioning of deeply held beliefs about students with exceptionalities, upon which many school practices are based. Without a disruption of our basic beliefs and a refocusing on what inclusion is intended to and can achieve, as Fraser and Shields suggest, new ideas for the improvement of instruction will be nearly impossible to design, implement, and sustain over the long term. Without a consideration for sustainability, inclusion is at risk of becoming a fad, both in spirit and in practice.

We must remember, however, that schools function within the administrative framework established by the school district, and to some extent, are limited by the district in what they can do. Instead of this being a negative characteristic, some school districts have used their influential role to reshape how schools deal with inclusion. DiPetta, Woloshyn, Gallagher, DiBiase Hyatt, Dworet, and Bennett provide an example of such an initiative. They describe how one school district developed a strategy for implementing inclusive education in its schools and they describe the impact the initiative had on administrators and teachers. They also provide recommendations for others who may wish to undertake a similar approach. The Edmunds et al. final chapter further describes how principals used the underpinnings of inclusion to both critically examine their school's organizational approaches to inclusion for strengths and needs, and to make systemic changes as necessary based on sound principles rather than unsubstantiated claims.

Managing the Instructional Program

The principal needs to support teachers in their efforts to develop and deliver effective inclusive classroom practices. One of the best ways to demonstrate this support is to ensure that the school is safe, both psychologically and physically. Edmunds's chapter on managing student behavior provides insights into the underpinnings of behavior and suggests how principals can use school-wide approaches to help teachers to manage their classrooms as an instructional support for inclusion. There are two underlying themes. First, is that persistent/consistent disruptive student behavior significantly undermines the learning of all students, but particularly for students with exceptionalities. Second, is that all students, and especially students with exceptionalities, learn, thrive, and prosper within psychologically secure learning environments.

Principals are charged with the instructional leadership of their schools and can take on this crucial role in a number of ways, such as advocating for appropriate and timely psycho-educational assessment practices. In Edmunds's second chapter, he describes how principals can take an active role in supporting teachers' instruction by ensuring that an accurate assessment of a child's strengths and needs is conducted, and by helping teachers through various means to develop appropriate instructional programs based on that assessment. This information, combined with evidence from Renihan and Noonan's chapter on classroom assessment, gives principals a comprehensive overview of all aspects of assessment and describes how their school can benefit from these understandings.

CONCLUDING COMMENTS

No doubt, principals have difficult decisions to make when trying to ensure that their school is genuinely inclusive, both in practice and in fact. These decisions range from the allocation of scarce resources for program support to ensuring that teachers understand the implications of becoming truly inclusive and developing ways to encourage teachers to work to that end. The chapters in this book indicate that there are no formulaic solutions, no short term fixes, and no easy shortcuts to the development of an inclusive school. Leaders also need to realize and accept that the sustainability of such a culture requires that inclusion must be one of the cornerstones of the school's ethos and not dependent on one person's leadership (Hargreaves & Fink, 2006). To this end, we hope that all readers, especially those in formal and informal leadership roles, will gain insights into how they can develop and sustain their inclusive leadership practices.

REFERENCES

Baker, D. (2007). *The principal's contribution to developing and maintaining inclusive schooling for students with special needs.* Unpublished master's Thesis at the University of Western Ontario, London, Ontario, Canada.

Bunch, F., Lupart, J., & Brown, M. (1997). *Resistance and acceptance: Educator attitudes to inclusion of students with disabilities.* North York: York University.

Hargreaves, A., & Fink, D. (2006). *Sustainable leadership.* San Francisco, CA: Jossey-Bass.

Macmillan, R., & Meyer, M. (2006). Guilt and inclusion: The emotional fallout for secondary teachers. *Exceptionality Education Canada, 16*(1).

Reyes, P., & Wagstaff, L. (2005). How does leadership promote successful teaching and learning for diverse students? In W. Firestone & C. Riehl (Eds.), *A new agenda for research in educational leadership* (pp. 101–118). New York: Teachers College Press.

Ryan, J. (2006). *Inclusive leadership.* San Francisco: Josey-Bass.

Scruggs, T. E., & Mastropieri, M. A. (1996). Teacher's perceptions of mainstreaming/inclusion, 1958–1995: A research synthesis. *Exceptional Children, 63*(1), 59–74.

Williams, M., & Macmillan, R. (2005). Litigation in special education: From placement to programming. *Education & Law Journal, 15*(1), 31–60.

Williams, M., & Macmillan, R. (2003). Litigation in special education between 1996–1998: The quest for equality. *Education & Law Journal, 12*(3), 293–317.

Williams, M., & Macmillan, R. (2001). Litigation in special education between 1978–1995: From access to inclusion. *Education & Law Journal, 10*(3), 349–369.

DEBORAH F. G. FRASER AND CAROLYN M. SHIELDS

2. LEADERS' ROLES IN DISRUPTING DOMINANT DISCOURSES AND PROMOTING INCLUSION

INTRODUCTION

Many current practices in education persist because of long held and unquestioned assumptions about the nature of schooling and the respective roles of educators and students. Many of these assumptions made about people, their behavior, and their capabilities, emerge from taken-for-granted beliefs held by dominant groups in society. Foucault, the eminent French intellectual reminded us that these dominant groups are the major power brokers and decision makers. His theory of discourse analysis highlighted the ways in which "systems of ideas emerge as systems of power" (Sawicki, 1991, p. 12). Power resides with those whose social status places them in a privileged and superior position that is rarely questioned in any explicit fashion, but rather accepted as the normal state of affairs. These discourses, or taken-for-granted assumptions, attitudes, and beliefs shape and guide dominant social and educational practices in ways that often exclude members of minoritized groups, including those who may require some form of adaptive educational support. Because typical concepts of normality are pervasive, they are often disempowering for groups who fall outside what is deemed normal; as a consequence, these groups are regularly marginalized and silenced in education. For that reason, discourse theory is particularly pertinent to the inclusion of students whose success requires various forms of adaptive educational services.

Concepts of normality or normalcy go to the heart of the issue in the field of inclusion. While those with special educational needs fall outside certain "measures" of what might be considered normal or average, too often the underlying assumption is that those outside the norm are somehow abnormal. The cult of normalcy which underpins dominant discourses assumes there are certain acceptable ways to be a citizen, a learner, a friend, a student and that there are some who patently do not "fit" these normative patterns. Inclusion, however, is not about everyone fitting a certain mould in order to be accepted.

From a dominant discourse perspective, connotations of the opposite of normal tend to be derogative and include terms such as impaired, defective, faulty, damaged, deficient, incapacitated, or broken. Alternative, more positive discourses would recognize, instead, difference, uniqueness, and distinctiveness. They would emphasize that all children, those with disabilities and those who are non-disabled, must be treated with honor and respect and take their rightful place as valued members of classrooms, schools, and communities. To position children with special educational needs as distinct and unique is far more appropriate, more

A. L. Edmunds and R. B. Macmillan (eds.), Leadership for Inclusion: A Practical Guide, 07–18.
© *2010 Sense Publishers. All Rights Reserved.*

respectful and humane, than to view them as abnormal and somehow 'faulty.' The ramifications of negative or deficit assumptions are far reaching; hence, it is the school leader's job to ensure that inclusion is more than lip service. School leaders can easily perpetuate (sometimes unknowingly) those discourses that continue to disempower, dehumanize and denigrate those with special needs. Unless detrimental attitudes, beliefs, and systems are recognized and questioned wherever they occur, then students with special needs will continue to be marginalized and disenfranchised despite formal policies of inclusion.

This chapter briefly outlines a number of dominant discourses that may under-gird a philosophy of inclusion. It illustrates these discourses and provides some brief examples of alternative discourses that emphasize the rights of children with exceptionalities, rights that their "normalized" peers already enjoy and which should not be withheld on any basis, let alone on moral, ethical, or legal grounds.

EXAMINING DOMINANT DISCOURSES

Despite a raft of legislation that affirms the rights of those with disabilities to a fair, just, and equitable education, a number of deficit discourses still dominate thinking about those with special needs. Although these discourses co-exist alongside a rights discourse, they continue to negatively influence the quality of life of those with exceptionalities. To illustrate the need for the school leader to be vigilant about the beliefs as well as the practices of all educators, three such discourses are outlined here: the lay, the medical, and the charity. We could just as easily have used terms such as deficit, pathologizing, or hegemonic discourses; the point is that when some students are singled out in unnecessary and essentializing ways, school leaders must be prepared both to speak and to act.

The Lay Discourse

The lay discourse assumes that life must be awful for those with disabilities and that having a child with a disability is a dreadful tragedy. The prevalent attitude from this perspective is that those with disabilities should be institutionalized (or at least hidden), kept away from the mainstream of society for everyone's benefit. In citing Taylor & Harrington's (2001) extensive research on interventions and services for students with exceptionalities, Edmunds & Edmunds (2008) provided a somber yet pointed reminder of this attitude;

> As unpalatable as it may be, we have to remember that the early forms and types of special education were not designed with the best interests of children with exceptionalities in mind. Rather, they were designed as convenient measures to thwart perceived threats to the education of normal students (p. 15).

For educators, the belief underpinning this attitude is that disability is shameful, embarrassing, and too difficult to address in regular schooling. From the lay perspective, people are victims of their disabilities, their lives are confined and restricted and their existence is assumed to be atypical, less meaningful, and less enjoyable than for those perceived to be normal. Although this attitude is now rarely explicit in public schooling, vestiges of it remain in the ways in which we offer services to those in need of assistance. For example, teacher aides who work with students with special needs sometimes block students' opportunities to integrate with their non-disabled peers and reinforce their differences in stigmatizing ways (Meyer & Bevan-Brown, 2005). The assumption, too often, is that the teacher aide "solves the problem" of having a student with special needs in the classroom. This discourse generally sees the teacher aide assigned to work one-on-one with the student on his or her particular remedial needs. If teacher aides become the "velcro aides," who are virtually attached to the side of their students, they may also symbolize over-protectiveness as they operate as a select adult tutor within the classroom. In such cases exclusion is manifest in what ostensibly appears to be an inclusive setting. This further isolates the student with special needs who has plenty of attention from one adult, but little interaction with the rest of his or her classmates. Nevertheless, the assumption is that his or her needs are being met.

In often subtle ways, underlying lay discourses continue to reinforce the view that the student is not really part of the class community and that the convenient option is to allocate a teacher aide to the student. Moreover, under the guise of teaching independent skills through adult tutelage, it can actually *increase* a student's dependence on the teacher aide to assist, translate, support, intervene, and guide (Meyer & Bevan-Brown, 2005). Opportunities for friendships and regular social interaction with the class community can be blocked if the teacher aide operates exclusively as personal tutor. Research has also found that non-disabled students often assume that their peers with special needs do not need friends as they have their teacher aide's abiding attention (MacArthur, Kelly & Higgins, 2005). In most circumstances, therefore, the school leader may be well advised to consider assigning teaching aides to specific classrooms or teachers rather than having them permanently associated with a specific student. A useful alternative is to have the teacher aide work with groups that include students with special needs so that they are facilitating social interaction as well as learning in ways that are less isolating and more focused on building the class community.

The Medical Discourse

The medical discourse positions disability as an illness that requires treatment. The emphasis from this perspective is on levels of impairment, degrees of severity, clinical descriptions, physiological symptoms, diagnosis, and treatment/therapeutic regimes. The assumption is that disability can and should be treatable, often with drugs and therapies, in an attempt to normalize people as much as possible. Education from this perspective focuses on treatment and remediation. Indeed, the medical discourse has contributed much to the deficit thinking surrounding people with disabilities as the pathological emphasis underscores the abnormal and undesirable (Skrtic, 1991). The assumption is that special needs are problematic, aberrant, unhealthy, and in need of specialized interventions in the "hope of curing" or of normalizing as much as possible. Shields, Bishop, and Mazawi (2005) use the term pathologizing for its utility in explaining social and cultural relationships that exist in schooling and classroom interactions. They define pathologizing as "a process where perceived structural-functional, cultural, or epistemological deviation from an assumed normal state is ascribed to another group as a product of power relationships, whereby the less powerful group is deemed to be abnormal in some way (p. x)." They then go on to say that pathologizing discourses and practices are ways of regulating, managing, and marginalizing others.

Obviously, schools need to know something about serious medical conditions that a student may have in order to keep a student from preventable harm. For example, children with cancer are particularly vulnerable to general childhood illnesses such as chicken pox when their immune system resistance is lowered during chemotherapy treatments. Children with severe allergies may also unexpectedly fall into anaphylactic shock. Thus, ongoing communication between school and home is required to keep students safe. However, it is rare that the medical discourse is actually used to describe a remediable condition; instead, it is often used to imply that students who need specific pedagogical interventions or adaptations are somehow ill and must be cured. Even when there are identifiable medical factors, the medical discourse often becomes so dominant that students' deficits, problems, and treatments are all encompassing and, conversely, their strengths, abilities and humanity are ignored.

For example, in the following description, Full Foetal Alcohol Syndrome (FAS) is identified by a number of highly specific criteria which are simultaneously present in the candidate. These include: 1) significant growth retardation before and after birth; 2) measurable mental retardation; 3) abnormal facial characteristics; 4) a range of other physical deformities and defects (Dorris, 1989). Here the emphasis is obviously on the negative physiological effects. When this is the only information teachers are given about a student diagnosed with foetal alcohol syndrome, it is not surprising that their view is one of deficit and that they are unlikely to expect much from such a student. The emphasis in this discourse on "deformity" and "defects" clearly signals this is repugnant and extremely unfortunate. Remediation in such cases is seen as the only hope, and given the permanent nature of the condition, thought to be a weak hope at best.

An alternative discourse would acknowledge the condition but consider what the student can do, not just what he or she cannot. For example, Tony, a seven-year-old student with FAS well-known to one of the authors, loves to be outdoors, enjoys dance and is learning to count on the abacus. His inclusion with his peers was enhanced on his birthday when his mother brought his favorite activity to school. At lunch time the playground was filled by Tony and his classmates blowing colored bubbles which drifted in multi-colored hues around the yard. Shrieks and giggles of delight were heard as Tony and his peers capered with glee after their incandescent and ephemeral creations. Moreover, this simple activity showed Tony interacting with his peers without experiencing negative judgments, sharing an activity in which they could all participate and succeed.

School leaders will need to attend to providing accurate and complete information for teachers and to facilitating excellent and necessary communication between home and school. In so doing, it becomes essential to find an appropriate balance between care and caution and nurturing the student's abilities, agency, and independence.

The Charity Discourse

The charity discourse positions people with disabilities as weak and powerless and in need of care and attention. This perspective assumes that those with disabilities should be nursed, cared for, protected and buffeted from a world in which they cannot cope. It fails to acknowledge or identify their agency, capabilities, and capacity; hence, their voices are rarely heard and less often sought either in the classroom or in policy debates. As with the other discourses, those with special needs are considered victims and their conditions thought to comprise terrible suffering, incapacity, and helplessness. This discourse appeals to those with benevolent intentions who believe they can alleviate suffering through helping actions and decision making of those so labeled.

The assumption underpinning this discourse is that students with exceptionalities, apart from the gifted, are not competent, do not have opinions worth considering, and should be grateful for the attention and assistance of those who are non-disabled. Assumption in fact goes to the heart of this discourse. For example, people who have low vision and use Braille canes are sometimes pulled across roads by well-meaning sighted people intent on helping, whether that assistance is welcomed or not. Students who use wheelchairs are pushed around the playground and school corridors by their peers and while this can sometimes be welcomed, sometimes it is not. Students who use wheelchairs for mobility obviously have their own wishes as to where they would like to go. From a charity discourse, students are treated as toys or as someone to look after, tend to, and protect. One author frequently recalls the words of a friend who typically described his son as the classroom "pet rock."

Actions emerging from this discourse reinforce feelings of inadequacy and helplessness. Students with disabilities are cosseted to the extent that they are not considered responsible for their behavior or decisions. Classrooms that operate from such a stance position students with exceptionalities as weak, needy, and beholden to those who deign to help, either as paid paraprofessionals such as teacher aides or as benevolent peers. Such classrooms often have rosters of 'buddies' wherein non-disabled students are paired up on a daily basis to help a student with a disability. The intention may be well meaning but too often the notion is that students with special needs require help all the time (which they do not) and that without a roster no one would bother with them. Moreover, the illusion of friendship is parodied when a roster proclaims on a public, daily basis who will be the 'buddy' today for student X. Real friendships are based upon a special alchemy that cannot be coerced (Van der Klift & Kunc, 1994) and are more likely to emerge through genuine, shared interests. Buddy systems that reinforce a one-way helper-helpee relationship effectively disempower and disenfranchise students with exceptionalities.

11

A charity discourse is complex as it obviously reflects the human trait of compassion, a desire to reach out and to help others who appear to be in need. However, the power dynamics always require consideration. Hence, a school leader should always ask, and encourage others to ask questions such as whose interests are being served? Who benefits from such help and who is left feeling undermined? Who, in fact, wanted the help in the first place? Who is really included and who has once again been marginalized—despite good intentions? A charity discourse can lead both educators and students to objectify, and dominate students with disabilities in ways that are unhealthy and dehumanizing. Consider, for example, the following report by a mother of a child with cancer:

> This girl became almost possessive of the fact that there was Natalie and she had no hair and she was "hers"…in fact the year that Natalie was off school [for various treatments] she'd say to the other kids "She's my friend" and she'd write Natalie cards saying you're my best friend, but she wasn't actually…and when Natalie did return to school she didn't want Natalie around her…the teacher came to me and said this girl doesn't want Natalie hanging around but she feels sorry for her…(Fraser, 2001, p. 21).

In this case the charity discourse was evident through the convenience of sending cards and proclaiming affection but not when it actually came to the demands of meaningful interaction and real friendship.

Summary

Discourses can thus be complex and multi-faceted, they can overlap and coalesce, with charity turning to lay discourse in the above situation. School leaders need to understand these discourses and the insidious ways in which they both dehumanize and disempower students with disabilities. Leaders must educate their staff about these discourses and how schools can, unconsciously, perpetuate these unethical attitudes. It is also the school leader's role to promote an alternative discourse, such as a rights discourse, that positions those with disabilities as people first and foremost; as capable of contributing to school and society and as worthy—as anyone—of dignity and respect. Here, they may find it helpful to promote among their school community, Starratt's (1991) notion of treating the other with "absolute regard," as they work to lead a community in which the complementary ethics of justice, caring, and critique are always present.

INCLUSION AS A RIGHT

An alternative to the three pervasive discourses described above is the rights discourse which emerged in the 1960s alongside various civil rights campaigns of the era including women's rights, the rights of war veterans, the rights of gays and the passage in 1964 in the United States of the Civil Rights Act. Many government and non-government organizations work to achieve political recognition and rights for those with disabilities and to promote positive images and attitudes

(Neilson, 2005). The aim is that people with disabilities have a legitimate right to the same privileges that the non-disabled take for granted such as access to jobs, social interaction, interdependence, independent living, respect, recognition, education, and the opportunities to which all who live in a thriving democracy are entitled. Increasingly, too, people with disabilities are defining just what rights mean for them rather than being told by well meaning organizations what their needs and rights are. In a recent interview about the Convention on the Rights of Persons with Disabilities adopted by the United Nations in 2006, Lex Grandia, head of the World Federation of the DeafBlind, stated that deaf/blind people are often not considered able to have a meaningful quality of life or to make a significant contribution to decisions made about them. He spoke about his experiences growing up in an institution, following the divorce of his parents when he was two years old, saying:

> When I grew up in institutions I had a number—number 49. I was not considered a person. Now I begin to get the feeling that I am a person with the possibility to make my own decisions. I have to learn that and I have to do it.... Access to information is very important for me also. It's the equality. It's the feeling of being a person like anybody else. And trying to change the attitude of people, of society is also very important... (Outlook BBC, 2007).

School leaders must take seriously Grandia's message about the importance of teaching people they are people with the right not only to make their own decisions but to make a contribution to the society in which they live. The following examples provide a few suggestions of ways in which schools can promote inclusive practices and honor the rights discourse in their practice.

Inclusive Geographies

The school and classroom are microcosms of society and will reflect dominant norms of power, privilege, and status unless school leaders devise and enact specific policies to ensure social justice. Some obvious ways in which those with physical disabilities are marginalized are the decisions made about access, space, and physical seating. Ramps for wheelchair access, or adaptations to bathrooms and drinking fountains are just a starting point. Some schools do virtually nothing beyond these basics which in themselves, do not provide inclusion. Inclusion is fostered when students with disabilities can participate alongside their non-disabled peers. This means that they are not isolated in the corner of the classroom with the teacher aide, separate from the rest of the class. It means instead that they are seated alongside their peers in academic and social groups that foster interaction, dialogue, and collaboration. It means that equipment in experiential classes such as physical education, art, and music is adapted to permit full participation. The playground is another site where inclusive geographies need to be evident. For health and safety reasons playground equipment is generally located in flat places where the ground surface is covered in soft materials to buffer and protect students from possible falls. Ensuring that the soft material does not inhibit the use of

13

calipers or wheelchairs promotes inclusion as does situating play areas so students with disabilities do not have to spend an inordinate amount of time and energy getting to them.

Structuring the classroom for inclusion also means ensuring that there is easy access to resources, seating, and movement around the room. It means that students with disabilities hold similar responsibilities in the classroom to those of their classmates whether they are being in charge of cleaning the board, taking attendance, distributing books and papers, or participating in a presentation. Having a responsible task disrupts the typical notion that students with disabilities always require help and assistance. It provides them a degree of power that positions students as authoritative and able to assist their non-disabled peers. It also facilitates social interaction as the supply of resources provides an authentic context for interaction. It is particularly important that students with special needs are not always on the receiving end of help (Meyer, Park, Grenot-Scheyer, Schwartz & Harry, 1998).

Although it is human to feel protective towards a student with obvious and severe special needs, sometimes we do students a disservice by protecting, buffeting, and "saving" them from opportunities to take risks and build resilience. For example, during a class excursion to an indoor, simulated rock climbing facility, Zaan, who had a brain tumor, was expected to watch and not participate. The tumor had affected his eyesight, coordination, and dexterity and so both parent and teacher assumed that it was better and safer if he did not take his turn in climbing the wall. However, Zaan pleaded to have a go and, with some trepidation, his teacher and parent relented. With the safety harness in place and the guidance of the climbing instructor, Zaan gingerly made his way up the wall watched by his peers, his mother and teacher. To everyone's surprise and delight he climbed to the top of the wall and stood there beaming with pride. His peers cheered and his mother smiled back with tears streaming down her face. It was one of those moments where assumptions were challenged and over-turned in a dramatic and unforgettable way.

Inclusive geographies require educators who do not block peer interaction, mixed instructional groups that include students with special needs, and physical inclusion of children with disabilities within the class milieu, not on the periphery. Thus, in inclusive schools, leaders constantly encourage teachers to provide opportunities for students to participate in all school activities alongside their peers.

Social Interaction and Friendships

Social interaction is particularly important for students with special needs. These students are more likely to be lonely, isolated, and lack authentic friendships. Lack of real friendships further isolates students with special needs and makes them more vulnerable to rejection or over-involvement (Fraser, 2001). As Cullingford (1991) argued "a school's virtues derive from the pleasures of friendship; its terrors from loneliness and isolation" (p. 48). There is often a tendency for students with special needs to be treated as ghosts (virtually ignored), guests (respected but not integrated), or pets (cosseted and pampered) in the classroom (Meyer & Bevan-Brown, 2005). Peer relationships can be enhanced through physical proximity, through cooperative group activities, through shared interests, and joint projects. Lack of friends can also increase the likelihood of teasing and bullying which in turn, creates a vicious cycle (MacArthur et al., 2005). Inclusive practices foster authentic relationships, and while friendship cannot be coerced the classroom should provide opportunities for positive peer relationships.

In addition to the emotional well-being that friends provide there is increasing evidence to suggest that social inclusion and friendships can enhance school achievement (Ladd, 1990; Newcomb & Bagwell, 1996; Peters, 2000). While having friends does not ensure academic progress, "friendships are associated with enhanced opportunities to exercise behaviors related to social, emotional, and cognitive growth" (Newcomb & Bagwell, 1996, p. 317). As previously stated, attention should be given to power dynamics so that students with special needs are not always on the receiving end of help from their peers.

When students have severe disabilities such as profound autism, social inclusion can be challenging. However, it is important to reframe perceptions of deficit as creative opportunities. For example, Imelda's vocalization consists of a loud gutteral utterance which she repeats at much the same volume and intensity. When her class performed a play, she had the role of signaling the change of scene through the expression of her utterance. Instead of framing her in deficit terms as non-verbal and thus unable to take a speaking role, she was framed as pivotal to the sequence of the play. Her role was not merely one of 'being a tree' or some similarly passive position amounting to background scenery. She was given power and prominence within the play. In another example, a student who was also non-verbal and had the habit of repeatedly putting marbles in a jar, became the centre of a process drama. Each time she placed a marble in the jar, it was the signal for her peers to change the focus of their drama and adopt a new genre. Such examples show how even repetitive behaviors that seem obsessive can be reframed in aesthetic terms and employed as central, not peripheral, to classroom programs.

High Academic Expectations

Achieving access and socialization do not ensure the presence of either an inclusive school or an inclusive classroom, but simply a kind of educational social club. School leaders are charged with a mandate to ensure that every child learns (consistent with his or her abilities) to high standards of academic excellence. Full inclusion for students whose academic programs may require some level of adaptation must nevertheless attend carefully to ensuring that students achieve appropriate and excellent academic learning—standards that understand and reject the limitations implicit in the discourses we examined earlier.

Fortunately, there has been considerable research to indicate that, here, it is the climate of expectations set by the school that makes the greatest difference. The long-standing studies of teachers who were told (falsely) that their classes comprised students of outstanding talent and aptitude, in which the students rose to the level of expectations such a belief implied, are well-known (Rosenthal & Jacobson, 1968). An important study (Wagstaff & Fusarelli, 1995) found that the single most important factor in the academic achievement of minoritized students was the *explicit* rejection of deficit thinking on the part of the school leader. In like fashion, a series of New Zealand studies of specific pedagogical interventions with Maori students also found that expectations were key (Bishop & Berryman, 2006) When Maori students were taught using relational and constructivist pedagogies that took account of their specific learning preferences and that assumed they were capable of initiative, agency, and academic excellence, they performed as well as their non-Maori peers. Although the previous two studies focused on students minoritized because of their ethnic group affiliation, there is good reason to believe that the same holds true for students minoritized for reasons related to some intellectual or physical limitations. Levy (1975) reviewed studies that demonstrated the ability of "severely retarded adults" to "perform complex industrial tasks" including the accurate insertion of electronic components into a printed or etched circuit board. Jones, Vaughn, and Roberts (2002) studied a similar phenomenon and found that because memory for spatial location appears to be not directly affected by the individual's level of intelligence, it is possible for those mentally impaired to learn complex tasks requiring spatial knowledge.

The key, not only to considering future employment for students with some kind of disability, but to considering appropriate academic expectations as well, is to focus not on the limitation, but on the capabilities and abilities of each student. Stereotyping what an individual may or may not be able to achieve is akin to earlier societal assumptions that some jobs were only suitable for male employees. Carla, a blind woman in one of the author's graduate classes in educational leadership, not only taught the instructor, but all of her peers this important lesson. When she had received the appropriate support, in terms of having her textbook material converted to an audio format, she was engaged, articulate, and perceptive in her classroom participation. However, when the university readers had failed to provide the audio material in a timely fashion, she was forced to sit quietly, unable to participate fully. Moreover, when I learned to accurately describe what appeared on an on-screen diagram or to adapt the rules of an assignment requiring visual manipulation, she again participated fully. The institution's recognition of its responsibility for making adequate and appropriate modifications was an essential prior condition to Carla's inclusion; taking responsibility for listening to and understanding the readings was, of course, Carla's part in assuring her ultimate success in graduate school. Had the lay, medical, or charity discourses dominated, Carla could never have achieved her potential. Providing her with the appropriate adaptations to which she was entitled was key. This is the critical responsibility of every school leader and administrator: ensuring that all students are provided with the instruction— academic, social, and physical—to which they have a legitimate and inherent right as citizens of a given community.

CONCLUSION

School leaders have a moral, legal and ethical obligation to provide for the education of those with special needs alongside their non-disabled peers in schools. Sometimes this requires that additional resources be allocated to physically adapt the environment so that all students may participate in meaningful ways. Sometimes, this requires an intentional focus on grouping and regrouping students in order to promote mutually beneficial and responsible social interaction. On occasion, it also requires modifications of learning goals and objectives. Here it may be useful for educational leaders to be aware of the findings of the President's Committee Job Accommodation Network, that on average 15% of accommodations cost nothing and 51% cost less than $500 (Walker, n.d.). If modification of the workplace is so cost effective, it is incumbent on educational leaders to take steps to allocate appropriate budgets to the task of creating an inclusive learning environment for all students.

At times, educators may be so paralyzed by the negative implications of dominant discourses that the task seems overwhelming. To ensure that inclusion fosters and enhances the learning and well-being of students requires that educational leaders constantly promote an understanding of alternative discourses and to challenge discourses that, although dominant, may be inappropriate. On the other hand, the rights discourse provided here presents a progressive framework for developing a respectful, engaging, humane, and thus, more inclusive education. The beliefs and values that accompany exclusionary discourses such as the lay, medical, and charity discourses, need to be recognized, "challenged, and replaced by more inclusionary paradigms" (Kearney & Kane, 2006, p. 216) as suggested here. Most importantly however, is the obligation to ensure that the human rights of every student are upheld in the educational processes and environments to which they are fully entitled.

REFERENCES

Bishop, R., & Berryman, M. (2006). *Culture speaks: Cultural relationships and classroom learning.* Wellington, New Zealand: Huia.
Dorris, M. (1989). *The broken cord.* New York: HarperCollins.
Edmunds, A. L., & Edmunds, G. A. (2008). *Special education in Canada.* Toronto, ON: McGraw-Hill Ryerson.
Erwin, P. (1993). *Friendship and peer relations in children.* Chichester, West Sussex: John Wiley & Sons.
Fraser, D. (2001). *The educational needs of children with cancer: A qualitative study of 12 families.* Hamilton, ON: Waikato Institute for Research in Learning and Curriculum.
Ladd, G. W. (1990). Having friends, keeping friends, making friends and being liked by peers in the classroom: Predictors of children's early school adjustment? *Child Development, 58,* 1168–1189.
Levy, S. M. (1975). The development of work skill training procedures for the assembly of printed circuit boards by the severely handicapped. *AAESPH Review, 1*(1), 1–10.
Kearney, A., & Kane, R. (2006). Inclusive education policy in New Zealand: Reality or ruse? *International Journal of Inclusive Education, 10*(2–3), 201–219.
MacArthur, J., Kelly, B., & Higgins, N. (2005). Supporting the learning and social experiences of students with disabilities: What does the research say? In D. Fraser, R. Moltzen, & K. Ryba (Eds.), *Learners with special needs in Aotearoa New Zealand* (3rd ed., pp. 49–73). Southbank, Victoria: Thomson.

Meyer, L., & Bevan-Brown, J. (2005). Collaboration for social inclusion. In D. Fraser, R. Moltzen, & K. Ryba (Eds.), *Learners with special needs in Aotearoa New Zealand* (3rd ed., pp. 168–192). Southbank, Victoria: Thomson.

Meyer, L., Park, H-S., Grenot-Scheyer, M., Schwartz, I., Harry, B. (Eds.). (1998). *Making friends: The influences of culture and development.* Baltimore: Paul Brookes.

Neilson, W. (2005). Disability: Attitudes, history and discourses. In D. Fraser, R. Moltzen, & K. Ryba (Eds.), *Learners with special needs in Aotearoa New Zealand* (3rd ed., pp. 9–21). Southbank, Victoria: Thomson.

Newcomb, A. F., & Bagwell, C. (1996). The developmental significance of children's friendship relations. In W. M. Bukowski, A. F. Newcomb, & W. W. Hartup (Eds.), *The company they keep: Friendship in childhood and adolescence* (pp. 289–321). Cambridge, USA: Cambridge University Press.

Outlook BBC. (2007). *UN disabilities convention.* London: British broadcasting Systems. Retrieved from www.bbc.co.uk/worldservice/programs/outlook.html

Peters, S. (2000, December). *"I didn't expect that I would get tons of friends...more each day." Children's experiences of friendship during transition to school.* Paper presented at the New Zealand Association of Research in Education conference, Hamilton, New Zealand.

Rosenthal, R., & Jacobson, L. (1968). *Pygmalion in the classroom: Teacher expectations and pupils' intellectual development.* New York: Holt, Rinehart & Winston.

Van der Klift, E., & Kunc, N. (1994). Friendship and the politics of help. In J. S. Thousand, R. A. Villa, & A. I. Nevin (Eds.), *Creativity and collaborative learning: A practical guide to empowering students and teachers* (pp. 391–401). Baltimore: Paul Brookes.

Sawicki, J. (1991). *Disciplining foucault: Feminism, power and the body.* New York: Routledge.

Shields, C. M., Bishop, R., & Mazawi, A. E. (2005). *Pathologizing practices: The impact of deficit thinking on education.* New York: Peter Lang.

Skrtic, T. M. (1991). *Behind special education. A critical analysis of professional culture and school organization.* Denver, CO: Love.

Starratt, R. J. (1991). Building an ethical school: A theory for practice in educational leadership. *Educational Administration Quarterly, 27*(2), 155–202.

Taylor, G. R., & Harrington, F. (2001). Incidence of exceptionality. In G. R. Taylor (Ed.), *Educational interventions and services for children with exceptionalities* (2nd ed., pp. 3–13). Springfield, IL: Charles C. Thomas Publisher.

Wagstaff, L., & Fusarelli, L. (1995). *The racial minority paradox: New leadership for learning communities of diversity.* Paper presented at the annual meeting of the University Council for Educational Administration, Salt Lake City, Utah.

Walker, S. (n.d.) Dispelling myths about people with disabilities. Retrieved January 2008, from http://www.disaboom.com/Career-Center/For-Employers/Articles/Dispelling-Myths-about-People-with-Disabilities.aspx

ALAN L. EDMUNDS

3. MANAGING SCHOOL-WIDE BEHAVIOR FROM THE PRINCIPAL'S OFFICE

INTRODUCTION

There is no doubt that academic excellence is facilitated by, even ameliorated by, well managed and psychologically secure learning environments. Marzano & Marzano's (2003) meta-analysis clearly demonstrated that classroom management vastly out-distances both instructional and curricular variables as the single-most important contributor to academic performance. By contrast, learning is seriously impeded and behaviour tends to deteriorate in classrooms and schools that feel chaotic (Johnson & Edmunds, 2006; Levin & Nolan, 2000). The escalation of small annoyances into significant problems primarily occurs because without clear boundaries and limitations, and the required support structures to operate within them, students do not know how to properly govern themselves. While these basic behavioural principles apply to all students in all classrooms, they are particularly important for students with exceptionalities in inclusive classrooms because most have learning difficulties and co-occurring attentional, behavioural, and social adjustment problems that often contribute to disruptive behaviors (Edmunds & Edmunds, 2008). Even more important to this discussion is the fact that teachers and administrators work harder and longer with students who demonstrate problematic behaviours, but get very little reward for their efforts. Educators' feelings of exploitation are worsened by the substantial emotional commitment they invest when trying to help troubled children, only to end up feeling distraught and abused when this commitment is only rewarded by continued bad or worse behaviour.

The primary objective of this chapter, then, is to outline how principals and administrators can support teachers in their creation of well managed classrooms and, by extension, create well-managed schools. More importantly, the chapter outlines the vital role principals must play in the day-to-day management of all spaces in their school, including classrooms, the playground, cafeteria and hallways, but mostly doing so from the comfort of their own office. While classroom management is distinctly different from instructional and assessment activities, teachers and administrators must integrate an overarching philosophy of classroom and behavior management into their school's agenda in order for all their efforts to be effective. Educators who leave good management to chance, have little chance of good management. To establish a functional management philosophy and to implement effective management practices administrators need to understand: a) what causes disruptive behaviour; b) how to design and implement

A. L. Edmunds and R. B. Macmillan (eds.), Leadership for Inclusion: A Practical Guide, 19–31.
© *2010 Sense Publishers. All Rights Reserved.*

a comprehensive approach that simultaneously diminishes problematic behavior, encourages and supports good behavior, and enhances learning; and c) what specific actions they can take to support this process.

Three underlying premises form the foundation for this chapter, all derived from exemplary research in the discipline: 1) The research is unequivocally clear that the absence of appropriate student behavior is merely a performance deficit problem; it is definitely not a skill deficit problem (Maag, 2004); problematic students have good behaviour skills, they just don't use them; 2) While most disruptive and problematic behaviours are not allowed, they are *permitted*. Permission occurs because existing rules are not clear, different teachers have different rules and tolerances for behaviour, and students are expected to implicitly learn/interpret the existing rules. Strangely, many educators expect that students will somehow learn the rules by osmosis; they often comment that "they should have learned that by now" as if other experiences will teach students the intricacies of a teacher's unique personality and way of conducting their classroom. Unfortunately, nothing good comes from this expectation. It absolves educators of the responsibility to explicitly outline the rules and, in the absence of such direct communication, it allows students to interpret whatever rules exist, or whatever rules they *think* exist. This tacit permission provides students with a litany of excuses for their actions and it contributes immensely to their non-accountability for those actions. In a distorted sense, this permissiveness actually condones problematic behaviour; 3) Finally, the research is also clear that disruptive behaviors in schools can be mitigated by improving teachers' and administrators' management knowledge and skills so they can implement an approach that properly motivates and reinforces students for appropriate behavior.

Facts about Behaviour

1) All behaviour has meaning, it is not random or arbitrary. People behave as they do for two reasons, and for two reasons only – they are either trying to get something, or they're trying to avoid something. Find the right reinforcer and you can get anyone to behave as you want them to;
2) Human behaviour is not instinctive; all human behaviour is learned and all behaviour is predicated by thinking. Therefore, all behaviour can be changed, but not without changing the thinking that drives it. Student self-regulation is more powerful and long term than teachers regulated student behaviour;
3) Behaviour is contextual; it is a direct manifestation of the environment within which it occurs. Change the rules of a particular environment, and behaviour will change;
4) Behaviour is reciprocally determined; it is not an isolated act. Individuals are constantly engaged in two-way interactions that determine the quality and type of all subsequent interactions.

Because all behaviour is geared toward getting or avoiding something, proper *motivation* in the form of rewards and consequences is imperative. Because changing behaviour requires changing the thinking behind it, explicit *awareness* of the rules and the encouragement of student self-regulated behaviour is imperative. Because behaviour is contextual and because appropriate behaviour is a performance deficit issue, structuring the environment to *elicit suitable behaviour* is imperative. Finally, because all behaviour is reciprocal, it is imperative that educators purposefully engage students in *two-way interactions* to co-determine the rules, rewards, and consequences that will govern their shared environment.

Causes of Disruptive Behaviours

There are three primary causes of problematic behaviours in schools: psychological issues, learning difficulties, and the learning environment. The main psychological cause of problematic behavior stems from children's inherent need to be liked and accepted by others. They have the misperception that they can get admiration and acceptance by engaging in improper behaviour to: 1) gain attention; 2) conceal inadequacy; 3) gain power or control over people or situations; and/or, 4) exact retribution or revenge from real or perceived injuries or slights (Dreikurs and Cassel, 1992). Students can also be antagonistic towards adults because they mistrust them and they do not feel that adults have their best interests at heart (Canter & Canter, 1993). To remedy both issues, teachers have to include students in co-designing classroom management principles so as to replace their mistaken perceptions with appropriate behavioral objectives and to re-establish students' trust of adults. The neurological factors associated with oppositional defiance, conduct disorder, inattentiveness, hyperactivity, and impulsivity also contribute to behavior problems. Finally, temperament contributes to behavior problems when the intensity of a person's emotional reactions reduces their behavioral control and renders them inconsolable by others (Berk, 1996; Thomas & Chess, 1977). Despite all of the above, educators would be wrong to conclude that children are inherently bad or that their misbehaviour is purposefully willful. While all behaviour has a purpose, it can be changed. The key is to direct students towards positive ends and away from negative ends.

Learning difficulties cause behavior problems primarily because of the frustration and embarrassment endured by students who do not experience sufficient academic and/or behavioural success, if they experience any success at all. Many students do not know how to properly remedy their persistent frustration, anxiety, and tension over these matters and they act/react inappropriately because of the absence of appropriate alternatives. Therefore, to cope, students develop a plethora of task avoidance strategies/excuses because it is psychologically safer to rationalize their academic failures as something they did not do, rather than as something they tried to do, but failed at. Ironically, because educators usually see students' ongoing task avoidance actions and rationales as facile excuses or even lies, it is difficult for educators to continually offer to help someone they suspect is trying to pull the wool over their eyes. Children, even adolescents, cannot be left to their own devices to come up with adult-approved and socially acceptable behavioural solutions.

Finally, the learning environment is also a factor that can significantly cause/exacerbate problematic behaviors in a variety of ways. While it is rare that an educator directly causes student bad behavior, educators would be well served to remember that they are part of the social interactive process and that they might be doing something that inadvertently sets the student off. According to Edmunds & Edmunds (2008), teachers mostly cause problematic student behaviors by failing to "…positively control nearly all the factors that contribute to problematic behaviour and non-efficient learning environments" (p. 37).

The following section presents a comprehensive approach to classroom management that administrators can implement in their school to significantly reduce problematic behaviour in classrooms and enhance the overall behavioural tone of their building. If behaviour is well managed, both behavior and learning will improve. Unfortunately, the reciprocal corollary is not true.

A COMPREHENSIVE MANAGEMENT APPROACH

Classroom management is not a "bag of tricks" nor is it a way of "controlling" students; rather, it is a coherent set of behavioural principles and classroom management skills that are applied and integrated into the everyday activities of teachers and students who interact and work together. *The Invitation*, an approach to classroom management developed by this writer (Edmunds & Edmunds, in press; Edmunds & Edmunds, 2008; Johnson & Edmunds, 2006), was designed to address all of the underlying issues mentioned above. It incorporates the five global principles contained in the gold standard in the discipline: *Handbook of Classroom Management: Research, Practice, and Contemporary Issues* (Evertson & Weinstein, 2006):
1) develop caring, supportive relationships with and among students;
2) organize and implement instruction in ways that optimize students' access to learning;
3) use group management methods that encourage students' engagement in academic tasks;
4) promote the development of students' social skills and self-regulation; and,
5) use appropriate interventions to assist students with behaviour problems (p. 5).

As a result, the four fundamental understandings used in *The Invitation* to direct teacher's actions have a history of strong empirical support (Gettinger & Kohler, 2006):
1) It emphasizes *positive behavioural support*: the use of universal, primary behaviour prevention methods while at the same time including a continuum of intervention supports for students with chronic behavioural concerns (Sugai, Horner, Dunlap, Hieneman, Lewis, Nelson, Scott, Liaupsin, Sailor, Turnbull, Turnbull, Wickham, Ruef, & Wilcox, 2000).
2) It emphasizes *classroom discourse research* because how teachers construct and maintain order in their classroom is as important as order itself (Nucci, 2006; Fallona & Richardson, 2006). There is an emphasis on explanatory teacher-student conversations that collaboratively and explicitly establish

classroom rules and routines, including the use of reminder mechanisms so rules and routines do not become invisible/diminish over time (Morine-Dershimer, 2006).

3) Classrooms are far too socially interactive and complex for teachers to be the only ones responsible for behaviour. The motivational dynamics of *self-regulated behaviour* advocate strongly that teachers collectively engage students in explicit strategies for: making behavioural choices; reflecting on the meaningfulness of choices; seeing choices through to completion; and reflecting on the outcomes of their actions. These conversations draw disparate perceptions of good and bad behaviour out and, through discussion, promote more universally student-accepted responsibilities, promote commitment to the rules, and impede behavioural impulsivity. Students award or suffer self-determined consequences for increased good, or reduced bad, behaviours (McCaslin, Bozak, Naploeon, Thomas, Vasquez, Wayman & Zhang, 2006).

4) Teachers use specific types of *discourses to convey their intentions* to manage their classroom and regulate student behaviour. To diminishes student passivity and/or compliance-only attitudes there is an emphasis on an exact clarification of what students are expected to do. To diminish punishment-based management and remove the implication that the only owner/enforcer of rules is the teacher, collaborative before-the-fact problem prevention is stressed while after-the-fact discipline is only used as needed. To increase the coherence and continuity of all classroom actions, management is discussed as an integral part of instruction; not as a disconnected element of teacher practice.

The Invitation places the teacher in a proactive mode of purposefully managing education rather than in a disciplinary mode that reacts to educational occurrences (Paintal, 1999). This process allows more class time to be spent on learning activities, it causes less time to be spent on non-goal-directed activities, and it prevents day-to-day functions from becoming a competition between the desires of the teacher and the non-complementary actions of students. *The Invitation* is designed to be easily implemented by all teachers in all classrooms, and with all students and it is adaptable to all teaching styles, personalities, and school settings.

The following section outlines how *The Invitation* is to be enacted by teachers and what, specifically, administrators and principals are to do to within the process to directly support their teachers' actions. These recommendations are based on the repeated successes experienced by administrators/principals in ongoing school interventions.

Recommendation #1. Principals should meet with the entire teaching staff and all other adults in the school (support staff, custodians, itinerant teachers, etc…) to decide three issues: 1) What are the primary behavioural problems that must be addressed? 2) What are the behavioural objectives of the school? and 3) What are the non-negotiable, universal rules that will be implemented school-wide and in every classroom?

Recommendation #2. Conduct a school-wide meeting with all students, all teachers, all support staff including custodians, and all itinerant professionals to outline the behavioural direction of the whole school. Describe the non-negotiable universal rules (from #1 above) that will underpin this process and state clearly that all teachers will engage all students in a rule-generating procedure (The Invitation) that complements the school rules.

Universal rules reduce/eliminate the tacit permissiveness fomented by ambiguous and disparate rules. When made explicit, theses universal rules become a deterrent to problematic behaviour because all students will know that all school personnel know all the rules and the differences between acceptable and unacceptable behaviour. In essence, knowing that all adult eyes will be watching them in all parts of the school leaves them nowhere to hide.

The Invitation

The multi-functional purpose of *The Invitation* is intended to eliminate or minimize misunderstandings, eliminate/minimize problematic behaviours, and create an exemplary environment that increases student learning and promotes positive student behaviours. The four steps of *The Invitation* are illustrated below (adapted from Edmunds & Edmunds, 2008; Johnson & Edmunds, 2006). While they are purposefully specific in meaning, they are easily adaptable. The teacher's spoken message is accompanied by an explanation of its implications. *The Invitation* starts the moment a teacher says hello and welcomes students into the classroom for the very first time. The purpose is to set a positive, engaging, and determined tone that says that each and every student will have successful learning and behavioural experiences.

1. *Welcome to my classroom! Let's walk down the path of education together. I will do my very best to make your time in my classroom both productive and enjoyable.*

   Making this mostly implicit message <u>very explicit</u> has a significant impact on students because it spells out the teacher's genuine purpose and it establishes that the teacher will be accountable for good learning and good behaviour.

2. *I really want all of you to be very successful and get along with each other and I will help you accomplish both objectives.*

   Expressing success in this way allows the teacher to set the stage for excellence and high standards. It also eliminates a common student perception that "My teacher wants me to struggle or fail" or "I will be made to feel stupid if I say I need help".

Teachers then <u>explicitly</u> state and explain all the critical elements that will operationalize how the classroom will be managed, including the non-negotiable universal rules mentioned above. The reason for this explicitness is that the major cause of problems between individuals is the misunderstandings they have of each other. Typically, misunderstandings occur because someone has expectations that go unfulfilled, or because one party *"thinks"* the other person fully understands what was implicitly inferred. Constant and significant social problems are likely.

The step-wise rationale for *The Invitation's* explicitness is that non-explicitness causes misunderstandings; misunderstandings causes conflict and problematic behaviours; conflict and problematic behaviours cause chaotic classrooms; and, chaotic classrooms cause more/worse conflict and problematic behaviours.

3. *However, in order for success to happen, we all have to agree on a set of rules, rewards for following the rules, and consequences for breaking the rules.*

This establishes that there will be rules, that the rules will be out in the open, that the students have the right to help design those rules, and that the teacher also will live by established rules.

This statement sets a tone of collaboration and cooperativeness, rather than having a dictatorial flavor. It also emphasizes that good behaviour is preferred and will be rewarded. The point of this is that in the absence of clearly understood messages, students will infer actions that directly contravene the teacher's intentions and will defend their disruptive/negative behaviours with what appear to be completely valid reasons of non-clarity and/or non-awareness. This part of the conversation also establishes that along with their right to have input into the rule-making process, students must also assume a responsibility for properly fulfilling their obligations.

4. *Now that we have agreed on what our roles and rules will be, let's post the rules, rewards, and consequences on the wall so that we can all refer to them when necessary. Once we see how well they work, we can make changes if needed.*

This statement conveys three things: 1) that the rules will be obvious and explicit, as opposed to "only in the teacher's head"; 2) that the rules will be used and referred to, as opposed to rules that are susceptible to forgetfulness or manipulation; and, 3) that the rules can be changed or modified, as opposed to being rigid or inflexible.

It is advised that the posted rules be written large enough to be seen from anywhere in the classroom. In light of the mutually agreed upon rules posted for all to see, problematic actions and excuses become indefensible. Educators are cautioned to not consider the posting of the rules as inappropriate for older students. In several interventions, the physical presence of the rules acted as a deterrent regardless of student age.

Setting the Class Rules

The best approach to establishing rules is for teachers to announce that everyone will participate in determining what they will be. First, students will devise rules in small groups, then they all engage in an entire class discussion led by one or two students. Every aspect of classroom functioning is up for discussion and the final rules, rewards, and consequences are decided democratically. *Participatory decision-making* (Lickona, 1987) is a collective process amongst teachers and students that holds students accountable for decisions that influence the quality of classroom life. This means not only being part of the rule making, but also being genuinely involved in the welfare of the classroom and taking responsibility for the actions of all students. During the initial stages, teachers should make students acutely aware of the non-negotiable universal rules of the school that are not up for discussion. This enables them to situate their own rules accordingly. There are six suggested universal rules with explanations of their significance (adapted from Edmunds & Edmunds, in press; 2008).

Rule #1: All our rules will be fair and reasonable and will be democratically decided upon. The rules will be posted on the wall for everyone to see and they will be enforced.

Rule #2: Absolutely No Disrespectful Behaviour.
There are three main reasons for this rule: 1) most disrespectful acts are directed at other students – this rule reduces feelings of threat, intimidation and victimization; 2) disrespect is the antithesis of the intent of The Invitation; and 3) there are no positive outcomes from disrespectful behaviour.

Rule #3: No Touching Other People or Their Things
Like disrespectful acts, most unwanted and unnecessary touching is directed towards other students – this causes conflict and usually escalates rapidly into confrontation. Also, there are no positive outcomes from touching others or their belongings.

Rule #4: Talking - Part A: Other than when I am teaching, speaking to someone, or giving directions, you are allowed to talk.
Students talking or not paying attention to the teacher is natural; these acts only become problems when the teacher needs their attention and can't get it, or when the teacher has something to say and students won't listen. This rule is an indicator of mutual respect: the teacher understands students' need to talk and the students understand the teacher's need to get their attention for instructional purposes. It also states there is a reasonable rationale for why the teacher will want their attention as opposed to student silence to satisfy an arbitrary moral or social convention.

Rule #4: Talking - Part B: When you talk, it will be at a reasonable noise level.
This allows for a reasonable amount/level of talking when appropriate but requires self-regulation.

Rule #5: The principal will be aware of all class rules. He/She will support us for our good behaviour and will deal with our bad behaviour according to the rules of the classroom/school.
This rule accomplishes two important objectives: it ensures that class rules are consistent with the overall school rules and it makes sure that students know that the principal knows how their classroom is supposed to function.

Establishing Rewards and Consequences

It makes little sense to design a set of rules if they are not matched with rewards for preferred behaviour, and consequences for bad behaviour. The key is to allow students responsibility for the decision-making as this increases students' commitment to schooling. After the rules have been decided, the entire class is asked to complete the following statements:

– *A reasonable and fair consequence for breaking this rule is ...*
– *A reasonable and fair reward for adhering to this rule is ...*

A serious and pointed discussion and a democratic vote for finalization will quickly reveal preferred rewards and consequences. It should be made clear that rewards and consequences will be used for a set period, then reviewed as needed. Extra school work as a consequence for misbehaviour and better grades for good behaviour are inappropriate and undermine the intended social climate. Contravening or adhering to the classroom's social contract only warrant social or behavioural remedies.

Recommendation #3. Once the rules, rewards, and consequences process has been completed, principals should visit every class and listen as the two designated students explain what the rules, rewards, and consequences of each classroom are, and how those decisions were accomplished.

Students who misbehave and draw the ire of various educators often take psychological refuge in the admiration of their peers. The collective discussion and democratic vetting process involved in the rule-making process, along with the explanation of such to the principal, will serve to eliminate this place of refuge.

Rule Enforcement

While *The Invitation* encourages student participation in establishing the classroom rules, rule enforcement always falls to teachers and principals. Therefore, teachers and principals should make it very clear that they will immediately and consistently enforce all rules and apply the matching rewards and consequences. Clear student understandings and expectations enhance psychological security and reduce anxiety; students will sense that their overall well being is important and is being protected. More importantly, it conveys that educators are willing to act on their convictions. As a result, students see themselves as being in a safe place and as accountable to each other. Moreover, not only is there is no refuge amongst their peers if they misbehave, they may even suffer further social ramifications for their actions.

Behaviour as Problem-Solving Exercise; Not Simply Doling Out Punishment

The six-step model for behaviour problem-solving requires students to acknowledge that a problem exists and that they are part of the solution, thus, removing the burden typically foisted upon teachers to sustain the lone vested interest in classroom harmony. Each step is accompanied but an important message.

Six Steps to Behaviour Problem-Solving (Edmunds & Edmunds, 2008)

1) *STOP!! What is the problem "we are having"?* Indicates that there is an inconsistency between what the teacher expects, what the rules state, and what the student is doing.
2) *Which of our rules is being broken?* Forces the student to acknowledge that there are rules that everyone agreed upon and that he/she broke one of them.

3) What did we agree would be the consequence(s) for breaking that rule? Forces the student to acknowledge that the consequences were also collectively agreed to, and that the consequences are just and fair.

4) What can we do about it? Sends the message that the student will have to do something to pay for his or her actions but that the teacher is supportive and will not belittle him or her.

5) Let's do what we have decided. Sends the message that the consequence has been mutually decided or agreed to and that there is a plan of action.

6) Let's check in later and see how we did. Indicates that there will be supportive follow-up.

While this process is effective, in most instances teachers will inevitably come to a point where they need support from their principal. Again, the fact that this back-up plan exists should be explicitly conveyed to students, not merely implied. This makes it clear that teachers are prepared for out-of-hand problems. Teachers should clearly state that they have had advanced discussions about such support with you, the principal, something like the following;

> There probably will come a time when I will have tried everything I can to resolve a behavioural problem, or it may be that too much time has been spent on a disciplinary issue, and we need to move along. In those instances, I will ask you to go see the principal. However, the principal and I have an understanding that when I send you to see him/her, it is because you will not agree to help me resolve the issue and that he/she will handle it from this point on (Edmunds & Edmunds, 2008; p. 79).

Recommendation #4. Principals should discuss with all teachers the intricacies of the potential disciplinary actions that could be instituted when a student is sent to their office.

Unfortunately, one of the major causes of problems in schools is that principals and teachers often do not properly process a student's return to the classroom. Students usually leave the principal's office unescorted, are expected to return directly to their classroom, and are expected to properly convey to the teacher what was discussed and what consequence was meted out, if any. This faith in students is misguided and simply opens the door to additional problems. Having been admonished by both the teacher and the principal, who probably invoked an unwanted consequence, the student is likely in an agitated and uncooperative state. Given that the student has already engaged in behaviour problematic enough to be sent to the office, it makes no sense whatsoever to rely on the student to now conduct themselves in an appropriate manner. On the contrary – in most instances students are likely to engage in various forms of misbehaviour during transit and probably will not return to their classroom promptly, if at all. Not only that, the student is probably in a foul mood when they finally arrive back at the classroom. This untenable situation undermines the authority of the teacher and sets up an unnecessary power struggle because the teacher is now beholding to the student for the information he/she possesses. The teachers does not know what happened in the principal's office, does not know if or when the student was supposed to be back in class, and does not know what disciplinary action was taken. This completely nullifies any previous arrangements the teacher made with the administrator regarding disciplinary support.

Recommendation #5. Principals should always personally return students to their classrooms. With the student present, they should discuss with the teacher what happened and what was done about it. This makes sure everyone knows what is going on.

Teachers should then take the following steps to provide the student with a smooth transition back into the classroom.

Steps for Classroom Re-entry
(adapted from Edmunds & Edmunds, 2008; p. 80)

1) The teacher indicates to the student that he/she is welcome back into the class. This diminishes the student's feelings of isolation and rejection.
2) The student has a private conversation with the teacher and they go over the six steps in the behaviour problem-solving model. This refocuses the student's attention on the importance of the issue rather than on the consequence. One of the most common student reactions to teacher reprimands is not to focus on what they did wrong, it is to insist that "the teacher doesn't like me." Teachers can mitigate this attempt to personalize the issue (and draw attention away from the offending behaviour) by focusing on the problem, and not on the student per se. The teacher should state "I really like you but I don't like what you did."
3) The teacher indicates that he/she is confident that the student will govern themselves better from now on. This reconfirms the student's sense that they can do it and reconfirms the teacher's expectation that it will be done.
4) The teacher makes it clear that he/she will be keeping an eye on the student to see how <u>well</u> they are doing, not whether he/she steps out of line again.
5) A very short timeline is set (1–2 class maximum) to review how things are going. This allows the student to prove themselves and be acknowledged by the teacher; it also provides another opportunity to review the class rules together.

CONCLUSIONS

Schools that are unpredictable, unstructured, and without established routines feel chaotic and significantly exacerbate problematic behaviours, furthering a school's state of chaos. Haphazard or incomplete behavioural structures increase psychological insecurities, increase learning inefficiencies, and contribute to increasingly problematic behaviours.

The results emanating from the process and recommendations outlined above are in line with the tenets of productive educational environments detailed throughout the literature. This approach has been demonstrated to enhance psychological security and reduce the potential for problematic behaviours. More importantly, higher degrees of social comfort allow students to better manage sudden and/or substantial changes to school routines and/or the disruptive behaviours of their peers. Therefore, the behavioural structures and processes implemented throughout a school must convey the same sense of structure that is demonstrated in well thought out, well prepared, and well executed teaching. While most schools institute behaviour and classroom management systems, such systems are usually devoid of the understandings of behaviour and the explicitness and comprehensiveness of the program described here. Obviously, those systems are also devoid of the influential roles of the principal recommended in this chapter. This is not because principals do not engage in similar actions; rather, it is because they do not engage in them in exactly the same way, or with the same intent and purpose as the research evidence suggests. The five recommendations for principals provided here are logical complements to what their teachers will be doing in all classrooms. The teachers' roles are to design and manage exemplary behavioural systems within their classrooms. The principal's role is to facilitate teachers' constructions of exemplary classrooms, thereby constructing an exemplary and effective behaviour management system for the entire school.

REFERENCES

Berk, L. E. (1996). *Infants and children: Prenatal through middle childhood*. Boston: Allyn & Bacon.

Canter, L., & Canter, M. (1993). *Succeeding with difficult students: New strategies for reaching your most challenging students*. Santa Monica, CA: Lee Canter & Associates.

Dreikurs, R., & Cassel, P. (1992). *Discipline without tears* (2nd ed.). New York: Plume.

Edmunds, A. L., & Edmunds, G. A. (in press). *Educational psychology in Canada*. Toronto, ON: Oxford University Press.

Edmunds, A. L., & Edmunds, G. A. (2008). *Special education in Canada*. Toronto, ON: McGraw-Hill Ryerson.

Evertson, C. M., & Weinstein, C. S. (2006). *Handbook of classroom management: Research, practice, and contemporary issues*. Mahwah, NJ: Lawrence Erlbaum Associates.

Fallona, C., & Richardson, V. (2006). Classroom management as a moral activity. In C. M. Evertson & C. S. Weinstein (Eds.), *Handbook of classroom management: Research, practice, and contemporary issues* (pp. 1041–1062). Mahwah, NJ: Lawrence Erlbaum Associates.

Gettinger, M., & Kohler, K. M. (2006). Process-outcome approaches to classroom management and effective teaching. In C. M. Evertson & C. S. Weinstein (Eds.), *Handbook of classroom management: Research, practice and contemporary issues* (pp. 73–96). Mahwah, NJ: Lawrence Erlbaum Associates.

Johnson, F. L., & Edmunds, A. L. (2006). *From chaos to control: Understanding and responding to the behaviors of students with exceptionalities*. London, ON: The Althouse Press.

Levin, J., & Nolan, J. F. (2000). *Principles of classroom management: A professional decision-making model* (3rd ed.). Boston: Allyn & Bacon.

Lickona, T. (1987). Character development in the elementary school classroom. In K. Ryan & G. F. McLean (Eds.), *Character development in the schools and beyond*. New York: Praeger. Retrieved from http://www.crvp.org/book/Series06/VI-3/chapter_vii.htm

Maag, J. W. (2004). *Behavior management: From theoretical implications to practical applications* (2nd ed., pp. 151–197). Belmont, CA: Thompson Wadsworth.

Marzano, R. J., & Marzano, J. S. (2003). The key to classroom management. *Educational Leadership, 61*(1), 6–13.

McCaslin, M., Bozak, A. R., Napoleon, L., Thomas, A., Vasquez, V., Wayman, V., et al. (2006). Self-regulated learning and classroom management: Theory, research and considerations for classroom practice. In C. M. Evertson & C. S. Weinstein (Eds.), *Handbook of classroom management: Research, practice and contemporary issues* (pp. 223–252). Mahwah, NJ: Lawrence Erlbaum Associates.

Morine-Dershimer, G. (2006). Classroom management and classroom discourse. In C. M. Evertson & C. S. Weinstein (Eds.), *Handbook of classroom management: Research, practice and contemporary issues* (pp. 127–156). Mahwah, NJ: Lawrence Erlbaum Associates.

Nucci, L. (2006). Classroom management for moral and social development. In C. M. Evertson & C. S. Weinstein (Eds.), *Handbook of classroom management: Research, practice, and contemporary issues* (pp. 711–734). Mahwah, NJ: Lawrence Erlbaum Associates.

Paintal, S. (1999). Banning corporal punishment of children. *Childhood Education, 76*, 36–40.

Sugai, G., Horner, R. H., Dunlap, G., Hieneman, M., Lewis, T. J., Nelson, C. M., et al. (2000). Applying positive behavioral support and functional behavioral assessment in schools. Washington, DC: OSEP Center of Positive Behavioral Interventions and Support.

Thomas, A., & Chess, S. (1977). *Temperament and development*. New York: Bruner/Mazel.

.

KENNETH LEITHWOOD

4. THE NATURE OF SUCCESSFUL LEADERSHIP PRACTICES

INTRODUCTION

This chapter describes practices common to successful leaders in many different situations and sectors, but especially in schools. We begin by acknowledging the substantial diversity within the academic literatures about the nature of successful leadership. The plural "literatures" is used, because there is only occasional acknowledgement of research and theory across school and non-school sectors; transformational leadership is the most obvious exception to this general claim with significant numbers of adherents in both camps who interact in print about their work.

For the most part, educational leadership researchers are exclusively concerned with leadership in school organizations. While they occasionally draw on evidence collected elsewhere, they rarely show any interest in extending their own work to other settings. In contrast, leadership researchers working in non-school contexts have typically worried about how well their theories and evidence travel across organizational sectors, although schools have been a relatively minor focus of their attention.

A recent series of related research summaries have described the central elements or the "core practices" or "basics" of successful school leadership (Leithwood & Jantzi, 2005; Leithwood & Riehl, 2005; Leithwood, Seashore-Louis, Anderson, & Wahlstrom, 2004). The four broad categories of practices we identified include:
1) Setting Directions;
2) Developing People;
3) Redesigning the Organization; and
4) Managing the Instructional Program.

Each encompasses a small number of more specific leadership behaviors (14 in total). The bulk of available evidence indicates that these categories are a significant part of the repertoire of successful school leaders whether working in an elementary or secondary school, in a school or a school district/LEA, or in a school in England, the United States, Canada or Hong Kong.

These core practices originated in several different models of transformational leadership – the early work of Burns (1978) and the follow-up empirical work of Podsakoff, MacKenzie, Moorman and Fetter (1990) and Bass (1985). But considerable work with this approach to leadership in district and school contexts has led to the current formulation. We have counted more than 40 published and some 140 unpublished studies focused on many of these leadership practices in

A. L. Edmunds and R. B. Macmillan (eds.), Leadership for Inclusion: A Practical Guide, 33–51.

school and district contexts since about 1990 (e.g., Leithwood & Jantzi, 2005; Leithwood & Sun, 2009). This considerable evidence tells us a good deal about their relative contribution to organizational improvement and student learning. Core practices are not all that people providing leadership in schools do. But they are especially influential on organizational goals. Their value lies in the focus they bring to what leaders attend.

JUSTIFYING THE CORE LEADERSHIP PRACTICES

In this section, we compare other formulations of consequential leadership practices with our core practices in order to further justify our claims about their validity and comprehensiveness. The first set of comparisons is restricted to school-related conceptions of effective leadership practice while the second set looks more broadly in other organizational sectors.

Core Practices and Comparators Based on Research in School Contexts

Although our core practices were developed from a broad array of empirical evidence collected in school contexts, we justify their validity and comprehensiveness by comparing them with behaviors included in the most fully tested model of instructional leadership available in the literature (Hallinger, 2003) and a meta-analysis of empirical evidence about the practices of leaders which demonstrably contribute to student achievement (Marzano et al., 2005).

Hallinger's model of instructional leadership. Instructional leadership has been mostly used as a slogan to focus administrators on their students' progress, but a small number of efforts have attempted to give the term a more precise and useful meaning, including book-length descriptions of instructional leadership (e.g., Andrews & Soder, 1987; Duke, 1987). However, Hallinger (2000), Hallinger and Murphy (1985), and Heck, Larson, and Marcoulides (1990) provide the most fully specified model and by far the most empirical evidence concerning the nature and effects of that model in practice. By one estimate, this evidence now runs to 125 studies reported between 1980 and 2000 (Hallinger, 2003). Three categories of practices are included in the model, each encompassing a total of 10 more specific practices:

1) *defining the school's mission* includes framing and communicating the school's goals;
2) *managing the instructional program* includes supervising and evaluating instruction, coordinating the curriculum, and monitoring student progress; and
3) *promoting a positive school learning climate* encompasses protecting instructional time, promoting professional development, maintaining high visibility, and providing incentives for teachers and for learning.

Hallinger's (2003) review of instructional leadership found that mission-building activities by principals are the most influential set of leadership practices.

Marzano, waters, and McNulty's meta-analysis. A paper and subsequent book (2005) by these authors report the results of a meta-analysis of 70 empirical studies reported over a 30 year period which included objective measures of student achievement and teacher reports of leadership behaviors. The main product of the analysis is the identification of 21 leadership "responsibilities" which contribute significantly to student achievement. These responsibilities are exercised in degree; the more the better. We consider 17 of these to be "behaviors" while the remaining four are traits or dispositions (Knowledge of curriculum, ideals/beliefs, flexibility, situational awareness).

Table 1 summarizes the relationship between our core practices, the behaviors included in Hallinger's (2003) instructional leadership model, Marzano, Waters, and McNulty's (Marzano et al., 2005) meta-analysis. All behaviors included in the two comparators are encompassed by our core leadership practices with the exception of a category called "Communication" (establishes strong lines of communication with teachers and among students) in the Marzano et al. analysis. Communication is an undeniably important skill and behavior for people in many walks of life – certainly for those in leadership roles – but we have chosen to focus on behaviors relatively unique to those in leadership roles.

Table 1. Core practices of successful school leaders compared with successful practices reflected in other school-related sources

Core Leadership Practices	Hallinger's Model of Instructional Leadership	Marzano et al. Meta-analysis
Setting Directions		
Vision	Developing a clear mission focused on students' academic progress	Inspires and leads new & challenging innovations
Goals	Framing the school's goals Communicating the school's goals	Establishes clear goals and keeps them in forefront of attention
High performance expectations		
Developing People		
Individualized support/consideration	Providing incentives for teachers	Recognizes & rewards individual accomplishment Demonstrates awareness of personal aspects of teachers and staff
Intellectual stimulation	Promoting professional development	Is willing to, and actively challenges, the status quo Ensures faculty & staff are well informed about best practice/fosters regular discussion of them

Table 1. (continued)

Modelling	Maintaining high visibility	Has quality contacts & interactions with teachers and students)
Redesigning the Organisation		
Building a collaborative culture		Fosters shared beliefs, sense of community, cooperation Recognizes and celebrates school accomplishments & acknowledges failures Involves Ts in design and implementation of important decisions and policies
Structuring the organization to facilitate work	Providing incentives for learning	
Creating productive relations with families & communities		Is an advocate & spokesperson for school to all stakeholders
Connecting the school to its wider environment		
Managing the Instructional Programme		
Staffing		
Providing instructional support	Supervising & evaluating instruction Coordinating the curriculum	Establishes set of standard operating procedures & routines Provides materials necessary for job Directly involved in design & implementation of curriculum, instruction and assessment practices
Monitoring	Monitoring student progress	Monitors the effectiveness of school practices & their impact on student learning
Buffering	Protecting instructional time	Protects teachers from issues & influences that would detract them from their teaching time or focus

Core Practices and Comparators Based on Research in Non-school Contexts

Substantial evidence demonstrates the value of our core leadership practices in school, in non-school contexts, and in quite diverse national cultures. While the fourth and most recently added category, Managing the Instructional Program, seems unique to schools, it is easily applicable to other organizations, slightly reworded, as Managing the Organization's Core Technology. Evidence in support of this claim in school contexts can be found in Geijsel, Sleegers, Leithwood and Jantzi. (2003). See Bass (1985) for evidence of this claim in the business and military sectors.

In this section, we compare the core practices with two other sources of evidence about key leadership practices justified by evidence primarily collected in non-school organizational contexts – Yukl's (1994) taxonomy of managerial behaviors and a synopsis of a significant selection of alternative leadership "models" or theories.

Yukl's taxonomy. This classification of important leader or manager behaviors synthesizes seven earlier behavioral taxonomies, each of which built on quite substantial empirical and/or theoretical foundations. Yukl (1994) found many points of agreement across these taxonomies and identified 14 managerial behaviors reflecting these areas of agreement. Table 2 compares our four core practices of successful school leadership with Yukl's "managerial behaviors". Described in some detail by Yukl (1989, 1994), these behaviors included planning and organizing, problem solving, clarifying roles and objectives, informing, monitoring, motivating and inspiring, consulting, delegating, supporting, developing and mentoring, managing conflict and team building, networking, recognizing, and rewarding.

Alternative leadership theories. A recent review (Yammarino, Dionne, Chun, & Dansereau, 2005) of leadership theories largely developed in non-school contexts pointed to 21 approaches or models that have been the object of considerable, though quite varying, amounts of theoretical and empirical development. Seventeen of these approaches have attracted an impressive amount of research attention. We provide a brief synopsis of the main theories prior to comparing the behaviors they highlight with our core leadership practices.

Ohio State model. This highly durable, two-dimensional conception of leadership includes two leadership "styles" - initiating structure (a task-oriented and directive style) and consideration (a friendly, supportive style). Each style is considered to be differentially effective depending on such variables as the size of the organization, how clear people are about their roles, and how mature people are in their jobs.

Contingency theory. This two-dimensional conception of leadership explains differences in leaders' effectiveness in terms of a task or relationship style (as with the Ohio State model) and the situation in which leaders find themselves.

Task-oriented leaders are predicted to be more successful in high- and low-control settings, whereas relationships-oriented leaders are predicted to be more successful in moderate- control settings. To be most effective, then, leaders' styles need to match the setting.

Participative leadership model. This approach is concerned with how leaders select among three distinct approaches to their colleagues' participation in organizational decisions: an autocratic approach allows for almost no member participation; a consultative approach restricts participation to providing information and; a more extensive and inclusive form of participation called "collaborative sharing". The choice among these forms is based on achieving such goals as improving decision quality, increasing the development of those to be involved and minimizing decision costs and time.

Situational leadership. Also oriented to the level of follower's development, this approach varies the extent to which the leader engages in task-oriented and relationship-oriented practices (Hersey & Blanchard, 1984). According to this theory, as follower maturity develops from low to moderate levels, the leader should engage in more relations behaviors and fewer task behaviors. Decreased behaviors of both types are called for as followers move from moderate to maximum levels of maturity; leadership should be delegated with considerable autonomy for its performance.

Path-goal theory. Yukl describes this motivational approach to leadership as consisting of "....increasing personal payoffs to subordinates for work-goal attainment and making the path to these payoffs easier to travel by clarifying it, reducing roadblocks and pitfalls, and increasing the opportunities for satisfaction en-route" (1989, p. 99). Organizational members make the effort to succeed only if they believe valued outcomes can be accomplished through serious effort. Depending on the situation, leadership may contribute to such beliefs by being supportive, directive, participative or achievement-oriented.

Vertical dyad linkage model, leader-member exchange (LMX) theory and individual-ized leadership theory. Beginning with vertical dyad concepts and developing into LMX, this approach recognizes that leaders treat members of the same group differently. Until its development, the common assumption was that all members of the organization experienced the same relationship with leaders. Leader-member exchanges can result in some members becoming part of an "in-group", enjoying the trust and confidence of leaders, or an "out-group", experiencing a more distant and formal relationship with leaders. Leaders and their individual colleagues, more generally, develop unique, one-to-one relationships as they influence each other and negotiate the role of the follower. This individual, rather than group, focus led to the development of individualized leader theory. Each leader/follower dyad involves investments by the leader in and returns from the follower as well as followers' investments in and returns from the leader. Leaders secure followership, for example, by supporting a follower's feelings of self-worth.

Transformational and charismatic leadership. These closely related approaches to leadership are defined in terms of leaders' influence over their colleagues and the nature of leader-follower relations. Transformational leaders (e.g., Dumdum, Lowe, & Avolio, 2002) need not be charismatic (e.g. Kim, Dansereau, & Kim, 2002), although some argue that it is the key component of such leadership and the only quality that accounts for extraordinary or outstanding leadership. Typical of both forms are such behaviors as communicating a compelling vision, conveying high performance expectations, projecting self confidence, role modelling, expressing confidence in followers' abilities to achieve goals, emphasizing collective purpose and identity. Charismatic leaders engender exceptionally high levels of trust, loyalty, respect, and commitment. But some of these outcomes depend on whether the charismatic leadership is socialized or personal. Socialized charismatic leaders are also transformational; that is, they help bring about desirable improvement in the organization. They acquire the commitment through the compelling nature of their vision and ideas, and through their genuine concern for the welfare of their colleagues. Personalized charismatics are unlikely to be transformational. They are attributed charismatic stature by virtue of their attractive personal qualities, for example. But they are prone to exploiting others, to serving their own self interests and to having a very high need for power.

Substitutes for leadership. This conception of leadership, introduced by Kerr and Jermier in 1978, has enjoyed a significant following in spite of difficulties in producing evidence confirming its central propositions. From this perspective, leadership can be a property of the organization as much as something engaged in by a person. Furthermore, features of the organizational setting either enhance or neutralize the influence of people attempting to function as leaders – engaging in either task or relationship-oriented functions. Routine and highly standardized tasks that provide their own outcome feedback, cohesive work groups, no control over rewards and spatial distance between leaders and followers are among the conditions hypothesized to neutralize task-oriented leadership. Relationship-oriented leadership, theorists argue, is neutralized by colleagues' need for independence, professional orientation and indifference to organizational rewards (Yammarino et al., 2005).

Romance of leadership. This follower-centric view of leadership (Meindl, 1998) is premised on the claim that leadership is an overrated explanation for organizational events. Its attraction may be a function of the simple, if incorrect, explanation it provides for quite complex and difficult to understand organizational events. Furthermore, there is a social contagion associated with leadership attributions; people begin to persuade one another of the importance of leadership quite apart from any other evidence that it matters. As Yammarino and his coauthors explain "Heroic social identification, articulation of an appealing ideology, symbols, rituals and rites of passage all play a role in this process" (2005, p. 900).

Self leadership. The focus of this theory and research concerns the strategies that individuals and groups can use to improve their own leadership capacities (Markham & Markham, 1998). To the extent that such strategies are available and have the desired effect, self management and self leadership has the potential to increase employee empowerment and reduce the resources devoted to traditional sources of leadership and supervision.

Multiple linkage. Developed by Yukl and his colleagues (e.g., Yukl, 1998), this approach includes the fourteen managerial behaviors identified in Table 1, along with a set of intervening and situational variables, along the lines of the framework used for our review. According to Yammarino, "The model proposes that leaders institute short-term actions to deal with deficiencies in the intervening variables and positively impact group performance in the long term" (2005, p. 901).

Table 2. Core practices of successful school leaders compared with successful practices identified in non-school organizational contexts

Core Leadership Practices	Yukl's taxonomy of managerial behavior	Alternative leadership theories
SETTING DIRECTIONS		
Vision	Motivating and inspiring	Charismatic and Transformational theory
Goals	Clarifying roles and objectives Planning and organizing	Substitutes theory
High performance expectations		Charismatic & Transformational theory
DEVELOPING PEOPLE		
Individualized support/consideration	Supporting Developing and mentoring Recognizing Rewarding	Ohio State, Contingency Model, Path-goal theory Transformational theory LMX, Individualized leadership
Intellectual stimulation		Transformational theory
Modelling		Charismatic and Transformational theory
REDESIGNING THE ORGANIZATION		
Building a collaborative culture	Managing conflict and team building Delegating Consulting	Participative Leadership,

Table 2. (continued)

Structuring the organization to facilitate work		Ohio State, Contingency Model, Participative Leadership, Path-goal theory
Creating productive relations with families & communities		
Connecting the school to its wider environment	Networking	
Managing the Instructional Programme		
Staffing		
Resources		
Monitoring	Monitoring	
Buffering		

Table 2 indicates considerable endorsement for our core practices from both Yukl's taxonomy and our selection of leadership theories. Only one practice or function identified in these two sources is not reflected in the core practices, Yukl's problem solving "behavior". Expertise in problem solving makes a crucial contribution to a leader's success. In this review, however, we treat it not as a behavior, but as a cognitive activity leading to behavior. Evidence about successful leaders' problem solving is reviewed as part of our treatment of the roots or antecedents of successful leadership practice.

Our selection of leadership theories includes much more about leadership than simply behaviors; for example, propositions about how behaviors and elements of the context interact to produce favorable outcomes. These additional features go beyond our purposes here, however.

A THEORETICAL (BUT PRACTICAL) PERSPECTIVE ON THE CORE PRACTICES

Lists of things - like leadership practices - are not very meaningful unless some underlying idea holds them together. The great advantage of leadership theories, for example, as compared with the many lists of leadership standards, is that the theories possess a conceptual glue almost entirely missing from the standards. This glue offers an explanation for how and why things work as they do and so builds understanding. We limit ourselves here to a type of glue which aims to explain why each of the main categories of our core practices is important to exercise if leaders are to have a substantial and positive impact.

The extent to which educational policies and other reform efforts improve what students learn finally depends on their consequences for what teachers do. And what teachers do, according to a particularly useful model for explaining workplace performance (O'Day, 1996; Rowan, 1996) is a function of their motivations, abilities, and the situations in which they work. The relationship among these variables can be represented in the deceptively simple formula of

$$Pj = f(Mj, Aj, Sj)$$

where P stands for a teacher's performance, M stands for the teacher's motivation (in Yukl's, 1989, Multiple Linkage model of managerial effectiveness, M includes the effort to engage in a high level of performance as well as demonstrating a high degree of personal responsibility and commitment to the organization's goals), A stands for the teacher's abilities, professional knowledge, and skills (in Yukl's model, such performance also includes their understanding of their job responsibilities), and S represents their work settings – the features of their school, and classroom.

Relationships among the variables are considered to be interdependent. This means two things. First, each variable has an effect on the remaining two (for example, aspects of teachers' work environments are significant influences on their motivations). Second, changes in all three variables need to happen in concert or performance will not change much. For example, neither high ability and low motivation, nor high motivation and low ability foster high levels of teacher performance; neither does high ability and high motivation in a dysfunctional work environment. Furthermore, a dysfunctional work setting will likely depress initially high levels of both ability and motivation.

The implications for leadership practice of this account of workplace performance are twofold. First, leaders need to engage in practices with the potential to improve all elements in the formula – teachers and other staff members' abilities, motivations and the settings in which they work. Second, leaders need to engage in those practices more or less simultaneously. The overall function of successful leaders, according to this formulation, is to improve the condition of all three variables.

Setting Directions

This category of practices carries the bulk of the effort to motivate leaders' colleagues (Hallinger & Heck, 1998). It is about the establishment of "moral purpose" (Fullan, 2003; Hargreaves & Fink, 2006) as a basic stimulant for one's work. Most theories of motivation argue that people are motivated to accomplish personally important goals for themselves. For example, such goals are one of four sources of motivation in Bandura's theory of human motivation (1986).

Three more specific sets of practices are included in this category, all of which are aimed at bringing a focus to both the individual and collective work of staff in the school or district. Done skillfully, these practices are one of the main sources of motivation and inspiration for the work of staff.

Building a shared vision. Building compelling visions of the organization's future is a fundamental task included in both transformational and charismatic leadership models. Bass's (1985) "inspirational motivation" is encompassed in this practice, and which Podsakoff defines as leadership behavior "aimed at identifying new opportunities for his or her unit....and developing, articulating, and inspiring others with his or her vision of the future" (1990, p. 112). Silins and Mulford (2002b) found positive and significant effects of a shared and monitored mission. Harris and Chapman's small scale qualitative study of effective leadership in schools facing challenging circumstances reported that:

> Of central importance ... was the cooperation and alignment of others to [the leader's] set of values and vision ... Through a variety of symbolic gestures and actions, they were successful at realigning both staff and pupils to their particular vision. (2002, p. 6)

Locke (2002) argues that formulating a vision for the organization is one of eight core tasks for senior leaders and a key mechanism for achieving integration or alignment of activities within the organization. After Locke, we include as part of vision building, the establishment of core organizational values. Core values specify the means by which the vision is to be accomplished.

Fostering the acceptance of group goals. While visions can be inspiring, action typically requires some agreement on the more immediate goals to be accomplished to move toward the vision. Building on such theory, this set of practices aims not only to identify important goals, but to do so in such a way that individuals come to include the organization's goals among their own. Unless this happens, the organization's goals have no motivational value; leaders can spend a lot of time on this set of practices, but giving short shrift misses the point entirely. This set of practices includes leader behaviors "....aimed at promoting cooperation among [teachers] and getting them to work together toward a common goal" (Podsakoff et al., 1990, p. 112).

In district and school settings, strategic and improvement planning processes are among the more explicit contexts in which these behaviors are manifest. One of the eleven effective managerial behaviors included in Yukl's Multiple Linkage model, "planning and organizing", encompasses a portion of these practices. Planning and organizing include "Determining long-range objectives and strategies..., identifying necessary steps to carry out a project or activity..." (1989, p. 130).

High performance expectations. This set of practices is part of direction setting because it is closely aligned with goals. While high performance expectations do not define the substance of organizational goals, they demonstrate "the leader's expectations of excellence, quality, and/or high performance" (Podsakoff et al., 1990, p. 112) in the achievement of those goals. Demonstrating such expectations is a central behavior in virtually all conceptions of transformational and charismatic leadership.

Developing People

The three sets of practices in this category contribute significantly to motivation and primarily aim at capacity building by building not only the knowledge and skill staff need to accomplish organizational goals, but also the dispositions to persist in

K. LEITHWOOD

applying that knowledge and skill (Harris & Chapman, 2002). Individual teacher efficacy is arguably the most critical of these dispositions and it is a third source of motivation in Bandura's (1986) model. People are motivated by what they are good at. And *mastery experiences*, according to Bandura, are the most powerful sources of efficacy. Building capacity leading to a sense of mastery is also highly motivational.

Providing individualized support/consideration. Bass and Avolio include, as part of this dimension, "knowing your followers' needs and raising them to more mature levels...[sometimes through] the use of delegation to provide opportunities for each follower to self-actualize and to attain higher standards of moral development" (1994, p. 64). This set of behaviors should communicate the leader's respect for colleagues and concerns about their personal feelings and needs (Podsakoff et al., 1990). This is a set of practices common to all of the two-dimensional models of leadership discussed above, and includes task orientation and *consideration for people.* This set of practices includes "supporting", and "recognizing and rewarding" managerial behaviors associated with Yukl's (1989) Multiple Linkage model, with Hallinger's (2003) model of instructional leadership and with the Marzano's et al. (2005) meta-analysis. This set of leadership behaviors has likely attracted more leadership research outside of schools since the 1960s than any other.

Intellectual stimulation. Behaviors in this dimension include encouraging colleagues to take intellectual risks, re-examine assumptions, look at their work from different perspectives, rethink how it can be performed (Avolio, 1994; Podsakoff et al., 1990), and otherwise "induc[e]...employees to appreciate, dissect, ponder and discover what they would not otherwise discern..." (Lowe, Kroeck, & Sivasubramaniam, 1996, p. 415–416). Marzano et al (2005) include "challenging the status quo" among the practices contributing to leader effects on students.

This is where the leader's role in professional development is key, especially for leaders of schools in challenging circumstances (Gray, 2000). *Intellectual Stimulation* recognizes the many informal, as well as formal, ways development occurs, and reflects our current understandings of learning as constructed, socially and contextually. All models of transformational and charismatic leadership include this set of practices. A considerable amount of the educational literature assumes such practices on the part of school leaders, especially the literature on instructional leadership which places school leaders at the centre of instructional improvement efforts (e.g., Hallinger, 2003; Stein & Spillane, 2005).

Providing an appropriate model. This category entails "leading by example," a general set of practices associated with models of "authentic leadership" (Avolio & Gardner, 2005), demonstrating transparent decision making, confidence, optimism, hope, resiliency and consistency between words and deeds. Locke (2002) claims that core values are established by modelling core values in one's own practices.

44

Both Hallinger (2003) and Marzano et al (2005) note the contribution to leader effects of maintaining high visibility in the school, a visibility associated with high quality interactions with both staff and students. Harris and Chapman found that their successful heads "modeled behavior that they considered desirable to achieve the school goals" (2002, p. 6).

Also encompassed by this dimension is Bass's "idealized influence," a partial replacement for his original "charisma" dimension: Avolio (1994) claims that leaders exercise idealized influence when they serve as role models with the appropriate behaviors and attitudes required to build trust and respect in followers. Such modeling on the part of leaders "…sets an example for employees to follow that is consistent with the values the leader espouses" (Podsakoff et al., 1990, p. 112).

Redesigning the Organization

This is the "S", or situation, or working conditions variable in our equation for predicting levels of performance described earlier. Little is to be gained by increasing peoples' motivation and capacity if working conditions will not allow their effective application. In Bandura's (1986) model, beliefs about the situation is a fourth source of motivation; people are motivated when they believe the circumstances in which they find themselves are conducive to accomplishing the goals they hold to be personally important. The three practices included in this category are about establishing the conditions of work which allow staff to make the most of their motivations and capacities.

Building collaborative cultures. A large body of evidence has accumulated since Little's (1982) early research which unambiguously supports the importance of collaborative cultures in schools as central to school improvement, the development of professional learning communities and the improvement of student learning (e.g., Louis & Kruse, 1998; Rosenholtz, 1989). Additional evidence clearly indicates that leaders are able to build more collaborative cultures and suggests practices that accomplish this goal (e.g., Leithwood, Jantzi, & Dart, 1990; Marzano et al., 2005). For leaders of schools in challenging circumstances, creating more positive collaborative and achievement-oriented cultures is a key task (West, Ainscow, & Stanford, 2005).

Connolly and James (2006) claim that the success of collaborative activity is determined by the capacity and motivation of collaborators along with opportunities for them to collaborate. Success also depends on prior conditions. For example, a history of working together will sometimes build trust, making further collaboration easier. Trust is increasingly recognized as a key element in encouraging collaboration: individuals are more likely to trust those with whom they have established good relationships (Bryk & Schneider, 2002; Louis & Kruse, 1995). Participative leadership theory and Leader-member exchange theory are concerned with the nature and quality of collaboration in organizations and how to manage it productively.

Leaders contribute to productive collaborative activity in their schools by being skilled conveners of that work. They nurture mutual respect and trust among those involved in collaborating, ensure the shared determination of group processes and outcomes, help develop clarity about goals and roles for collaboration, encourage a willingness to compromise, foster open and fluent communication, and provide adequate and consistent resources in support of collaborative work (Connolly & James, 2006; Mattessich & Monsey, 1992).

Restructuring. This is a function or behavior common to virtually all conceptions of management and leadership practice. Organizational culture and structure are two sides of the same coin. Developing and sustaining collaborative cultures depends on putting in place complementary structures, typically something requiring leadership initiative. Practices associated with such initiatives include creating common planning times for teachers, and establishing team and group structures for problem solving (e.g., Hadfield, 2003). Hallinger and Heck (1998) identify this variable as a key mediator of leaders' effects on students. Restructuring also includes distributing leadership for selected tasks and increasing teacher involvement in decision making (Reeves, 2000).

Building productive relationships with families and communities. Shifting the attention of school staffs from an exclusively inside-the-school focus to one which embraces a meaningful role for parents and a close relationship with the larger community was identified during the 1990s as the biggest change in expectations for those in formal school leadership roles (e.g., Goldring & Rallis, 1993). More recently, Muijs, Harris, Chapman, Stoll and Russ (2004) identified this core practice as important for improving schools in challenging circumstances. Attention to this focus has been encouraged by evidence of the contribution of family educational cultures to student achievement (e.g., Coleman, 1966; Finn, 1989), the increase in public accountability of schools to their communities through the widespread implementation of school-based management (Murphy & Beck, 1995), and the growing need for schools to actively manage public perceptions of their legitimacy (e.g., Mintrop, 2004).

Connecting the school to its wider environment. School leaders spend significant amounts of time in contact with people outside of their schools, seeking information and advice, staying in tune with policy changes, anticipating new pressures and trends likely to have an influence on their schools. Meetings, informal conversations, phone calls, email exchanges and internet searches are examples of opportunities for accomplishing these purposes. The extensive number of Network Learning projects facilitated by the National College of School Leadership in England provides especially powerful opportunities for connecting one's school to its wider educational environment (Jackson, 2002). Bringing in external support may also be a productive response by schools engaged in significant school improvement projects (Reynolds, Hopkins, Potter, & Chapman, 2001).

Considerable time is spent by school leaders on this function, but we are unaware of any research, to date, that has inquired about its contribution to improving pupil learning and/or the quality of the school organization. However, research has been conducted about the effects of this practice in non-school organizations. Referring to it as "networking", Yukl includes it in his Multiple Linkage model of leadership as one of eleven critical managerial practices. He describes this practice as "Socializing informally, developing contacts with people who are a source of information and support, and maintaining contacts through periodic interaction, including visits, telephone calls, correspondence, and attendance at meetings and social events" (1994, p. 69).

Managing the Instructional Program

There is some potential confusion about the effects of this set of practices. Surprisingly, Hallinger's (2003) review suggested that those management practices involving close association with the classroom and supervision of what happens in the classroom appear to have the least effect on students. On the other hand, when managerial behaviors have been included in other recent research on school leadership effects, they have explained almost as much as did leadership behaviors (e.g., Leithwood & Jantzi, 1999). These behaviours are important, especially those that create stability and strengthen the infrastructure, but those of a more supervisory nature seem not to be.

Staffing the program. Although not touched on by Hallinger (2003) or Marzano et al. (2005), this has proven to be a key function of leaders engaged in school improvement. Finding teachers with the interest and capacity to further the school's efforts is the goal of this activity. Recruitment and reteention is a primary task when leading schools in challenging circumstances (Gray, 2000).

Providing instructional support. This set of practices, included by Hallinger (2003) and Marzano et al. (2005), encompasses "supervising and evaluating instruction", "coordinating the curriculum" and providing resources in support of curriculum, instruction and assessment activity. For leaders of schools in challenging contexts, focusing on teaching and learning is essential (West et al., 2005), including controlling behavior, boosting self-esteem, and talking and listening to pupils. It also may include urging pupils and teachers to put a strong emphasis on pupil achievement, thus creating an "academic climate" that makes significant contributions to achievement (De Maeyer, Rymenans, Van Petegem, van der Bergh, & Rijlaarsdam, 2006).

Monitoring school activity. The analysis by Marzano et al. (2005) associated leadership effects on students with leader monitoring and evaluating functions, especially those focused on student progress. The purposeful use of data is reported by West et al. (2005) to be a central explanation for effective leadership in failing schools. Hallinger's (2003) model includes a set of practices labelled "monitoring student progress". Monitoring operations and environment is one of Yukl's (1989) eleven effective managerial practices, and Gray (2000) reports that tracking student progress is a key task for leaders of schools in challenging circumstances.

Buffering staff from distractions to their work. A long line of research has reported the value of leaders who prevent staff from being pulled in directions incompatible with agreed on goals. This buffering function acknowledges the open nature of schools and the constant bombardment of staff with expectations from parents, media, special interest groups and government. Internal buffering is also helpful, especially buffering teachers from excessive pupil disciplinary activity.

The four sets of leadership practices in this category provide the coordination for initiatives stimulated by the other core leadership practices. They help provide the stability necessary for improvement to occur.

CONCLUSION

Four broad categories of leadership practices – and fourteen more specific categories – capture our review of the evidence about what effective leaders do. They do not do all of these things all of the time, of course; you don't have to create a shared vision everyday. And the way you go about each set of practices will certainly vary by context. If your school has been labelled as "failing," you likely do more selling of your vision to staff than developing it collaboratively – so you can get on with your turnaround mission. So what is contingent about leadership is not the basic or core practices, but the way they are enacted. The enactment must be sensitive to context, not the core practices themselves. The core practices provide a powerful source of guidance for leaders, and a framework for their initial and continuing development.

Significant sections of this chapter are based on Leithwood, K., Day, C., Sammons, P., Harris, A., & Hopkins, D. (2006). *Successful school leadership: What it is and how it influences student learning.* Nottingham: Research Report 800 prepared for the National College of School Leadership and the Department for Education and Skills.

REFERENCES

Andrews, R., & Soder, R. (1987). Principal leadership and student achievement. *Educational Leadership, 44,* 9–11.

Avolio, B. J. (1994). The alliance of total quality and the full range of leadership. In B. M. Bass & B. J. Avolio (Eds.), *Improving organizational effectiveness through transformational leadership* (pp. 121–145). Thousand Oaks, CA: Sage.

Bandura, A. (1986). *Social foundations of thought and action.* Englewood Cliffs, NJ: Prentice Hall.

Bass, B. M. (1985). *Leadership and performance beyond expectations.* New York: The Free Press.

Bass, B. M., & Avolio, B. J. (1994). *Improving organizational effectiveness through transformational leadership.* Thousand Oaks, CA: Sage.

Bryk, A. S., & Schneider, B. (2002). *Trust in schools: A core resource for improvement.* New York: Russell Sage Foundation.

Burns, J. M. (1978). *Leadership.* New York: Harper & Row Publishers.

Coleman, J. S. (1966). *Equality of educational opportunity.* Washington, DC: Government Printing Office.

Connolly, M., & James, C. (2006). Collaboration for school improvement: A resource dependency and institutional framework of analysis. *Educational Management Administration and Leadership, 34*(1), 69–87.

De Maeyer, S., Rymenans, R., Van Petegem, P., van der Bergh, H., & Rijlaarsdam, G. (2006). *Educational leadership and pupil achievement: The choice of a valid conceptual model to test effects in school effectiveness research.* Unpublished paper: University of Antwerp.

Duke, D. L. (1987). *School leadership and instructional improvement.* New York: Random House.

Dumdum, U. R., Lowe, K. B., & Avolio, B. J. (2002). A meta-analysis of transformational and transactional leadership correlates of effectiveness and satisfaction: An update and extension. In B. J. Avolio & F. J. Yammarino (Eds.), *Transformational and charismatic leadership: The road ahead* (pp. 35–66). Oxford, UK: Elsevier Science Ltd.

Finn, J. D. (1989). Withdrawing from school. *Review of Educational Research, 59*(2), 117–143.

Fullan, M. (2003). *The moral imperative of school leadership.* Thousand Oaks, CA: Corwin Press.

Geijsel, F., Sleegers, P., Leithwood, K., & Jantzi, D. (2003). The effect of teacher psychological and school organizational and leadership factors on teachers' professional learning in Dutch schools. *Journal of Educational Administration, 41*, 228–256.

Goldring, E., & Rallis, S. (1993). *Principals of dynamic schools.* Newbury Park, CA: Corwin Press.

Gray, J. (2000). *Causing concern but improving: A review of schools' experience.* London: Department for Education and Skills.

Hadfield, M. (2003). Building capacity versus growing schools. In A. Harris, C. Day, D. Hopkins, M. Hadfield, A. Hargreaves, & C. Chapman (Eds.), *Effective leadership for school improvement* (pp. 107–120). New York: RoutledgeFalmer.

Hallinger, P. (2000). *A review of two decades of research on the principalship using the Principal Instructional Management Rating Scale.* Paper presented at the annual meeting of the American Educational Research Association, Seattle, WA.

Hallinger, P. (2003). Leading educational change: Reflections on the practice of instructional and transformational leadership. *Cambridge Journal of Education, 33*(3), 329–351.

Hallinger, P., & Heck, R. (1998). Exploring the principal's contribution to school effectiveness: 1980–1995. *School Effectiveness and School Improvement*, (9), 157–191.

Hallinger, P., & Murphy, J. (1985). Assessing the instructional management behavior of principals. *Elementary School Journal, 86*, 217–247.

Hargreaves, A., & Fink, D. (2006). *Sustainable leadership.* San Francisco: Jossey-Bass.

Harris, A., & Chapman, C. (2002). *Effective leadership in schools facing challenging circumstances.* Nottingham, UK: National College for School Leadership (NCSL).

Heck, R. H., Larsen, T. J., & Marcoulides, G. A. (1990). Instructional leadership and school achievement: Validation of a causal model. *Educational Administration Quarterly, 26*, 94–125.

Hersey, P., & Blanchard, K. H. (1984). *The management of organizational behavior* (4th ed.). Englewood Cliffs, NJ: Prentice Hall.

Jackson, D. (2002). *The creation of knowledge networks: Collaborative enquiry for school and system improvement.* Paper presented at the CERI/OECD/DfES/QCA ESRC Forum 'Knowledge Management in Education and Learning', Oxford, UK.

Kerr, S., & Jermier, J. M. (1978). Substitutes for leadership: Their meaning and measurement. *Organizational Behavior and Human Performance, 22*, 375–403.

Kim, K., Dansereau, F., & Kim, I. (2002). Extending the concept of charismatic leadership: An illustration using Bass (1990) categories. In B. Avolio & J. F. Yammarino (Eds.), *Transformational and charismatic leadership: The road ahead* (pp. 143–172). Oxford, UK: Elsevier Science.

Leithwood, K., & Sun, J. P. (2009). Transformational school leadership effects on schools, teachers and students. In W. Hoy & M. DiPaola (Eds.), *Studies in school improvement* (pp. 1–22). Charlotte, NC: Information Age Publishers.

Leithwood, K., & Jantzi, D. (2005). A review of transformational school leadership research: 1996–2005. *Leadership and Policy in Schools, 4*(3), 177–199.

Leithwood, K., & Jantzi, D. (1999). The relative effects of principal and teacher sources of leadership on student engagement with school. *Educational Administration Quarterly, 35*(Suppl.), 679–706.

Leithwood, K., Jantzi, D., & Dart, B. (1990). Transformational leadership: how principals can help reform school cultures. *School Effectiveness and School Improvement, 1*(4), 249–280.

Leithwood, K., & Riehl, C. (2005). What we know about successful school leadership. In W. Firestone & C. Riehl (Eds.), *A new agenda: Directions for research on educational leadership* (pp. 22–47). New York: Teachers College Press.

Leithwood, K., Seashore-Louis, K., Anderson, S., & Wahlstrom, K. (2004). *How leadership influences student learning: A review of research for the Learning from Leadership Project.* New York: The Wallace Foundation.

Little, J. (1982). Norms of collegiality and experimentation: Workplace conditions of school success. *American Educational Research Journal, 19,* 325–340.

Locke, E. A. (2002). The leaders as integrator: The case of Jack Welch at General Electric. In L. L. Neider & C. Schriesheim (Eds.), *Leadership* (pp. 1–22). Greenwich, CT: Information Age Publishing.

Louis, K., & Kruse, S. (1995). *Professionalism and community: Perspectives on reforming urban schools.* Newbury Park, CA: Corwin Press.

Louis, K. S., & Kruse, S. D. (1998). Creating community in reform: Images of organizational learning in inner-city schools. In K. Leithwood & K. S. Louis (Eds.), *Organizational learning in schools* (pp. 17–45). Lisse, The Netherlands: Swets & Zeitlinger.

Lowe, K. B., Kroeck, K. G., & Sivasubramaniam, N. (1996). Effectiveness correlates of transformational and transactional leadership: A meta-analytical review of the MLQ literature. *Leadership Quarterly, 7*(3), 385–425.

Markham, S. E., & Markham, I. S. (1998). Self-management and self-leadership reexamined: A levels-of-analysis perspective. In F. Dansereau & F. Yammarino (Eds.), *Leadership: The multi-level approaches Part A* (pp. 193–210). Stamford, CT: JAI Press Inc.

Marzano, R. J., Waters, T., & McNulty, B. A. (2005). *School leadership that works: From research to results.* Alexandria, VA: Association for Supervision and Curriculum Development.

Mattessich, P. W., & Monsey, B. R. (1992). *Collaboration: What makes it work?* St. Paul, MN: Amherst H. Wilder Foundation.

Meindl, J. R. (1998). The romance of leadership as follower-centric theory: A social constructionist approach. In F. Dansereau & F. Yammarino (Eds.), *Leadership: The multi-level approaches Part B* (pp. 285–298). Stamford, CT: JAI Press Inc.

Mintrop, H. (2004). *Schools on probation: How accountability works (and doesn't work).* New York: Teachers College Press.

Muijs, D., Harris, A., Chapman, C., Stoll, L., & Russ, J. (2004). Improving schools in socieconomically disadvantaged areas—A review of research evidence. *School Effectiveness and School Improvement, 15*(2), 149–175.

Murphy, J., & Beck, L. (1995). *School-based management as school reform.* Thousand Oaks, CA: Corwin Press.

O'Day, J. (1996). Incentives and student performance. In S. Fuhrman & J. O'Day (Eds.), *Rewards and reform: Creating educational incentives that work.* San Francisco: Jossey-Bass.

Podsakoff, P., MacKenzie, S., Moorman, R., & Fetter, R. (1990). Transformational leader behaviors and their effects on followers' trust in leader satisfaction and organizational citizenship behaviors. *Leadership Quarterly, 1*(2), 107–142.

Reeves, J. (2000). Tracking the links between pupil attainment and development planning. *School Leadership and Management, 20*(3), 315–332.

Reynolds, D., Hopkins, D., Potter, D., & Chapman, C. (2001). *School improvement for schools facing challenging circumstances: A review of research and practice*. London: Department for Education and Skills.

Rosenholtz, S. J. (1989). *Teachers' workplace: The social organization of schools*. New York: Longman.

Rowan, B. (1996). Standards as incentives for instructional reform. In S. Fuhrman & J. O'Day (Eds.), *Rewards and reform: Creating educational incentives that work*. San Francisco: Jossey-Bass.

Silins, H., & Mulford, W. (2002). Schools as learning organizations: The case for system, teacher and student learning. *Journal of Educational Administration, 40*, 425–446.

Stein, M., & Spillane, J. (2005). What can researchers on educational leadership learn from research on teaching: Building a bridge. In W. Firestone & C. Riehl (Eds.), *A new agenda for research in educational leadership* (pp. 28–45). New York: Teachers College Press.

West, M., Ainscow, M., & Stanford, J. (2005). Sustaining improvement in schools in challenging circumstances: A study of successful practice. *School Leadership and Management, 25*(1), 77–93.

Yammarino, F., Dionne, S., Chun, J., & Dansereau, F. (2005). Leadership and levels of analysis: A state-of-the-science review. *Leadership Quarterly, 16*, 879–919.

Yukl, G. (1989). *Leadership in organizations* (2nd ed.). Englewood Cliffs, NJ: Prentice Hall.

Yukl, G. (1994). *Leadership in organizations* (3rd ed.). Englewood Cliffs, NJ: Prentice-Hall.

DAVID C. YOUNG

5. THE PHILOSOPHY AND POLICIES OF INCLUSION: AN ADMINISTRATOR'S GUIDE TO ACTION

INTRODUCTION

When conducting undergraduate, continuing education, and graduate courses dealing with the education of students with exceptionalities, I often ask those I am teaching to think about their own views on inclusion. In almost every circumstance, there is unanimous agreement that including children with exceptionalities in regular classrooms is laudable and that this should be the ideal that all schools and educators strive towards. This viewpoint is hardly atypical; such sentiments are held by the vast majority of those involved in education. In fact, "teachers, educational assistants, and principals in neighbourhood schools – the people who deal with inclusion on a daily basis – have pretty much discarded the notion that [inclusion] is still a controversial issue" (Weber and Bennett, 2004; p. 19). In spite of this uniformity of agreement concerning the merits of inclusion, I do not want to imply that issues or concerns about inclusion no longer exist. In fact, beginning and seasoned teachers often lament that they experience tremendous difficulties creating truly inclusive classrooms. It appears, however, that a large part of this difficulty stems from the fact that educators often struggle with two important and related elements: 1) understanding the philosophy of inclusion; and 2) understanding the policies that govern its implementation. I would argue, therefore, that in order to make classrooms inclusionary, a recognition and appreciation of what inclusion is, as well as the procedures and protocols associated with it, is crucial.

Given the above, this chapter will outline the philosophy, or *terra firma*, upon which inclusion rests. In doing so, specific attention will be devoted to situating the philosophy of inclusion within the major polices in use throughout the United States and Canada. In addition, this chapter will outline some of the problems and issues that teachers experience with inclusion. Some of these problems are real, such as a lack of physical resources, while others are more about perceptions, such as teachers feeling alone in their struggle to enact inclusion. Although the actual implementation of inclusion is eventually left to individual teachers in their own classrooms, it is important to recognize that ultimately, the responsibility for inclusion falls under the leadership purview of the principal. Therefore, the primary focus of this chapter is to describe how school administrators can assist educators to better understand and implement the philosophy and policies of inclusion. This will make for better educational experiences for their students.

A. L. Edmunds and R. B. Macmillan (eds.), Leadership for Inclusion: A Practical Guide, 53–63.
© *2010 Sense Publishers. All Rights Reserved.*

THE PHILOSOPHY OF INCLUSION

When I enrolled in teachers' college some years ago, I was expected, as part of the degree requirements, to complete a course examining the philosophy of education. I can vividly recall internally recoiling against the notion that such a course would ever serve me in my professional practice. As a prospective teacher, I was only concerned with the "how-tos" of teaching and issues such as philosophy held little interest. I know this naïve perspective was widespread, as I often heard classmates voicing similar sentiments. In retrospect, I now see that my position was not entirely surprising since "the word philosophy calls up images of concepts, hypotheses, and notions of impracticality" (Ryan, 2007; p. 44). However, with age and experience, I have come to not only realize the crucial role that philosophy plays in education, I have also come to appreciate how philosophy is the groundwork upon which much of the practice of education rests. Yet, for some teachers philosophy remains an elusive concept; thus, it falls to principals to instil within these reluctant pedagogues an understanding and appreciation of how much of the practice of education rests on philosophical principles and ideals. This understanding may be accomplished via a principal's gentle reminders or by direct instruction by the school administrator on what philosophy entails, as well as its obvious importance. In both cases, the key point is that principals must assist staff members in recognizing and accepting the philosophy of inclusion.

In thinking about inclusion, it is important to recognize that it is first and foremost a philosophy and that the policies which have been subsequently developed for its implementation have stemmed from, and built upon, this philosophy. It is also vital to recognize that the road towards modern conceptions of inclusion, which have unfolded primarily during the course of the last two decades, has been a long and bumpy one, with periods of both major and minor reforms (see Edmunds and Young, 2007). As Winzer (2008; p. 43) points out, within the current context "a single, universal, or generally accepted version of inclusion does not exist." Rather, disagreement and a lack of clarity of what the term actually entails abounds, and thus, "it is probably more apt to talk about inclusions rather than a single inclusion (p. 43)." This divergence of opinion is troubling, especially for teachers and administrators who are striving to create inclusive classrooms. If one is unsure of what inclusion means, it logically follows that creating learning environments that are inclusive is extremely difficult, if not virtually impossible. Thus, what is required is to search for and understand the commonalities that exist among competing definitions. In doing so, one is left with the realization that:

> The philosophical basis for inclusion…is a belief that all students should be included within the regular classroom, and that any removal of a student to other educational settings must be justified on the basis of individual learning needs (Andrews and Lupart, 1993; p. 44).

While the foundational principle underlying this definition is the notion that regular classrooms should serve as the most desired placements for the provision of services for students with exceptionalities, it is also important to recognize that some children, because of their condition, may need to be educated in settings other than the regular classroom. As Edmunds and Edmunds (2007) point out, "to think that the regular classroom is the only option for students with exceptionalities is an abuse of the fundamental tenet of inclusion which is to provide an appropriate education for all students (p. 22–23)."

Inclusion, due to its roots within the civil rights movement, is inextricably linked with the related principles of equity and fairness. That is, each student, regardless of ability or inability, is entitled to receive the type of education that he or she needs to grow and prosper academically and socially. "Inclusion, therefore, means more than simply placing students with disabilities in general education classrooms. It means giving students the opportunity to participate, as members, in all school activities and affirming their right to such opportunity" (Smith, Polloway, Patton, Dowdy, and Heath, 2001; p. 36–37). This issue is reinforced in Lavoie's (1989) *F.A.T. City Workshop* where he points out that in thinking about students with exceptionalities, fairness for all students does not mean sameness; rather, fairness means each student receiving what he or she needs to succeed. As a result, inclusion must involve providing all students with the means and opportunity to participate fully in their own education. At the same time, inclusion also involves the removal of all practices that are exclusionary.

Closely related to issues of equity and fairness, is the notion of educational change. As Armstrong (2003) puts it, "inclusion refers to a set of principles, values and practices which involve the social transformation of education systems and communities (p. 2)." This view is echoed by Winzer (2008) who claims that "inclusion is a radically different way of conceptualizing schools and the children they serve. Inclusion represents a fundamental change in who does what, to whom it is done, where it is done, and how resources support what is done (p. 44)." This change of perspective within education harkens back to the *raison d'être* of inclusion – providing an appropriate education for all students.

Although the primary purpose of this chapter is not to chronicle the benefits associated with inclusion, for they are many, it is worth noting that there is a myriad of research lauding the positive impact that the inclusion movement has had on education. Among the most notable advantages is the social and academic benefits afforded to all students, exceptional and otherwise. Another overwhelmingly positive outcome is that teachers who are engaged in inclusive educational programs have consistently reported highly beneficial professional outcomes from the experience (Stanovich, 1999). While these examples are not exhaustive, they add credence to the view that "inclusion is the best philosophical approach we have...to direct the education of students with exceptionalities" (Edmunds and Edmunds, 2008; p. 24).

It is clear from the preceding that in thinking about the philosophy of inclusion, the common and universal reference amongst the different views is to a set of values and beliefs. Although there is continuing disagreement about the specifics of implementing inclusion, it is clear that in order for inclusion to be successful, all members of the school community - teachers, administrators, other school staff, students and parents - must embrace its central tenets (Friend, 2005). To some degree, a teacher's or administrator's commitment to inclusion is a personal choice.

THE POLICIES OF INCLUSION

It is important to recognize that there are policies that guide and direct the implementation of the philosophy of inclusion. As educators, it is incumbent to adhere to them even though this may well result in a clash between what teachers believe and what teachers are required to do. For principals, the task then becomes to first communicate to his or her staff the values and benefits associated with inclusion. If an administrator can convince reluctant teachers, and/or those who are not fully informed, to accept the philosophy of inclusion, then related policies are more readily embraced. With this conundrum between philosophy and policies in mind, attention will now be devoted to discussing the various policies and frameworks that affect inclusion.

In 1963, Cunningham commented that "policy is like an elephant - you recognize one when you see it, but it is somewhat more difficult to define (p. 229)." In the current educational context, policy continues to defy easy explanation but as Levin & Young (1998) point out, a policy typically describes a general approach that is intended to guide behaviour and which has broad implications within particular settings, whether it be a country, province, state, or school.

> Policies shape the structure of schools, the resources available in schools, the curriculum, the teaching staff, and, to a considerable extent, the round of daily activities. Policies determine how much money is spent, by whom, and on what, how teachers are paid, how students are evaluated, and most other aspects of schools as we know them (Levin & Young, 1998; p. 60–61).

It is obvious that educators cannot underestimate the importance that policies play in the educational enterprise because, without exaggeration, policies overwhelmingly govern and shape the way education systems are organized and operated. A complete examination of the various American and Canadian polices dealing with inclusion would leave one exhausted and perhaps confused as it is quite easy to become lost in the veritable plethora of international, federal, state, provincial, school board, and school-specific documents containing such guidelines. The overall point which is clear, however, is that policies governing the implementation of inclusionary practices vary greatly between jurisdictions, and even between schools in the same jurisdiction. Other than this, it is virtually impossible to make broad conclusions about the nature and degree to which inclusion has been implemented in either country. As a result, educators are left with the troubling realization that no all-encompassing snapshot of inclusion policies exists. Instead, individual portraits, each telling a somewhat different tale, are the norm. Any effort to provide a complete profile of the numerous intricacies regarding inclusion that exist across the United States and Canada is fraught with difficulty, and certainly well beyond the scope of this writing. As a result, attention will be devoted to detailing the larger, macro-level policies that seem to directly impact on inclusion in both countries.

As early as 1948, the entire realm of education was receiving special international attention. The *Universal Declaration of Human Rights* adopted by all members of the United Nations stipulated that education was a fundamental human right. Although it stopped short of addressing the rights of the disabled *per se*, this document is nonetheless important because it brought to the attention of the international community the importance of education. Building on this, the United Nations in 1975 released the *Declaration of Rights of Disabled Persons* which stated that the disabled had the same rights as all other individuals (Hutchinson, 2007) and while it did not specifically address the issue of inclusion by name, it did bring attention and focus to the issue of providing an appropriate education for those deemed to have exceptionalities.

In the United States, the march towards inclusive education is tied closely to the civil rights movement. The 1954 *Brown v. Topeka Board of Education* decision declared that segregation based on race was unconstitutional. This caused many professionals, both inside and outside education, to question whether separate educational facilities were appropriate venues for the provision of services for persons with disabilities. Coupled with this debate were various court challenges in which parents of children with exceptionalities won the right to a free and appropriate education for their children (see Friend, 2005 & Salend, 2005). In response to these judicial decisions and mounting pressure from advocacy groups, the U.S. federal government passed the *Education for All Handicapped Children Act* in 1975. Commonly referred to as P.L. 94–142, this legislation guaranteed all children with exceptionalities a free and appropriate education in the least restrictive educational environment. This landmark piece of legislation has been expanded several times since its passage by the 1990 *Americans with Disabilities Act* (P.L. 101–336) and the 1990 *Individuals with Disabilities Education Act* (P.L. 101–476). And yet, it is more than somewhat perplexing that in spite of these amendments and the tremendous progress that has been made in regards to the education of students with exceptionalities that "inclusion is a state-of-the art term; it is not mentioned in federal law or in state statutes" (Winzer, 2008; p. 54). This lack of specific statutory expression might lead one to dismiss the importance of inclusion within America's schools. However, it is wise to avoid such a temptation because although inclusion lacks *de jure* status, it is, in the vast majority of jurisdictions, *de facto* policy. In fact, the 1997 amendment (P.L. 105–17) to the *Individuals with Disabilities Education Act* "did not mandate inclusion but strongly encouraged consideration of educational placements in general classrooms" (Winzer, 2008; p. 54). As such, it appears that while the United States has adopted the fundamental tenets of inclusion, its polices have yet to catch up with its philosophical position.

In Canada, the responsibility for education is vested almost entirely with the provincial and territorial governments. Of course, this is very much unlike the United States which has a strong federal presence in special education. This is not to imply that Canadian federal policies have not impacted on education. For example, the 1982 Canadian *Charter of Rights and Freedoms* does guarantee rights to people with disabilities but, as the Supreme Court of Canada pointed out in the 1997 case of *Eaton v. Brant County Board of Education*, there is no presumption in favor of inclusion in the *Charter*. In spite of this, much progress has been made in the area of inclusive education in Canadian schools. In fact, because "…nearly all

Canadian provinces have adopted the philosophy of inclusion, most students with exceptionalities receive their specialized programs in regular classroom settings" (Edmunds and Edmunds, 2008; p. 22). Still, like the United States, "the implementation of inclusionary practices varies widely from province to province and even among neighbouring school boards" (Winzer, 2009; p. 49). For example, the provinces of New Brunswick and Nova Scotia have enacted legislation that stipulates full inclusion, and while inclusion in Ontario is to be the norm in all schools, no official policy has yet been enacted which explicitly states this.

> Other jurisdictions treat inclusion programs as one more choice, albeit the most important one, on the education menu. They have chosen to maintain a continuum of services and typically approach inclusion on a one-to-one basis. It is held that case-by-case decisions are consistent with the essence of special education; rather than a blanket policy, the special needs of each pupil must be carefully assessed and the most appropriate educational placement for that child judged. Opting for participation in any program is justified only if such programming meets the needs, wishes, and interests of a student (Winzer, 2008; p. 49).

Therefore, in examining the Canadian policy landscape in the area of inclusion, it would appear that it mirrors almost exactly the American situation. While the philosophy of inclusion has been openly embraced, the policies enacted to address the issue are quite divergent and thus the legislated practice of inclusion varies widely.

With constant changes occurring in the domain of special education, it is obvious that the notion of inclusive schooling will continue to be prevalent. As policies emerge and evolve, we may see more willingness on the part of governments to achieve a balance or symmetry between the philosophy of inclusion and the legislation that enacts it. In the interim, given the widespread variation in the form and practice of inclusion across the United States and Canada, it is important that we avoid dichotomies that classify education systems in terms of best or worst. Rather, we must recognize that there is no "one best" approach to inclusive schooling. Education policies are, to some measure, responses to *local* conditions and, consequently, are directed at meeting the needs of students within specific jurisdictions (Winzer, 2008). Local policies dictate the manner in which special education unfolds in schools and although teachers do have concerns about teaching students with exceptionalities, administrators can and should play an important role in making sure their school is inclusionary.

MAKING INCLUSION WORK: THE SCHOOL ADMINISTRATOR'S ROLE

In most educational jurisdictions in North America, an introductory course in special education is a minimum requirement for prospective teachers. The scope and duration of such courses vary greatly but some of the typical issues addressed include: a) details about what special education is; b) the characteristics associated with various exceptionalities; c) and types of teaching strategies that can be utilized to help teachers help students learn to their potential. The key is that these are often "survey" courses which provide but a glimpse into the topic. Perhaps it stems from these types of courses that many teachers feel they do not possess an adequate understanding of exceptionalities, nor do they believe they have the skills required to teach children with special needs (Chang, Early, & Winton, 2005; Cook, 2002). Thinking back on my own training, I too felt a great degree of trepidation, uncertainty, and confusion about how to include students with exceptionalities in my classroom. At the same time, I readily admit that I had little if any knowledge about what inclusion really meant and I had even less understanding about the regulations and policies that were in place. I suspect my experiences are not atypical and that many educators lack the further appreciations about inclusion that I have gathered throughout my career. This is not surprising given that the interactions between the theory and practices of inclusive schooling are complex and multi-faceted. To a degree, this dilemma might be alleviated by teacher education programs. In a recent study, it was reported that teacher candidates felt that an extended mandatory course in special education would be advantageous (Woloshyn, Bennett, and Berrill, 2003); however, in the absence of such comprehensive courses, the responsibility for fostering inclusion rests with the school administration, and, most particularly, with the principal.

Leadership studies often point to the school principal as an instructional leader, as well as being a resource for teachers. If teachers are to embrace inclusion, principals must ensure that each member of the school community understands the nature of inclusion, including all its relevant polices. Principals must therefore become acclimatized with the fundamental features of inclusive schooling and should be prepared to brief their staff on them. This can be accomplished through in-service sessions or it might simply occur through meaningful discussions in the staff room. At any rate, principals should always be visible and should be readily available to serve as a sounding board for all staff and teachers. It is also useful for principals to apprise staff of emerging or changing polices or issues related to inclusion. Providing teachers with pamphlets or brochures is often well-received and most appreciated. If need be, school administrators should seek out and solicit advice and assistance from other principals, school district administrators, or education department officials if new or changing policies appear to have several interpretations. If a principal feels that his or her staff would benefit from having a guest lecturer brief teachers on various topics regarding inclusion, then this course of action should be followed. According to John Colbert, Principal of Holcomb Elementary School in Fayetteville, Arkansas, one of the greatest barriers to inclusion is teachers who do not support having students with exceptionalities included in their classrooms. For Colbert, the key is to have these teachers speak with other educators who have had successful experiences. As he states: "I can talk to them [reluctant teachers] all day long, but they really don't think I know the problems created by some of these students. On the other hand, when they talk to other teachers who have had success, they tend to believe them" (as cited in Smith, Polloway, Patton, and Dowdy, 2004; p. 10). The related research by Edmunds (2003) clearly indicates that teachers are quite interested in learning the skills which will allow them to be successful in inclusive classrooms, and that principals can certainly assist educators in this regard.

In addition to their role as instructional leaders and acting as a resource for teachers, school principals are the primary source from which teachers take their educational direction. That is, teachers often look to administrators to gauge the school climate and principals, through their words and deeds, dictate whether inclusion will receive a warm or chilly welcome. In this regard, research by Stanovich & Jordan (1998) is telling; according to their findings, the most successful teachers are those whose principals advocate having children with exceptionalities included in mainstream classrooms. The conclusion we can draw from this is clear – inclusion works best when it is supported by principals. It logically follows, therefore, that school administrators must create environments in which inclusion is the accepted norm. At the same time, principals must establish conditions which foster the acceptance of inclusion by all staff members. To achieve this end, principals must openly support both the philosophy and polices of inclusion and take steps to develop school goals and mission statements that set these commitments down in writing. It is advisable that in developing such statements, attention is devoted to ensuring that all members of the school community, including teachers, other staff, parents, and students are afforded a voice in the development process. Also, it is always advantageous to look to other schools that have already undergone this process for guidance and support. According to Smith & Andrews (1989):

> A clear vision for the school is articulated by the principal to the point of redundancy. Through slogans, themes, logos, and reminders, the principal makes it known that everyone in this school is headed in the same general direction. Individual teachers may choose different means of achieving this, emphasizing different strengths and interests, but the overarching direction supersedes individual whim (p. 46).

Thus, the principal must be the voice that helps in the establishment of an inclusive school climate.

My final point addresses the issue of support for teachers who are implementing inclusive practices. A recent study (Edmunds, Halsall, MacMillan, and Edmunds, 2000) found that seventy-seven per cent of Nova Scotia teachers felt they lacked the necessary resources to professionally facilitate inclusion. A distinct lack of a variety of different types of support were cited as the culprits. For example, some teachers indicated that in order for inclusion to succeed, class sizes must be reduced. Others argued that additional personnel needed to be hired in order that the varying needs of students could be adequately met. And, yet others have lamented the fact that they lack the curricular materials and equipment necessary to do their jobs (Scruggs & Mastropieri, 1996). These complaints, while entirely justified are, to a large degree, beyond the control of the principal and most likely stem from funding cutbacks initiated by state, provincial, and local education authorities. This is indeed troubling and it undeniably has an impact on the quality of services provided in community schools. While principals have little real power to resist or reverse funding decisions, this does not suggest that positive or progressive steps cannot be taken. On the contrary, school administrators must be active spokespersons on behalf of their schools and this mostly means lobbying school districts and education-related agencies for resources and support. At the same time, administrators should work closely with school personnel to arrive at satisfactory solutions. Perhaps part of the solution lies in efforts directed at team-building. By fostering a team approach to inclusion, principals may alleviate some of the pressures felt by individual teachers. This is not difficult to accomplish and the long-term gains associated with collaborative approaches to teaching students with exceptionalities in inclusive settings have proven to be many and widespread. Team-building begins and ends with the school principal and it is through their efforts that such a climate can be produced – one that benefits all members of the school.

SUMMARY

Although "...the topic of inclusion was once guaranteed to brew up a storm, the winds are now relatively calm" (Weber and Bennett, 2004; p. 19). In fact, the philosophy of inclusion is now a generally accepted part of education throughout North America, with educator surveys revealing that teachers hold positive attitudes towards inclusion and towards students with exceptionalities (Edmunds, 2003). Despite inclusion being embraced and fostered, polices aimed at its direct implementation are varied. While some jurisdictions have enacted legislation that mandates inclusion, others have been reticent to provide specific statutory expressions for inclusion. This results in somewhat of a disconnect between philosophy and policy. Still, at a minimum, most jurisdictions in the United States and Canada accept inclusion as *de facto* government policy. Consequently, teachers operate in an environment where students with exceptionalities will be included in regular classrooms. To create school climates that accept inclusion, school administrators must themselves embrace the tenets of inclusion. At the same time, they must work openly and actively with their teachers and other staff. This can be accomplished by assuming the role of instructional leader as well as providing support for the school community.

Finally, it is rightfully acknowledged that creating a truly inclusive school is difficult and time-consuming. However, the reality is that inclusion is the preferred approach to educating students with exceptionalities and it appears here to stay. Therefore, a healthy understanding of the philosophy and polices of inclusion will help create and promote schools that respect and embody the fundamental premise of inclusion – that all children will receive an education appropriate to their unique needs. A laudable goal indeed!

REFERENCES

Allen, K. E., Paasche, C. L., Cornell, A., & Engel, M. (1998). *Exceptional children: Inclusion in early childhood programs* (2nd Canadian ed.). Toronto, ON: ITP Nelson.

Andrews, J., & Lupart, J. (1993). *The inclusive classroom: Educating exceptional children.* Scarborough, ON: Nelson Canada.

D. C. YOUNG

Armstrong, F. (2003). *Spaced out: Policy, difference and the challenge of inclusive education*. Boston: Kluwer.

Bélanger, N. (2001). Solicitude and special education policies. *Cambridge Journal of Education, 31*(3), 337–348.

Byrnes, M. (2008). *Taking sides: Clashing views in special education* (3rd ed.). Dubuque, IA: McGraw-Hill/Duskin.

Change, F., Early, D. M., & Winton, P. J. (2005). Early childhood teacher preparation in special education at 2- and 4-year institutions of higher education. *Journal of Early Intervention, 27*, 110–124.

Cook, B. G. (2002). Inclusive attitudes, strengths, and weaknesses of pre-service general educators enrolled in a curriculum infusion teacher preparation program. *Teacher Education and Special Education, 25*, 262–277.

Crockett, J. B., & Kauffman, J. M. (1999). *The least restrictive environment: Its origins and interpretations in special education*. Mahwah, NJ: Lawrence Erlbaum.

Cunningham, G. (1963). Policy and practice. *Public Administration, 41*, 229–238.

Daniel, Y. (2005). The textual construction of high needs for funding special education in Ontario. *Canadian Journal of Education, 28*(4), 763–783.

Edmunds, A. L. (2003). The inclusive classroom—Can teachers keep up? A comparison of Nova Scotia and Newfoundland & Labrador perspectives. *Exceptionality Education Canada, 13*(1), 29–48.

Edmunds, A. L., & Edmunds, G. A. (2008). *Special education in Canada* (1st ed.). Toronto, ON: McGraw-Hill Ryerson.

Edmunds, A. L., Halsall, A., MacMillan, R. B., & Edmunds, G. A. (2000). *The impact of government funding cuts on education: Report from a teacher survey*. Halifax, UK: Nova Scotia Teachers' Union.

Edmunds, A. L., & Young, D. C. (2007). The evolution of special education policy in Ontario: 1968 to present. In T. G. Ryan (Ed.), *The reflexive special educator* (pp. 57–72). Calgary, AB: Detselig.

Emanuelsson, I., Haug, P., & Persson, B. (2005). Inclusive education in some Western European countries: Different policy rhetorics and school realities. In D. Mitchell (Ed.), *Contextualizing inclusive education: Evaluating old and new international perspectives* (pp. 114–138). London: Routledge.

Friend, M. (2005). *Special education: Contemporary perspectives for school professionals*. Boston: Pearson.

Hallahan, D. P., & Kauffman, J. M. (2003). *Exceptioanl learners: Introduction to special education* (9th ed.). Boston: Pearson.

Hardman, M. L., Drew, C. J., & Egan, M. W. (2005). *Human exceptionality: School, community and family* (8th ed.). Boston: Allyn and Bacon.

Hehir, T. (2005). *New directions in special education: Eliminating ableism in policy and practice*. Cambridge, MA: Harvard Education Press.

Holtermann, S. (2003). Costing the future. In M. Nind, J. Rix, K. Sheehy, & K. Simmons (Eds.), *Inclusive education: Diverse perspectives* (pp. 264–273). London: David Fulton.

Hutchinson, N. L. (2007). *Inclusion of exceptional learners in Canadian schools: A practical handbook for teachers* (2nd ed.). Toronto, ON: Pearson.

Jordan, A. (2001). Special education in Ontario, Canada: A case study of market-based reforms. *Cambridge Journal of Education, 31*(3), 349–372.

Kochhar, C. A., & West, L. L. (1996). *Handbook for successful inclusion*. Gaithersburg, MD: Aspen.

Kugelmass, J. W. (2004). *The inclusive school: Sustaining equity and standards*. New York: Teachers College Press.

Lavoie, R. D. (1989). *Understanding learning disabilities: How difficult can this be? The frustration, anxiety, tension (F.A.T.) city workshop* [Video]. United States: PBS.

Levin, B., & Young, J. (1998). *Understanding Canadian schools: An introduction to educational administration*. Toronto, ON: Harcourt Brace.

Lipsky, D. K., & Gartner, A. (1997). *Inclusion and school reform: Transforming America's classrooms*. Baltimore: Paul H. Brookes.

MacKay, A. W., & Sutherland, L. (2006). *Teachers and the law* (2nd ed.). Toronto, ON: Emond Montgomery.

McLaughlin, M. J., & Jordan, A. (2005). Push and pull: Forces that are shaping inclusion in the United States. In D. Mitchell (Ed.), *Contextualizing inclusive education: Evaluating old and new international perspectives* (pp. 89–113). London: Routledge.

Mitchell, D. (2005). Sixteen propositions on the contexts of inclusive education. In D. Mitchell (Ed.), *Contextualizing inclusive education: Evaluating old and new international perspectives* (pp. 1–21). London: Routledge.

Ornstein, A. C. (2003). *Pushing the envelope: Critical issues in education.* Upper Saddle River, NJ: Pearson.

Ryan, T. G. (2007). The reflexive educators philosophical orientation. In T. G. Ryan (Ed.), *The reflexive special educator* (pp. 43–56). Calgary, AB: Detselig.

Salend, S. J. (2005). *Creating inclusive classrooms* (5th ed.). Upper Saddle River, NJ: Pearson.

Scruggs, T. E., & Mastropieri, M. A. (1996). Teacher perceptions of mainstreaming/inclusion, 1958–1995: A research synthesis. *Exceptional Children, 63*(1), 59–74.

Smith, T. E. C., Polloway, E., Patton, J. R., & Dowdy, C. A. (2004). *Teaching students with special needs in inclusive settings* (4th ed.). Boston: Pearson.

Smith, T. E. C., Polloway, E., Patton, J. R., Dowdy, C. A., & Heath, N. L. (2001). *Teaching students with special needs in inclusive settings* (Canadian ed.). Toronto, ON: Pearson.

Smith, W. F., & Andrews, R. L. (1989). *Instructional leadership: How principals make a difference.* Alexandria: Association for Supervision and Curriculum Development.

Stanovich, P. J. (1999). Conversations about inclusion. *Teaching Exceptional Children, 31*(6), 54–58.

Stanovich, P. J., & Jordan, A. (1998). Canadian teachers' and principals' beliefs about inclusive education as predictors of effective teaching in heterogeneous classrooms. *Elementary School Journal, 98*, 221–238.

Thomas, G., & Loxley, A. (2001). *Deconstructing special education and constructing inclusion.* Philadelphia: Open University Press.

Tymochenko, N. (2002). Special education in Ontario: Is it workable? *Education & Law Journal, 12*(2), 213–241.

Ware, L. (2000). Sunflowers, enchantment and empires: Reflections on inclusive education in the United States. In F. Armstrong, D. Armstrong, & L. Barton (Eds.), *Inclusive education: Policy, contexts and comparative perspectives* (pp. 42–59). London: David Fulton.

Weber, K., & Bennett, S. (2004). *Special education in Ontario schools* (5th ed.). Palgrave: Highland Press.

Winzer, M. A. (2008). *Children with exceptionalities in Canadian classrooms* (8th ed.). Toronto, ON: Pearson.

Winzer, M. A. (1999). The inclusion movement in Canada: Philosophies, promises and practice. In H. Daniels & P. Garner (Eds.), *Inclusive education* (pp. 99–106). London: Kogan Page.

Woloshyn, V., Bennett, S., & Berrill, D. (2003). Working with students who have Learning disabilities—teacher candidates speak out: Issues and concerns in preservice education and professional development. *Exceptionality Education Canada, 13*(1), 7–28.

JACQUELINE A. SPECHT AND GABRIELLE D. YOUNG

6. HOW ADMINISTRATORS BUILD SCHOOLS AS INCLUSIVE COMMUNITIES

INTRODUCTION

Children learn many things in school besides the academic curriculum. They learn about their competencies, skills, and strengths. They learn social skills, how to relate to peers and adults, and the importance of friendships and belonging. They learn how to approach challenges and new learning situations. They learn how to make contributions to teams and to their broader school community. Other "school success" outcomes include the development of competencies and interests that go beyond the curriculum, through involvement in after-school sports or clubs, and the development of solid values and belief systems. Children who receive special education services, like all children, need opportunities to explore different roles in school settings and to pursue their interests and develop their skills. Schools currently are much better suited to children of privilege than students who are marginalized (Cassidy & Bates, 2005) and students with disabilities can be one such group. Research studies consistently find the same factors to be important in promoting children's resilience, success in school, and success in life.

This chapter will highlight practical tips based on the current research that will assist administrators in creating inclusive communities that allow all children to develop to their full potential. Successful implementation of any program depends on support from administration and school personnel, especially when it is not a top-down initiative but rather a collaborative partnership (Burnstein, Sears, Wilcoxen, Cabello, & Spagna, 2004; Milson, 2006). Therefore the strategies recommended in this chapter are meant to be implemented by administrators in conjunction with their school staff. These strategies provide a means for educators to work together to create an inclusive school community.

CREATING SUPPORTIVE ENVIRONMENTS

Supportive environments are created by promoting feelings of acceptance through a welcoming school atmosphere and a school culture that accepts different kinds of behaviours. School environments that are caring and that show respect for individual differences are related to more adaptive patterns of cognition, affect and behaviour (Roesner, Midgely, & Urdan, 1996). The positive social, emotional and academic development of children and adolescents depends, to a considerable degree, on whether the contexts in which they develop,

A. L. Edmunds and R. B. Macmillan (eds.), Leadership for Inclusion: A Practical Guide, 65–72.

including schools, are reliable sources of caring relationships (Noddings, 2002; Rauner, 2000). Patrick, Turner, Meyer, and Midgley (2003) observed 20 classrooms on the first few days of school and were able to classify them into three categories: (a) *supportive environments* in which teachers expressed enthusiasm for learning, were respectful, used humor, and voiced expectations that all students would learn; (b) *ambiguous environments* in which teachers were inconsistent in their support and focus on learning, and exercised contradictory forms of management and (c) *non-supportive environments* in which teachers emphasized extrinsic reasons for learning, forewarned that learning would be difficult and that students might cheat or misbehave, and exercised authoritarian control. Students in supportive classrooms reported less avoidant behaviours (specifically not completing school work and being disruptive) than the other two groups of classrooms, which did not differ from each other. In the non-supportive environment, students used avoidance behaviours to protect themselves from anticipated failure; they attempted to save face by not participating in the activity in the first place. Avoidant behaviours mentioned in the literature (i.e., Patrick et al.) and commonly seen in today's classrooms include: not trying; not asking for help even though students may need it; acting out and being disruptive; and cheating.

Recommendation #1. The first days of school predict the classroom environment for the rest of the school year. Therefore, educators should be made aware that being supportive is important and that this message needs to be conveyed to the students from the very first day.

Arter (2007) notes that there are four functions of behaviour: avoidance, attention, revenge, and power. It is important to understand the function of the behaviour that the student engages in if it is to be remedied. If a student misbehaves because she is avoiding schoolwork, suspension will probably exacerbate rather than diminish the behaviour. If she gains attention for the behaviour (even negative attention), and this is what she wants, she is being reinforced, not punished. Cassidy and Bates (2005) note that students who have been viewed as "the most troubled" (e.g., drug abusers, drop-outs, and those engaged in criminal activity) flourish in an environment where they are provided the opportunity to have the needs of their behaviours met. If the child wants attention, positive attention should be provided. In writing about a school geared towards "troubled youth" Cassidy and Bates describe an incident where a student punched a hole in the wall. In order to reconcile the situation the student and one of the guidance counsellors went to a hardware store and bought the materials to fix the hole. As they were fixing the hole, they discussed alternate ways of getting rid of anger. In this scenario, the student was repairing the mistake that he made and learning some other ways to deal with anger. Cassidy and Bates note that suspensions are not methods of discipline at this school and that consequences should be logical or natural in nature. In this specific instance, suspension would not have provided an opportunity for growth, rather it would have only enabled the student to avoid being at school.

Being treated with respect reduces acting out behaviour (Cassidy & Bates, 2005). In school we need to care for all aspects of students' lives; not just their academic performance. In environments that are caring, students discuss feeling psychologically, physically, and emotionally safe. Students start to care more about themselves because of the support and care that they receive in school. In some schools, students are expected to give respect even if teachers do not provide it. This cannot work. Respect needs to be reciprocal. Students need to be provided with respect for they give back what they learn.

Characteristics of the classroom environment have an impact on student motivation and engagement (Ryan & Patrick, 2001). Students engage in more adaptive patterns of behaviour in classrooms when they are encouraged to interact with and help classmates; feel their ideas are respected; do not feel belittled; and feel that the teacher does not publicly identify their relative performance. Active and cooperative actions between teachers and students are seen in positive classroom environments (Shin & Koh, 2007).

Recommendation #2.   Encourage staff to engage in positive behavioural supports. Yelling at students, humiliating them, and suspending them are not ways in which students learn that they belong and are cared for.

Recommendation #3.   Implore teachers to create an environment of respect for different levels of accomplishment. One way to create this environment is by accepting the best work from each child according to his/her abilities, and to not compare the work of children.

DEVELOP RELATIONSHIPS BY EXPOSING STUDENTS TO ROLE MODELS

We learn a great deal from watching others (Bandura, 1986). Edwards (2001) notes that the most frequently encountered role model outside of the family circle is a teacher. Dominguez (2003) determined that co-curricular activities (e.g., school clubs, teams and service learning) with positive adult role models help students see the relevance of their school work. Building relationships with students helps them buy into what they are learning. These relationships are best built in supportive environments as we have outlined earlier in this chapter.

Teacher-student relationships often reflect administrator-teacher relationships. To provide the support and encouragement adolescents require, teachers and staff must feel supported and encouraged by their school administrators. Therefore administrators need to take care that they foster the same respectful and positive relationships with teachers and staff that they would like teachers and staff to form with students (Harvey, 2007). In secondary school, teachers and administrators must have the same rules so that they are consistent across settings.

Recommendation #4.   Encourage consistency in expectations for students across school settings.

Recommendation #5. Encourage staff in their efforts to create a caring and supportive environment. Model the respect that you would like to see. If teachers or other staff members are engaging in behaviours that run counter to supportive and inclusive environments, administrators need to provide support and encouragement to get them to engage in more acceptable behaviour.

PARTICIPATION

It is important for educators to provide opportunities for all students to participate in activities that allow them to understand societal expectations; to acquire the physical and social competencies needed to function in their school, home, and larger community; and to gain an understanding of their strengths and inter-relationships with others. The International Classification of Functioning, Disability, and Health (ICF) defines participation broadly as, "involvement in life situations" (World Health Organization, 2001, p. 7). Repeatedly, participation has been shown as key to the healthy adjustment of individuals. Unfortunately, children with disabilities have been found to engage in recreational and leisure activities less than children without disabilities (Brown & Gordon, 1987; Law, Haight, Milroy, Willms, Stewart, & Rosenbaum, 1999; McWilliam & Bailey, 1995), thus putting them at risk for negative life outcomes such as low self-esteem, depression, and anxiety.

"Mental health is a foundation for well-being and effective functioning for an individual, and for a community, and is created and compromised in everyday life, in families and schools" (Herman & Jane-Llopis, 2005, p. 42). Simovska and Sheehan (2000) reflect on the health promoting schools paradigm as a framework for building school environments which support mental and emotional health. They call for "genuine student participation, both within the classroom and in the broader school environment" (p. 216). By genuine participation, we mean that students must be given meaningful opportunities. Such meaningful opportunities, rather than busy work, provide a sense of empowerment rather than alienation (Edwards, 2001). Promoting children's participation in school through opportunities such as involvement in classroom lessons, games, sports, and social events, leads to a greater likelihood of successful experiences (Lauver & Little, 2005). Harvery (2007) promotes offering different types of activities (e.g., intramurals, yoga, and other non-competitive physical activities). In low income communities these programs may be the only way that children are exposed to the arts, workplace skills, social skills, and safe physical activities.

Participation is especially relevant in adolescence and specifically secondary school where students with disabilities tend to spend less time with typically developing peers and more time with adults and peers with disabilities (Carter & Kennedy, 2006). We need to provide opportunities for students with and without disabilities to interact in meaningful, socially relevant ways. The more opportunities that a school can create for students to participate in positive healthy groups activities, the more opportunity these students have to combat negative peer pressure (Paterson, 2007).

Recommendation #6.   Administrators should do a needs assessment to find out what participation opportunities the community needs or would like to see offered, as well as what students want or what parents want for their children. This assessment should determine if flexible drop-in programs would work better than requiring students to sign up for a particular day or time.

PROMOTE COMPETENCE

Ableism is a form of prejudice that is common in our schools (Storey, 2007). It is the belief that is better to be without a disability than to have one. Although we promote multiculturalism and acceptance of differences in our schools, we often overlook the prejudices that occur because one has a mental, physical, or emotional disability. Curricular documents must show individuals with disabilities and exceptionalities as contributing members of society partaking in everyday life events. Students with disabilities must partake in everyday life events. We need to get rid of the "us-versus-them" mentality and promote competence amongst students with disabilities so that they learn to value themselves and develop a strong sense of self-worth and self-esteem.

Simply placing children with disabilities in the classroom is not inclusion. This is true for all disabilities and not just those that are emotional or behavioural in nature. Coster and Haltiwanger (2004) found that 40% of children with physical disabilities who had no known cognitive disabilities performed below criterion on social skills. It was not that these children did not know the correct ways of behaviour, only that they did not implement them consistently throughout the day. Students and teachers need to be taught to include all children in all aspects of the school day. Similarly, students need to learn how to develop positive peer relationships as successful peer relationships contribute to healthy school adjustment and higher academic achievement (Berndt & Keith, 1995; Parker & Asher, 1987). Students need specific skill instruction or social interaction will remain less than optimal (Carter & Hughes, 2005).

Recommendation #7.   Educators need to pay particular attention to the social and behavioural skills limitations for all children on Individual Education Plans as social competence is a strong predictor of healthy life outcomes in adulthood.

Edwards (2001) indicates that students who fail see themselves as worthless, whereas students who feel appreciated and are successful start to see themselves as worthy of contribution. Instructional practices of teachers contribute to the psychological environment of the classroom because they send messages to the student about the importance of school work (Patrick et al., 2003). The majority of respondents in a survey of general educators did not believe that access to the general curriculum is appropriate for students with severe disabilities and that these students should not be held accountable to the same performance standards as typical peers (Agran, Alper, & Wehmeyer, 2002). Teachers should explore whether they hold the same high expectations for all students as these views are translated to children in the behaviours that teachers exhibit as demonstrated by the number and type of questions asked, and the response opportunities they provided for all children in the classroom (Killion, 2006). One must ask what message is being sent to students with and without disabilities if all are not included in the general curriculum? Research tells us that all students with exceptionalities, even students with intellectual disabilities, can access the general curriculum and meet standards if goal setting, self-monitoring and self instructional strategies are taught (Agran, Cavin, Wehmeyer, & Palmer, 2006). Harvey (2007) tells us that students need academic work where they can be successful. However, students must be challenged and find the work meaningful, as success when the tasks are too easy does not promote a sense of competency. Classrooms that are perceived as mastery focused have the lowest rate of academic avoidance (Kaplan, Gheen, & Midgley, 2002; Turner et al., 2002).

Recommendation #8. Require teachers to ensure that all students are being engaged in the curriculum at levels which they can appropriately access. Differentiated instruction allows all children to access the general curriculum in ways that match their understandings and abilities. All students must be challenged and allowed opportunities to demonstrate individual success.

CREATE A BOND BETWEEN HOME AND SCHOOL ENVIRONMENTS

Brofenbrenner's (1999) bioecological model is a useful theoretical framework in which to operate, as it allows educators and administrators to understand the bidirectionality of effects that occur between children and their environments. Bronfenbrenner suggests that while the environment influences a child's development, the interactions of that child *with* his/her environment are reciprocally influential in shaping development. It is especially important to understand the connection between the child, the home, and the school, as many failures that children have in school can often be attributed to one or more of these sources (Pianta & Walsh, 1998).

Bronstein and Kelly (1998) explain the need for advocates who can accompany families to school meetings, especially when the parents may have had negative experiences of school when they were younger. These advocates would help speak on behalf of families who may otherwise feel marginalized. Cassidy and Bates (2005) state that, "we can't successfully work with kids unless we're working with their families because whatever's going on at home is affecting what is happening here" (p. 77). Similarly, Dominguez (2003) notes that educators must be prepared to understand and promote the diversity of family involvement as many parents do not feel that they have the skills to help their children succeed at school. Parents who hear that the teacher took the time to get to know their children as individuals feel more comfortable with their children's experiences at school.

Recommendation #9. Work to engage families in the school, especially those who may feel marginalized. Personally invite parents to school events and interact with them for reasons other than negative feedback about their children. Allow and even facilitate the use of advocates for families who may have had a negative experience at school or whose culture is different from that of the mainstream.

CONCLUSION

In summary, a supportive school environment is certainly one of the key ingredients in facilitating school success. Creating such an environment is not done by administrators alone, but rather by all educators working together to meet the unique learning needs of each child. Nonetheless, school leaders have a unique and powerfully influential position from which to positively enact and maintain supportive environments. They can also, however, allow non-supportive environments to exist. Having said that, this chapter has attempted to indicate the importance of a positive school environment for all children and has provided some recommendations on how to do so. Often we forget about the children with disabilities when we focus on other marginalized groups. We need to show all of our students respect and care in order to create a positive environment where students and staff come together to celebrate each other and the learning process. Celebrating each other's strengths through positive relationships, providing opportunities to participate, and strong home and school bonds are the steps to creating inclusive communities where all feel and are welcomed.

REFERENCES

Agran, M., Alper, S., & Wehmeyer, M. (2002). Access to the general curriculum for students with significant disabilities: What it means to teachers. *Education and Training in Mental Retardation and Developmental Disabilities, 37,* 123–133.

Agran, M., Cavin, M., Wehmeyer, M., & Palmer, S. (2006). Participation of students with moderate to severe disabilities in the general curriculum: The effects of the self -determined learning model of instruction. *Research and Practice for Persons with Severe Disabilities, 31*(3), 230–241.

Arter, P. S. (2007). The positive alternative learning supports program: Collaborating to improve student success. *Teaching Exceptional Children, 40*(2), 38–46.

Bandura, A. (1986). *Social foundations of thought and action: A social cognitive theory.* Englewood Cliffs, NJ: Prentice Hall.

Berndt, T. J., & Keefe, K. (1995). Friends' influence on adolescents' adjustment to school. *Child Development, 66*(5), 1312–1329.

Bronfenbrenner, U. (1999). Environments in developmental perspective: Theoretical and operational models. In S. L. Friedman & T. Wachs (Eds.), *Measuring environments across the lifespan.* Washington, DC: American Psychology Association.

Bronstein, L. R., & Kelly, T. B. (1998). A multidimensional approach to evaluating school-linked services: A school of social work and county public school partnership. *Social Work in Education, 20*(3), 152–164.

Brown, M., & Gordon, W. (1987). Impact of impairment on activity patterns of children. *Archives of Physical Medicine Rehabilitation, 68,* 828–832.

Burnstein, N., Sears, S., Wilcoxen, A., Cabello, B., & Spagna, M. (2004). Moving toward inclusive practices. *Remedial and Special Education, 25*(2), 104–116.

Carter, E. W., & Hughes, C. (2005). Increasing social interaction among adolescents with intellectual disabilities and their general education peers: Effective interventions. *Research and Practice for Persons with Severe Disabilities, 30*(4), 179–193.

Carter, E. W., & Kennedy, C. H. (2006). Promoting access to the general curriculum using peer support strategies. *Research and Practice for Persons with Severe Disabilities, 31*(4), 284–292.

Cassidy, W., & Bates, A. (2005). Drop-outs and push-outs: Finding hope at a school that actualizes the ethic of care. *American Journal of Education, 112*(1), 66–102.

Coster, W. J., & Haltiwanger, J. T. (2004). Social-behavioral skills of elementary students with physical disabilities included in general education classrooms. *Remedial and Special Education, 25*(2), 95–103.

Dominguez, C. (2003). Involving parents, motivating students. *Principal Leadership, 4*(4), 43–46.

Edwards, C. H. (2001). Moral classroom communities for student resiliency. *The Education Digest, 67*(2), 15–20.

Harvey, V. S. (2007). Raising resiliency schoolwide. *The Education Digest, 72*(7), 33–39.

Herman, H., & Jane-Llopis, E. (2005). Mental health promotion in public health. *Promotion & Education Supplement, 2*, 42–47.

Kaplan, A., Gheen, M., & Midgley, C. (2002). Classroom goal structure and student disruptive behaviour. *British Journal of Educational Psychology, 72*, 191–211.

Killion, J. (2006). Staff development guide. *Principal Leadership, 6*(5), 53–54.

Lauver, S., & Little, P. M. D. (2005). Finding the right hook. *School Administrator, 62*(5), 27–30.

Law, M., Haight, M., Milroy, B., Willms, D., Stewart, D., & Rosenbaum, P. (1999). Environmental factors affecting the occupations of children with physical disabilities. *Journal of Occupational Science, 6*(3), 102–110.

McWilliam, R. A., & Bailey, D. B. (1995). Effects of classroom social structure and disability on engagement. *Topics in Early Childhood Special Education, 15*(2), 123–147.

Milson, A. (2006). Creating positive school experiences for students with disabilities. *Professional School Counselling, 10*, 66–72.

Noddings, N. (2002). *Educating moral people: A caring alternative to character education.* New York: Teachers College Press.

Parker, J. G., & Asher, S. R. (1987). Peer relations and later personal adjustment: Are low- accepted children at risk? *Psychological Bulletin, 102*, 357–389.

Paterson, J. (2007). Positive peer pressure. *Leadership for Student Activities, 36*(4), 23–25.

Patrick, H., Turner, J. C., Meyer, D. K., & Midgley, C. (2003). How teachers establish psychological environments during the first days of school: Associations with avoidance in mathematics. *Teachers College Record, 105*, 1521–1558.

Pianta, R. C., & Walsh, D. J. (1998). Applying the construct of resilience in schools: Cautions from a developmental systems perspective. *School Psychology Review, 27*(3), 407–417.

Rauner, D. M. (2000). *They still pick me up when I fall: The role of caring in youth development and community life.* New York: Columbia University Press.

Roesner, R. W., Midgley, C., & Urdan, T. C. (1996). Perceptions of the school psychological environment and early adolescents' psychological and behavioural functioning in school: The mediating role of goals and belonging. *Journal of Educational Psychology, 88*(3), 408–422.

Ryan, A. M., & Patrick, H. (2001). The classroom social environment and changes in adolescents' motivation and engagement during middle school. *American Educational Research Journal, 38*(2), 437–460.

Shin, S., & Koh, M. S. (2007). A cross-cultural study of teachers' beliefs and strategies on classroom behaviour management in urban American and Korean school systems. *Education and Urban Society, 33*, 421–442.

Simovska, V., & Sheehan, M. (2000). Worlds apart or like minds? Mental health promotion in Macedonian and Australian schools. *Health Education, 100*(5), 216–223.

Storey, K. (2007). Combating ableism in schools. *Preventing School Failure, 52*(4), 56–58.

Turner, J. C., Midgley, C., Meyer, D. K., Gheen, M., Anderman, E., Kang, Y., et al. (2002). The classroom environment and students' reports of avoidance behaviors in mathematics: A multi-method study. *Journal of Educational Psychology, 94*(1), 88–106.

World Health Organization. (2001). *ICF. International classification of functioning, disability, and health.* Geneva, Ill: World Health Organization.

ROBERT MACMILLAN

7. LEADERSHIP AS TRUST AND TEAM-BUILDING FOR INCLUSIVE PRACTICE

INTRODUCTION

In a previous chapter, Kenneth Leithwood discussed the current conceptualisations of leadership and the best practices associated with successful leaders. In a related manner, this chapter primarily focuses on issues affecting the development of an inclusive school environment, including teachers' difficulty with inclusion and principal's practices which encourage the development of the mutual trust required to enhance the development of a school culture based on inclusive practise. Its secondary focus is the provision of ideas about strategies that administrators can use to achieve all of the above in their schools.

The conception of inclusive leadership presented here is similar to Ryan's (2006) in that it is leadership that includes as many groups and people as possible, and its practices are designed to create an educational environment that assumes the needs of all students will be met. This conception moves the field forward by suggesting that the values and beliefs created by such leadership influence the school culture such that inclusivity becomes the basis for all decisions, and becomes the taken-for-granted way of operating. In effect, inclusion becomes so deeply embedded in all practices that discussion, and even thought, about its appropriateness no longer occurs. In schools which are considered to be successful, including those which have successfully adopted an inclusive model, the principals understand that no one single person is responsible for the care and supervision of included students: all staff are involved (Barth, 2003; Spillane, 2006). Leaders in these schools realize that the complexity of the task requires more time and energy than they have individually, especially if they wish to move from the transactional to the transformative styles of leadership that foster deep educational change (Hallinger, 2003).

If principals want teachers to be intimately involved with initiatives and/or changes, then teachers require a network of support made up of colleagues, resource teachers, the administration, and parents; all of whom focus on the improvement of the educational experiences of each child (Robinson & Carrington, 2002). This network builds into a collaborative, sustainable environment in which problems are seen as challenges to work through (Hargreaves & Fink, 2006). Support network coordination usually comes from the administration who provide the coherence, encouragement and resources for inclusion to work, and whose decisions are based on the principle of inclusion (Gurr, Drysdale, & Mulford, 2007).

A. L. Edmunds and R. B. Macmillan (eds.), Leadership for Inclusion: A Practical Guide, 73–82.
© 2010 Sense Publishers. All Rights Reserved.

The discussion to follow is divided into three parts and combines evidence from two previous research studies. The first part examines how teachers react when faced with having to develop inclusionary practices, especially if they do not feel supported in the development and implementation of inclusive practice. The second part explores the difference principals can make in their schools if they are trusted by their staffs. The combination of these two parts will give insights into the nature of inclusive leadership and the creation of an inclusive school culture, and the administrative practices that help to create such a culture. The last part makes suggestions about those practices that can/will lead to the development of inclusive leadership practices that foster the creation of an inclusive school culture and that recognise the needs of all students, regardless of background. For the purposes of this chapter, we focus on the inclusion of students with exceptionalities.

PART ONE: THE PROBLEM OF INCLUSION

Several studies have shown (e.g., Bunch, Lupart, & Brown, 1997) that teachers agree with the ideals of inclusion and the potential benefits for students. The problem for teachers is not in the concept, but in the practice. A few years ago, in the second of two studies examining the impact of financial cutbacks on schooling in the province of Nova Scotia (Macmillan, Meyer, Edmunds, A., Edmunds, G. & Feltmate, 2002), we asked a number of secondary teachers what they found to be the biggest issues for them surrounding inclusion and how they coped with these issues. The main issues, as one would anticipate, were: lack of resources, lack of support, and inadequate preparation (Macmillan & Meyer, 2006). Without resources, without support and without professional development, teachers did not believe that they could include all students without negatively affecting their teaching, or their professional and personal integrity.

Lack of resources encompassed a number of different categories, including pedagogical material, equipment, and educational support workers. The key factor was money; the provincial government had finite financial resources which were spread as widely as possible. In an attempt to allocate funding where it could address the greatest perceived need, the government and school districts developed a hierarchical list of categories of the anticipated range of student exceptionalities, then indicated which exceptionalities would receive funding. As a result of this governmental and school district triage, only the most severe, often behavioral, cases were granted financial support in the form of educational assistants and equipment, leaving those students with less severe needs with little or no support, and the classroom or subject teacher with the responsibility to seek out whatever help could be found. A critical factor in determining whether a school received funding was the degree to which the principal was proactive in securing favourable diagnoses of student needs and able to use the diagnoses to negotiate funding.

The second issue was lack of support. Teachers believed that they had been left to work with students without the professional, administrative and even emotional support from the system, generally, and from in-school administrators, specifically. Teachers said they felt as if they had been abandoned to their own devices after inclusion policies had been put in place by government and implemented by school districts, but with little or no thought to the classroom practicalities of these demanding policies. Teachers suggested the government and school districts assumed that teachers would know what to do, but they stated that their experience and training had not prepared them for the necessary shifts in classroom practice required by inclusion. As for the principals, teachers reported that some principals listened to teachers and tried to provide support in creative ways (e.g., asking the community to raise necessary funds), whereas other teachers reported that their principals took a hands-off approach, letting teachers proceed as they may and not even checking to determine whether the students' legally mandated IEPs were being followed. When the latter happened, teachers felt as if they were adrift with little direction as to how to proceed and that the work they put in to designing individualized plans was for naught.

The final issue identified by teachers was their lack of professional development, preparation, or training for working with students with special needs. While some teachers struggled to acquire the necessary knowledge and skills to teach all students well, regardless of individual needs, others stated that they often employed whichever instructional strategy they felt capable of using, regardless if the strategy was appropriate to meet individual student needs or not. While professional development and preparation to teach all students in their classroom could be construed as the responsibility of teachers, and some took on that responsibility, the availability and focus of professional development was haphazard, at best, and often not suited to the teachers' context (e.g., assumptions about the availability of funding for resources were inaccurate). We also heard from teachers that they often had to deal with students who had a specific need based on one aspect of a broad spectrum exceptionality (e.g., autism) or who had multiple exceptionalities (e.g., behavioural and intellectual disabilities combined), any one of which could have been the subject of a series of workshops or courses. Unfortunately, when the teachers felt comfortable working with one set of exceptionalities, students with these exceptionalities would move on and the teachers would find students with a different set of needs in their classrooms.

Teachers told us that they felt guilty that they could not meet student needs to the degree that they wished. The way that they addressed this guilt followed two general paths, one which we suggest was positive and the other which we believe was destructive, if not for the students, then certainly for the teachers, both professionally and personally. For those teachers who were on the first path, they developed positive strategies that enabled them to teach their students what they needed, regardless of what the rest of their classmates were doing, and, in some instances, regardless of the curriculum. Teachers rationalised this action by saying that the students who could not perform at level had deficits that needed to be addressed, and would not have been able to achieve the outcomes of the mandated curriculum anyway. These teachers believed that they carried out their professional responsibilities to their students to the best of their ability, and they appeared to be comfortable, or at least tolerably so, with the decisions that they made.

Teachers on the second path were of more concern for us because they appeared to be so unsure of the appropriate instructional paths to take that they seemed to be frozen; they could not decide about what they ought to do, or whether to carry on teaching as if they had no student with special needs within their classroom. This latter group stated that they had made few attempts to deal with inclusion, and often demonstrated their disregard for their responsibility to implement inclusion policies by ignoring their responsibility to read individualised learning plans or to discuss student needs with parents. These individuals related how they could not meet the needs of all students, so decided either to teach the way they felt most comfortable, or to teach to the majority of students, ignoring individual student needs entirely. In the latter instance, teachers said that they did not have the knowledge and skills to teach the students with exceptionalities, nor did they feel that they could teach all students well, even if they had the requisite knowledge and skills. Teachers on this path appeared to be least comfortable with their efforts, and experienced emotional and professional conflict as a result, part of which, they stated, could be addressed by better scheduling and by the provision of time to work together on instructional strategies and appropriate plans.

We contend that all of the above are symptoms of a deeper issue, specifically the issue of a school culture based on the perception that inclusion is a problem that cannot be resolved, instead of being based on a belief that inclusion is a challenge to be addressed. The responsibility for inclusion was left largely to the individual teacher, with little or no support from administration. For those teachers with more positive attitudes and approaches, the principal was essential to the construction of these positive perceptions about inclusion, especially if some concerted effort was taken by the principal to address the needs of all students and the concerns of the teachers.

PART TWO: BUILDING AN ENVIRONMENT OF TRUST

Research is consistent in describing the role of the principal as building cohesive school communities that foster inclusion for all students. Reyes and Wagstaff (2005) call principals the "integrative force" (p. 105) that helps to build cohesion among staff, students, and parents. But this cohesion does not occur instantaneously with the appointment of a principal: it takes time and trust in the administrator by teachers and trust in the teachers by the administrator (Tschannen-Moran, 2004). This brings into play evidence from our second study. In that research, while we looked at the impact of principal succession on teachers' work, our findings provided insight into the ways that principals can build positive school cultures through the development of mutual, collaborative trust between themselves and teachers during and after a succession event.

When we speak of trust, we mean that teachers and principals are able to predict with a large degree of certainty responses to events, and understand the decisions made by the each other because each is aware of the foundational values and beliefs upon which decisions are based. Trust is a reciprocal relationship in that to trust someone requires implied as well as overt agreement to rely on another, and to place oneself in a potentially vulnerable position. This may include the sharing of confidential information and contextual knowledge (Davenport & Prusack, 1998), the protection of each other from risk (Harmon & Toomey, 1999), and an expectation that appropriate action will be taken and that this action will fit the context (Kanter, 2004).

Consistency of decisions with beliefs and values and the perceived competency to carry out these decisions (Tschannen-Moran, 2004) is critical to building a relationship of trust between administrators and teachers. Without trust, neither can be certain that they will be supported in difficult situations (e.g., a conflict with a parent over an educational decision) nor can they be certain that the others' duties will be carried out in a professional manner and may lead to micro-management (Kouzes & Posner, 2006). This uncertainty negatively affects the ability to implement changes and can even shift the school culture away from collaboration and more toward individualism (Hargreaves, 1994), thus reducing the likelihood that inclusive education will be a pervasive part of the ethos of the school. Given teachers' reactions cited earlier and the inherent difficulties in implementing inclusive practices, teachers may not be willing to invest much time in developing inclusion strategies unless they know that they have, and can trust, the support of the principal.

In our research in 12 schools in Nova Scotia over a period of three years, we heard teachers describing the development of trust between themselves and the new administrator in such a way that we could easily conceptualise it as a continuum (Macmillan, Meyer & Northfield, 2004). In a few cases, significant levels of trust grew from a single event but, in most cases, trust grew over time with an accumulation of observations wherein principals' and teachers' actions contributed to an assessment of whether or not individuals could be trusted. This continuum for examining the growth of trust from the time of a principal's initial entry enabled us also to hypothesise about what that trust might look like if the principal remained *in situ* for an extended period (e.g., > 5 years). While this study also found instances of mistrust (uncertainty) and distrust (absence of trust), the focus here is on how trust can be built and maintained while establishing an inclusive school culture. The flip sides of trust are discussed only peripherally.

Based on what teachers and principals told us, we began to develop a picture of the development of trust during and after a succession event. We conceptualised the development of trust as a continuum with four nodes: *Role Trust, Practice Trust, Integrative Trust, and Correlative Trust*. We defined the beginning of the continuum as *Role Trust* which is characterised by the mandates given to teachers and principals. When new principals arrived, particularly those about whom nothing much was known, teachers expected the individual to act within the parameters described by the laws, regulations and policies which established and defined the duties, responsibilities and boundaries of the administrative role. Apart from the legal definitions of the principal's role, teachers' experiences, both as teachers and as students, also contributed to their own definition by setting the expectations for the new principal and his/her practices. This definition was also influenced by the context of the school and the practices and the trustworthiness of the incumbent's predecessors. Decisions made by the new principal were expected to be based within this generic conception of the role, with little expectation that the principal's decisions, at least in the initial period, would fall outside of these boundaries.

Our research suggests that principals who never move beyond this node of Role Trust execute their decisions within the legal definitions of the role and their conceptions of it. While teachers may be able to predict a principal's responses to various situations, the values and beliefs on which the actions are based are external to the school context, and thus not adapted to fit the reality of inclusion in that school. Due to the narrow confines of the role as defined by legal mandates, flexibility of practices based on context and circumstances will likely be lost as a result.

New principals often faced with the difficult task of reconciling the legal definition(s) of the role, teachers' expectations of the role, and their own experiences as administrators. Each decision they made was scrutinized by teachers in their attempt to determine the underlying values, assumptions and beliefs about schools on which the decision was made. As teachers gained knowledge of the principal, they built their understanding of the principal's decision making that led them to trust the principal in specific situations, which we called *Practice Trust* – trust based on a principal's practice. In effect, when teachers could predict with a significant degree of certainty how the principal would react in particular situations, they began to move beyond the legal expectations of the role to begin to trust the principal, but only in very specific circumstances. Inconsistency between action and espoused values and beliefs led teachers to expect the principal to treat each situation as new, without teachers being able to predict with any degree of certainty how the principal would react. This also meant that they were unsure of the support they might receive in a difficult situation involving students: different people were treated differently, even if they had similar issues.

The third node on the continuum, *Integrative Trust*, is a result of prolonged exposure to the principal's decision-making and practices such that the teachers were able to state clearly and succinctly the basis for the principal's actions. Teachers assured us that the principal's values and beliefs as espoused could be found in the decisions and practices, even if the principal did not give a rationale for a particular decision or practice. Teachers were able to predict how the principal would react, which gave them some degree of comfort in knowing when they would be supported and why, without necessarily asking in advance for support, especially if a difficult situation arose unexpectedly. While teachers may not have agreed with the principal's decisions in all cases, they at least appreciated that the principal had a clear basis for the decisions. Consequently, teachers were able to plan for and rely on the principal with a large degree of confidence.

The fourth node, for which we don't have direct evidence, but for which we suggest characteristics given the data from the teachers, is *Correlative Trust*. We hypothesise that this type of trust is one where the teachers and the principal function as a well choreographed team, each with her/his responsibilities, with little discussion needed to determine how the other will react to an initiative or a difficult situation. If quick decisions are to be made, then they are made without hesitation in anticipation that they will be supported. Teachers and principals with such a trust relationship share common values and beliefs, and work closely as a team to address the needs of all students, with the actual boundaries between administration and teaching becoming blurred. The advantage in having such a degree of trust is that everyone is working from the same premise, and working to achieve goals based on the same values and assumptions. In the case of inclusion, the enterprise is based on a team effort. One difficulty we could see in such instances might be when difficult decisions have to be made (e.g., reduction of staff due to financial constraints), teachers may feel that they have been betrayed even when the circumstances are beyond administrative control. Such a severe reaction would likely mean that trust is seriously damaged or destroyed.

PART THREE: SYNTHESIS

In this section, we bring together the findings from Parts One and Two with a view to extrapolating what these findings mean for a principal's practice and decision making relative to inclusion. The key point to be stressed here is that for a school to have a culture based on the principles of inclusion, teachers need to feel supported and they have to have the trust of, and in, the principal. For this to happen, the principal needs to use inclusive practices not only when working with students, but also when working with teachers (Gurr, Drysdale & Mulford, 2006), through decisions and practices based on inclusive values and beliefs. Through such actions, the principal will signal to teachers the importance of their work, provide support for their efforts, and thus help to build and sustain an inclusive school culture. We suggest three basic principles on which principals should function to build trust and to provide evidence of support for teachers.

Basic Principle 1: Principals need to be consistent between what they say and what they do. This principle may sound obvious, but our research suggests that not all administrators follow this principle. We found consistent evidence that principals made decisions or used practices that had little evident connection with their espoused values, or only tangentially so. When this happened, teachers expressed their uncertainty in the principal because they did not have a clear indication of the foundational values and beliefs upon which the principal based his/her decisions, nor could they believe that what the principal said was what the principal believed, given his/her actions.

This principle of consistency is important because teachers need to feel that they can predict how their administrator will function in various situations. Teaching is difficult enough without having to be tentative about the degree to which the principal will support teachers' decisions or to be concerned whether the principal will support them when they are faced with difficult situations. In our study, we found that only when teachers saw the consistency between the administrator's words and deeds did teachers have the ability to predict with certainty a principal's actions. At this point, trust in the administrator began to develop, and a solid working relationship established. To facilitate the building of trust, we suggest that principals consider the following practices:

1. Wherever possible, principals need to clarify and communicate the values and beliefs upon which they base their decisions and practices. This will entrench these values and beliefs in the minds of teachers and act as reference points for their analysis of a principal's actions.
2. Principals need to be consistent in their practices and decisions, and to point out, at least in the beginning, how these practices and decisions fit within their framework of values and beliefs. This will enable teachers to observe the patterns of actions and develop the ability to predict how the principal will react in any given situation.
3. Principals need to maintain consistent and clear lines of communication that involve both speaking and listening to teachers, and discussing with them in a professional manner any misconceptions that they may have about the principal's values and beliefs.

Basic Principle 2: Principals need to advocate for the inclusion of all students. This builds on the first principle. One of our graduate students (Baker, 2007) found an inclusive school culture had been created when the principal acted as the advocate for students with special needs. In this particular case, the principal's main set of values and beliefs was grounded in the principles of inclusion. He clearly stated this, and then focused his decisions on developing inclusionary practices and a school culture that embraced inclusion. His communication of his belief in inclusion and the consistency between this belief and his practices sent a strong message to teachers and support staff. To facilitate the building and maintenance of an inclusive school culture, we suggest that principals consider the following practices:

1. The establishment or maintenance of an inclusive school culture is dependent on how well the principal uses the principles of inclusionary practices for all members of the school community, including teachers and staff. For this reason, administrators need to reflect constantly on whether a decision or a practice is consistent with inclusionary principles, and to adjust decisions and practices accordingly if they do not fall within the framework of these principles.
2. Teachers need opportunities to discuss what an inclusive school culture means for their practice. Their concerns, suggestions and their reluctance need to be acknowledged and addressed in an inclusionary manner.
3. Teachers need support, which may include counselling, both professionally and personally. The teachers to whom we talked appreciated the time given by us because they felt as if they had someone who would listen to their concerns; whether we were able to do anything to address their concerns did not seem to be important. Principals need to be aware of teachers' concerns, to discuss ways to address these concerns, and to identify those resources that can be used to support the individual teachers' needs.

Basic Principle 3: Building and maintaining an inclusive school culture takes time. We found that trust evolved over time and could not be mandated by fiat or demanded. Those principals who were given a great deal of trust appeared to realise this fact early on, and planned for the long term. They developed strategic practices that consciously built on previous actions (A) to develop working policies (P) that were based on clearly identifiable values (V) (Northfield, Macmillan, & Meyer, 2008). The consistency of the interactions between and among the A-P-V framework helped teachers to analyse principal's practices and decisions. This is especially crucial for principals attempting to create and maintain inclusive school cultures, because, as teachers readily indicated in the first study, inclusion may be philosophically and morally sound, but putting it into practice can be extremely difficult. Over time, and with appropriate support from the administrator, inclusionary practices can be established and eventually permeate throughout the school, such that inclusion is not in question, but a natural state of the culture. To facilitate the creation and maintenance of inclusive school cultures, we suggest that principals consider the following practices:

1. The principal needs to arrange opportunities to collaborate that enable teachers not only to understand the issues surrounding the implementation of inclusion and the identification of best instructional practices, but also to share what works well with the specific students they meet. By providing these opportunities, teachers will build the network of support among their colleagues with the principal as an integral part in this network.

2. Teachers need professional development that is developmental in its approach. It should enable teachers to first gain understanding of the general principles behind program modification and instructional adaptation, and then progress to understanding the specific modifications that they can make to meet the needs of individual students. The principal is an essential partner in this professional development in that the administrator also needs to have similar knowledge as the teachers in order to be able to make informed decisions in support of teachers' efforts.

3. Principals need to think creatively when assigning workloads and schedules such that teachers have time to collaborate and to share ideas. Principals also need to adapt timetables to best meet the needs of individual students. For example, some students may respond better in mornings than afternoons, when dealing with specific courses.

FINAL COMMENTS

As mentioned at the beginning of this chapter, the research is consistent in its findings about the importance of the principal in school improvement. We suggest here that the principal plays an even more important role in developing an inclusive school culture, which may mean shifting the fundamental way that teachers teach and the way in which the school functions. Principals have to be the key advocates for students with special needs when working with teachers, while at the same time they must also advocate for teachers who are trying to understand the implications for including students. The task is not an easy one and requires time, effort, and a great deal of patience, but in the end if the principals are successful, the reward is a school which addresses the needs of all students, not just those with special needs.

REFERENCES

Baker, D. (2007). The principal's contribution to developing and maintaining inclusive schooling for students with special needs. Unpublished master's thesis at the University of Western Ontario, London, Ontario, Canada.

Barth, R. (2003). *Lessons learned: Shaping relationships and the culture of the workplace.* Thousand Oaks, CA: Corwin.

Bunch, F., Lupart, J., & Brown, M. (1997). *Resistance and acceptance: Educator attitudes to inclusion of students with disabilities.* North York: York University.

Davenport, T., & Prusack, L. (1998). *Working knowledge.* Boston: Harvard Business School.

Edmunds, A., Halsall, A., & Macmillan, R. (2000, April). *The impact of budgetary cuts on education: Report from a teachers' survey.* Halifax, NS: The Nova Scotia Teachers' Union.

Gurr, D., Drysdale, L., & Mulford, B. (2007). Instructional leadership in three Australian schools. *International Studies in Educational Administration, 35*(3), 20–29.

Gurr, D., Drysdale, L., & Mulford, B. (2006). Models of successful principal leadership. *School Leadership and Management, 26*(4), 371–395.

Hallinger, P. (2003). Leading educational change: Reflections on the practice of instructional and transformational leadership. *Cambridge Journal of Education, 33*(3), 329–351.

Hargreaves, A., & Fink, D, (2006). *Sustainable Leadership.* San Francisco: Jossey-Bass.

Hargreaves, A. (1994). *Changing teachers, changing times.* London: Cassell.

Harmon, R., & Toomey, M. (1999). Creating a future we wish to inhabit. In F. Hesselbein, M. Goldsmith, & I. Somerville (Eds.), *Leading beyond the walls* (pp. 251–259). San Francisco: Jossey-Bass.

Kanter, R. M. (2004). *Confidence.* New York: Crown Business.

Kouses, J., & Posner, B. (2006). *A leader's legacy.* San Francisco: Jossey-Bass.

Macmillan, R., & Meyer, M. (2006). Guilt and inclusion: The emotional fallout for secondary teachers. *Exceptionalities Education Canada, 16*(1), 25–44.

Macmillan, R., Meyer, M., & Northfield, S. (2004). Trust and its role in principal succession: A preliminary examination of a continuum of trust. *Leadership and Policy in Schools, 3*(4), 275–294.

Macmillan, R., Meyer, M., Edmunds, A., Edmunds, G., & Feltmate, C. (2002). *A survey of impact of government funding cuts on inclusion: Report to the NSTU.* Halifax, NS: Nova Scotia Teachers' Union.

Northfield, S., Macmillan, R., & Meyer, M. (2008). Succession and trust development. *The CAP Journal, 16*(1), 15–18.

Reyes, P., & Wagstaff, L. (2005). How does leadership promote successful teaching and learning for diverse students? In W. Firstone & C. Riehl (Eds.), *A new agenda for research in educational leadership* (pp. 101–118). New York: Teachers College Press.

Robinson, R., & Carrington, S. (2002). Professional development for inclusive schooling. *The International Journal of Educational Management, 16*(4/5), 239–248.

Ryan, J. (2006). *Inclusive leadership.* San Francisco: Jossey-Bass.

Spillane, J. (2006). *Distributed leadership.* San Francisco: Jossey-Bass.

Tschannen-Moran, M. (2004). *Trust matters: Leadership for successful schools.* San Francisco: Jossey-Bass.

remember all
of things could
we be doing

ELIZABETH A. NOWICKI AND BOBA SAMUELS

Kids
attitudes be
might be
observed

8. FACILITATING POSITIVE PERCEPTIONS OF
EXCEPTIONAL STUDENTS

parent
teacher
attitudes

INTRODUCTION

In this chapter, we describe the psychosocial challenges of inclusion and review programs which have focused on improving the social acceptance of children with exceptionalities. We begin with an overview of research on children's attitudes towards, and the psychosocial difficulties experienced by, children with cognitive or physical exceptionalities (i.e., disabilities). Before specific intervention programs and their outcomes are considered, it is important to be aware of how children with exceptionalities are seen through the eyes of their classmates. Research has shown that children with exceptionalities are not only at risk for academic difficulties but are also likely to face negative peer evaluations at school. Social difficulties experienced during the elementary school years can lead to further challenges in forming healthy relationships during adolescence and adulthood. Thus, our goal in the first part of this chapter is to inform administrators about the psychosocial challenges of inclusion so that they will understand the pressing need to implement programs which aim to enhance the social inclusion of children with exceptionalities. The second part of the chapter reviews evidence-based research on interventions which have demonstrated some success in facilitating children's positive perceptions towards peers with exceptionalities. We hope this chapter will guide administrators towards a deeper understanding of the social difficulties faced by children with exceptionalities. We also hope this chapter will encourage administrators to work with their school communities to ensure that children with exceptionalities experience positive social inclusion at school.

Children's Attitudes towards Peers with Exceptionalities

Attitudes are complex. They are determined by personal beliefs and characteristics, the beliefs and behaviours of others, and environmental or situational variables (Eagly & Chaiken, 1993). Although a number of studies have concluded that children have negative perceptions of peers with exceptionalities, recent research suggests that degree of bias can be influenced by a variety of factors such as type and severity of disability; amount and accuracy of knowledge about exceptionalities; interactions with age, race and gender; and the kinds of questions children are asked (e.g., Diamond, Hestenes, Carpenter, & Innes, 1997; Nowicki, 2006a, 2006b, Nowicki, 2007, 2008; Norwich & Kelly, 2004; Ring & Travers, 2005).

A. L. Edmunds and R. B. Macmillan (eds.), Leadership for Inclusion: A Practical Guide, 83–92.

Attitudes towards classmates with cognitive or physical exceptionalities. Children's attitudes towards classmates with physical exceptionalities are usually more favourable than their attitudes towards classmates with cognitive exceptionalities (Nowicki, 2006a; Norwich & Kelly, 2004; Ring & Travers, 2005). Children tend to hold classmates with physical signs of disability, such as Down syndrome or the use of a wheelchair, less accountable for their conditions than they do children who do not have external signs of disability (Lewis & Lewis, 1987). It may be that children have a tendency to believe that cognitive exceptionalities can be overcome through trying harder, paying attention in school, and getting help from teachers and family. Physical exceptionalities, on the other hand, are considered to be beyond the control of the child, family, or school (Nowicki, 2007). Severity of disability can also impact on whether attitudes are positive, negative, neutral or pronounced. Greater functional limitations are more likely to be associated with more negative biases (Harper, 1997).

Knowledge about exceptionalities. Children need to be better informed about cognitive exceptionalities, and to some extent, physical exceptionalities. Although children seem to be able to distinguish between sensory, physical, and learning exceptionalities, they have more knowledge about physical exceptionalities than cognitive exceptionalities (Magiati, Dockrell, & Logotheti, 2002). It is important to emphasize, however, that quality rather than quantity of knowledge is important, especially as children's knowledge informs the beliefs they come to hold. Some children hold misinformed beliefs which need to be replaced with accurate knowledge, otherwise negative stereotypes may persist and have an impact on successful inclusion (Nowicki, 2007). Providing descriptive information alone (i.e. describing the similarities between students with and without exceptionalities) may not be effective in improving attitudes towards children with exceptionalities (Campbell, 2007). A recent study concluded that inaccurate and stereotypical beliefs about people with exceptionalities can lead to stigmatization (Hamovitch, 2007). Children in a segregated middle school were interviewed about their views of students in a special education class. Children with exceptionalities were viewed as being different from the norm and were considered to be deviant and inferior. Not surprisingly, children who have regular and positive contact with people with exceptionalities tend to be better informed about exceptionalities in general and have more accepting attitudes (Lewis, 1993).

Gender, age, and racial bias. Although children *in general* have less than positive attitudes towards classmates with exceptionalities, the question arises as to whether some groups of children are more accepting than others. Are age, gender, and racial biases important considerations? Do age differences figure in degree of bias? What about gender biases in childhood or racial prejudice? How do these attitudes intersect with attitudes about classmates with exceptionalities? Few studies have directly investigated these interactions, but recent research is making some progress in acknowledging that children with exceptionalities also belong to other social groups which encompass gender, race, and age (e.g., Nowicki, 2006b, 2007, 2008). These demographic characteristics may have a bearing on how children with exceptionalities are viewed by their classmates.

Girls and boys do not differ much in their attitudes towards classmates with exceptionalities. When gender differences are reported in the literature, they are often weak or confounded by some other factor such as age, whether children are being asked to evaluate someone of the same or opposite gender (e.g., Powlishta, Serbin, Doyle & White, 1994), or they are being asked about specific situations. For example, boys may be less accepting than girls about having peers with cognitive exceptionalities on sports teams, an attitude which may be due to boys' more competitive attitudes towards sports rather than a lower acceptance of peers with exceptionalities (Townsend & Hassell, 2007).

The effect of age is more pronounced. One of the consistent research findings is that younger children seem to be more biased than older children. Children around four years of age tend to view the world in a global manner. They see the world in absolutes with very little in between (Powlishta et al., 1994). This, in turn, extends to how they evaluate those around them. They tend to be more polarized in their attitudes towards classmates such that someone who possesses one or two highly salient, positive characteristics tends to be viewed as globally good, whereas someone who has one or two highly visible negative characteristics tends to be seen in a less positive way. Several studies have shown that younger children's gender, racial, and disability biases are more pronounced than those of older children (Aboud, 2003; Nowicki, 2006a, 2006b; Powlishta et al.; Underwood, 2004). Further, a child who has an exceptionality and is of the opposite gender or of a different race may be at a double disadvantage in terms of peer acceptance, especially among younger children (Nowicki, 2008). Older children, however, and specifically those towards the end of middle childhood (e.g., 11 or 12 years of age) are able to consider multiple characteristics of a person, and realize that someone can have, to varying degrees, both positive and negative characteristics. This realization coincides with a moderation of attitudes such that biases in either direction become less pronounced.

The kinds of questions children are asked. An important factor that can have an impact on determining whether children's attitudes towards classmates with exceptionalities are positive or negative, weak or strong, is the way in which research questions are asked. For example, children may be asked about their beliefs, feelings, or behaviours. Indeed, there is some discussion that attitudes may be a combination of these aspects (Eagly & Chaiken, 1993). For example, a child may believe that a classmate with a cognitive exceptionality is kind, which may translate into positive feelings and wanting to play with him/her. However, it is not clear if these three aspects of attitudes exist in tandem during childhood. Recent research suggests that feelings and behaviours may be more closely aligned than beliefs (Nowicki, 2006 a, 2006b). For instance, a child may hold negative beliefs about cognitive exceptionalities yet have positive feelings about peers with such exceptionalities and may want to interact with them. This distinction might explain the possibly surprising finding that, despite their actions, younger children are more negatively biased towards classmates with exceptionalities than are older children. It is possible that a child may hold negative beliefs about individuals with exceptionalities yet may still want to play with them.

Psychosocial problems of children with exceptionalities. Given the more negative perception of children with exceptionalities by their classmates, there is an increased risk for psychosocial problems. Children's perceptions of classmates with exceptionalities often translate into behaviours that can make inclusion a challenge. Children with exceptionalities are more likely to be neglected or rejected by their peers than are children without exceptionalities (Hamovitch, 2007; Vaughn, Elbaum & Schumm, 1996). Peer rejection may lead to a preference for working or playing alone in order to avoid further negative experiences (Meadan & Halle, 2004). Isolation can, in turn, increase a child's chances of being bullied. It is not surprising, therefore, to find that children with exceptionalities are more likely to be targeted in bullying incidents (Faye, 2003). They are also more likely to be perceived by teachers and peers as a problematic subgroup within the class who are disengaged from their peers and their studies (Hamovitch, 2007). Negative peer experiences can impact on school success, self-esteem, and social-emotional adjustment later in life.

Research has also shown that quality of friendships and academic performance are closely related. Children who experience positive social relationships at school have better academic achievement than children who are rejected or neglected by their peers (Malecki & Elliot, 2002). Social skills may be a mediating factor in the relationship between quality of friendship and social success because children with cognitive exceptionalities often have difficulties in interpreting both social *and* academic information (Meadan & Halle, 2007). In addition, children with exceptionalities who have developed high levels of social skills are judged more positively by their peers than children with poorer social skills. Consequently, some children with cognitive exceptionalities will benefit from remedial instruction on social skills and academic learning.

Administrators need to be aware of the fact that children with exceptionalities are not only dealing with academic difficulties, but they may also be struggling with poor social acceptance, which in turn, can have long term consequences (Nowicki, 2003). The negative psychosocial aspects of inclusion therefore need to be overcome if children are to accept classmates with exceptionalities. There is ample evidence to suggest that children's attitudes towards classmates with exceptionalities are less positive than their attitudes towards classmates who do not have exceptionalities. Such negative attitudes towards classmates with exceptionalities can translate into exclusionary behaviours. Interventions which are aimed at facilitating inclusion should therefore focus on creating both attitude *and* behavioural changes.

Administrators need to understand the social difficulties faced by children with exceptionalities, and must be cognizant that these difficulties can have long-lasting effects on a child's psychosocial well-being. Thus, it is critical that inclusive schools are safe, welcoming, and without bias or prejudice. To accomplish this, administrators need to become informed about effective social intervention programs. With this knowledge, they will be in a better position to explain to their school communities why intervention programs are needed, and why the programs and strategies they have chosen to implement in their schools need to be successful.

A Review of Programs Designed to Enhance the Acceptance of Students with Exceptionalities

Full-time inclusion does not necessarily result in better acceptance of children with exceptionalities by their classmates unless specific interventions or policies are implemented (Gibb, Tunbridge, Chua & Frederickson, 2007). In the remainder of this chapter, we will review recent programs and strategies which have focused on improving children's acceptance of classmates with exceptionalities. These interventions have been chosen for review because they have been evaluated by experts and described in peer-reviewed academic journals. Thus, they have been closely scrutinized by educators and researchers who adhere to ethical research standards and practices.

Explicitly teaching everyday social interactions. Explicit instruction on how to encourage positive interactions between children with and without exceptionalities can benefit both teachers (Hundert, 2007) and children (Gibb et al., 2007). Strategies need not be complex to be effective. For example, teachers can use positive reinforcement when children with and without exceptionalities are interacting appropriately. When interactions are not prosocial, explicit instructions about what was inappropriate, why the behaviour was inappropriate, and what would have been appropriate behaviour need to be provided. Negative interactions should be met with informative feedback, and positive interactions need to be reinforced. Hundert also recommended that early years elementary classroom teachers should preplan play activities which require interactions between children with and without exceptionalities rather than leaving responsibility for objectives to resource teachers and paraprofessionals who tend to focus on individual objectives for children with exceptionalities. In early years classrooms, planning seating arrangements for circle time, using smaller circles, and planned interactive peer activities can be effective. Team meetings when teachers and paraprofessionals come together to plan and share ideas about how to better include children with exceptionalities can assist in the development and implementation of specific strategies. Team members need to make a concerted effort to plan activities which include all children, and to be vigilant about guiding prosocial behaviours.

Some of the social difficulties experienced by children with exceptionalities may stem from poor social skills or poor social competence. Children with exceptionalities are frequently rated by their peers and teachers as being lower in social competence than children without exceptionalities (Meadan & Halle, 2007).

Children with and without exceptionalities need to be explicitly taught social skills such as taking turns, reciprocity in conversing, initiating contact, and terminating social exchanges to facilitate positive and respectful interactions.

The open circle program. The Open Circle Program (Hennessey, 2007) is a school-wide intervention similar to Tribes (Gibbs, 2006), with a focus on socio-emotional learning. Although the Open Circle Program and Tribes do not specifically target the inclusion of children with exceptionalities, the underlying premise is that building positive relationships amongst children and staff will foster the inclusion of all children who may otherwise be unaccepted by their peers. These kinds of programs have been in use by many schools for several years, but not all have undergone formal program evaluations. The Open Circle Program is an exception, and was recently evaluated on a demographically diverse group of approximately 150 fourth grade students (Hennessey). Teachers implementing the Open Circle Program undergo formal training, much as they would for Tribes or other programs, and are mentored by a supervisor who helps them develop these skills in their own classrooms. Classroom implementation of the Open Circle Program requires children and their teachers to participate in a twice weekly circle meeting to work on prepackaged lessons which specifically address social and communication skills such as listening, including others, speaking up, conflict resolution, self-esteem, and controlling anger. The circle also allows children and teachers to discuss current classroom issues and how the lessons apply to the children's own experiences. It provides children with a positive and supportive environment in which to develop self-esteem, positive relationships, respectful communication, and solving social problems. Children are encouraged and expected to apply the lessons to their daily activities. Hennessey found that children who participated in the program for one school year showed improvements in social skills and decreased problem behaviours. Inclusion of children who were neglected or rejected by their peers also improved. These trends were relatively consistent across ability, ethnic, and gender groups.

Positive peer reporting and tootling. Another effective class-wide intervention which improves the acceptance of children with exceptionalities by their peers is positive peer reporting. Research has shown it to be an effective peer-mediated intervention which increases the social acceptance of children who are socially rejected or neglected by their peers, and decreases bullying, teasing, and other negative peer interactions (Morrison & Jones, 2004). Positive peer reporting takes place at daily meetings between children and their teachers with a focus on praising a target child for appropriate behaviour and classroom performance. The premise is that public, positive reinforcement of a child will promote positive behaviour within the child and will change how they are perceived by their peers.

Tootling, a word derived from 'tattling' and the phrase 'blowing your own horn' is similar to positive peer reporting but differs in that the focus is on any student rather than a specific target child. Another difference is that children privately record behaviours on index cards throughout the day. The index cards are gathered, screened by the teacher, and displayed. Tootling is effective in enhancing positive peer relationships and inclusion (Skinner, Cashwell & Skinner, 2002). Morrison and Jones (2004) combined tootling with positive peer reinforcement in two Grade Three inclusive classrooms. Children received explicit instruction on how to provide praise for good behaviour (e.g., look at the person, smile, describe what they said or did, then provide praise such as 'good job'). Once this skill had been learned, the Positive Peer Reporting Game was played. The game was based around a carnival-style wheel of chance. The teacher would spin the wheel to identify the first child to receive praise. Any child could volunteer to praise the selected child, or the teacher might call on a particular student. Appropriate praise was rewarded with a sticker. The game was played for fifteen minutes each day for several weeks. During the intervention, positive effects on behaviour were found. Problem classroom behaviours decreased and improvements generalized to lunchtime and transition times. There were also significant reductions in the number of socially neglected or isolated children. Children with exceptionalities were also included more by their peers. These improvements may have been due to providing unpopular children with the opportunity to give and receive praise; providing all children with explicit instruction on how to give praise; and providing a regular, structured, and positive environment in which to practice these skills.

Peer tutoring. Peer tutoring is one of the most popular interventions aimed at improving the acceptance of children with exceptionalities. It can provide both academic and social support. There are several kinds of peer tutoring including homogenous tutoring in which both tutee and tutor have the same level of ability, heterogeneous tutoring in which a child is tutored by a same-age peer of higher ability, cross-age tutoring which typically involves a tutee who is younger than the tutor, and reverse role tutoring whereby a child with exceptionalities tutors a student who does not have a exceptionality. Although each of these kinds of tutoring have been shown to be somewhat effective in evidence-based studies, the most effective in improving academic and social outcomes is heterogeneous tutoring (Stenhoff & Lignugaris/Kraft, 2007). However, in order for any tutee-tutor configuration to be effective, it is essential that the tutor receive explicit instruction in *how* to tutor and *what* to tutor. Important elements of tutor training include providing the tutor with highly structured lesson plans, modelling and role playing of appropriate tutor and tutee behaviour, monitoring tutoring sessions to provide feedback, providing opportunities for tutor and tutee to discuss progress and problems, carefully matching tutor and tutee on personal characteristics, and ensuring that tutor and tutee are sufficiently different in skill level.

Other school-wide interventions. Brigham, Morocco, Clay and Zigmond (2006) summarized the characteristics which make a school a good school for children with exceptionalities. Although their focus was on high schools, several of these characteristics can be applied to elementary schools. For example, creation of affinity groups allow students with exceptionalities to come together to discuss disability challenges. Providing opportunities for students with exceptionalities to undertake leadership roles, and actively promoting accessibility to school clubs can enhance a sense of community among all students. Arrangement for students to share and take notes with one another, and participation in high profile activities such as theatre productions need to be actively promoted. In addition, effective schools use a number of strategies which come from concerted school-wide efforts to build supportive and inclusive environments for all students regardless of disability status, ethnic or racial background, or gender. These schools allow students to develop a sense of identity and belonging so that students feel they belong regardless of whether or not they have a disability. Further, strong leadership from school administration ensures that special education teachers are not marginalized by other staff. Administrators also need to engender a sense of responsibility for all students which should be shared by the school community. Successful schools make a purposeful mission to provide an environment in which students with exceptionalities can succeed, and in doing so, create schools that serve all students well.

Summary of interventions. Evidence-based research has resulted in identifying interventions which can enhance the social inclusion of children with exceptionalities. Interventions can range from simple, everyday strategies used on an individual basis, to class-wide and school-wide initiatives. Using positive reinforcement when students engage in respectful behaviour, carefully planning inclusive activities, and providing children with opportunities to develop good social skills are within the reach of regular classroom teachers. Carefully structured, class-wide activities such as positive peer reporting, tootling, or a combination of both, are other ways to build inclusive classroom communities. Replacing misinformed beliefs about exceptionalities with accurate information can also reduce stigmatization and enhance acceptance. Peer tutoring can be effective, though it requires careful planning. Simply pairing children and expecting them to fit comfortably into the tutor – tutee relationship does not necessarily enhance inclusion. Finally, school-wide initiatives such as the Open Circle Program and adopting a school culture of inclusion for all students are showing promising results in the evidence-based studies.

The interventions and strategies discussed in this chapter have been shown to be effective in peer-reviewed research studies. Although teachers and administrators can use some of these interventions on a case by case basis, school-wide programs can promote a culture of inclusion among administrators, special education and regular teachers, children with or without exceptionalities, families, and other community members. Such school-wide initiatives require strong leadership and a dedicated school community. A shared vision to improve the social well-being of all students is necessary if children with exceptionalities are to be accepted by their peers.

Implementing such a vision, however, requires that sufficient financial resources for professional development and for classroom resources be in place (Forness & Kavale, 1996), which can be a challenge when budgets are tight. Nonetheless, when a child is dealing with academic and social difficulties, school can be a difficult place. Given the long term impact of social rejection or neglect by peers, children with exceptionalities must have positive learning *and* social experiences at school. Investing in children at the early stages of schooling by teaching prosocial behaviours and inclusive attitudes is a proactive way to offset social-emotional difficulties which may otherwise develop and persist throughout a child's schooling.

As facilitators of change, it is essential that school administrators become informed about the social issues faced by children with exceptionalities, and that they become informed about evidence-based intervention programs. It is also important that this knowledge base is shared with teachers who need to know why an intervention program is being implemented. Educating teachers about the unique psychosocial challenges faced by children with exceptionalities is a necessary preliminary step in program implementation. Earlier, we mentioned that children's attitudes and behaviours need to be changed so that their classmates with exceptionalities feel genuinely included at school. We also mentioned that knowledge can be effective in changing attitudes, and that positive attitudes can lead to positive behaviours. This also holds for administrators and teachers who need to know *why* change is needed, and *what* they can do to accomplish change. We hope this chapter will encourage administrators to reflect on the psychosocial challenges experienced by children with exceptionalities, to educate their school communities about these issues, and to implement effective social inclusion programs so that children with exceptionalities can develop healthy relationships at school and beyond.

REFERENCES

Brigham, N., Morocco, C. C., Clay, K., & Zigmond, N. (2006). What makes a high school a good high school for students with disabilities. *Learning Disabilities Research & Practice, 2*(3), 184–190.

Campbell, J. M. (2007). Middle school students' response to the self-introduction of a student with autism: Effects of perceived similarity, prior awareness, and educational message. *Remedial and Special Education, 28*(3), 163–173.

Eagly, A. H., & Chaiken, S. (1993). *The psychology of attitudes.* Fort Worth, TX: Harcourt Brace Jovanovich, Inc.

Diamond, K., Hestenes, L., Carpenter, E., & Innes, F. (1997). Relationships between enrolment in an inclusive class and preschool children's ideas about people with disabilities. *Topics in Early Childhood Special Education, 17*, 520–536.

Doyle, A., & Aboud, F. E. (1995). A longitudinal study of white children's racial prejudice as a social-cognitive development. *Merrill-Palmer Quarterly, 41*, 209–228.

Faye, M. (2003). Learning disabilities and bullying: Double jeopardy. *Journal of Learning Disabilities, 36*, 336–347.

Forness, S. R., & Kavale, K. A. (1996). Treating social skills deficits in children with learning disabilities. *Learning Disability Quarterly, 19*, 2–13.

Gibb, J. (2006). *Reaching all by creating tribes learning communities.* Windsor, CA: CentreSource Systems, LLC.

Gibb, K., Tunbridge, D., Chua, A., & Frederickson, N. (2007). Pathways to inclusion: Moving from special school to mainstream. *Educational Psychology in Practice, 23*(2), 109–127.

Hamovitch, B. (2007). Hoping for the best: "Inclusion" and stigmatization in a middle school. In S. Books (Ed.), *Invisible children in the society and in schools* (3rd ed., pp. 263–281). Mahwah, NJ: Lawrence Erlbaum.

Harper, D. (1997). Children's attitudes toward physical disability in Nepal. *Journal of Cross Cultural Psychology, 28*, 710–729.

Hennessey, B. A. (2007). Promoting social competence in school-aged children: The effects of the Open Circle Program. *Journal of School Psychology, 45*(3), 349–360.

Hundert, J. P. (2007). Training classroom and resource preschool teachers to develop inclusive class interventions for children with disabilities: Generalization to new intervention targets. *Journal of Positive Behavior Interventions, 9*(3), 159–173.

Lewis, A. (1993). Primary school children's understanding of severe learning difficulties. *Educational Psychology, 13*, 133–141.

Lewis, A., & Lewis, V. (1987). The attitudes of young persons towards peers with severe intellectual disabilities. *British Journal of Developmental Psychology, 5*, 287–292.

Magiati, I., Dockrell, J. E., & Logotheti, A. (2002). Young children's understanding of disabilities: The influence of development, context and cognition. *Journal of Applied Developmental Psychology, 23*, 409–430.

Malecki, C. K., & Elliott, S. N. (2002). Children's social behaviours as predictors of academic achievement: A longitudinal analysis. *Social Psychology Quarterly, 17*, 1–23.

Meadan, H., & Halle, J. W. (2004). Social perceptions of students with learning disabilities who differ in social status. *Learning Disabilities Research & Practice, 19*(2), 71–82.

Morrison, J. Q., & Jones, K. M. (2007). The effects of positive peer reporting as a class-wide positive behavior support. *Journal of Behavioral Education, 16*(2), 111–124.

Norwich, B., & Kelly, N. (2004). Pupils' views on inclusion: Moderate learning difficulties and bullying in mainstream and special schools. *British Educational Research, 30*, 43–65.

Nowicki, E. A. (2008). The interaction of attitudes toward racial membership and learning ability in school-age children. *Educational Psychology, 28*, 229–244.

Nowicki, E. A. (2007). Children's beliefs about learning and physical difficulties. *International Journal of Disability, Development, and Education, 54*(4), 463–473.

Nowicki, E. A. (2006a). A cross-sectional multivariate analysis of children's attitudes towards disabilities. *Journal of Intellectual Disability Research, 50*, 335–348.

Nowicki, E. A. (2006b). Children's cognitions, behavioural intent, and affect toward girls and boys of lower or higher learning ability. *Learning Disabilities: A Contemporary Journal, 4*, 43–57.

Nowicki, E. A. (2003). A meta-analysis of the social competence of children with learning disabilities compared to classmates of low and average-to-high achievement. *Learning Disability Quarterly, 26*, 171–188.

Powlishta, K. K., Serbin, L. A., Doyle, A., & White, D. R. (1994). Gender, ethnicity, and body type biases: The generality of prejudice in childhood. *Developmental Psychology, 30*, 526–536.

Ring, E., & Travers, J. (2005). Barriers to inclusion: A case study of a pupil with severe learning difficulties in Ireland. *European Journal of Special Needs Education, 20*, 41–56.

Stenhoff, D. M., & Lignugaris/Kraft, B. (2007). A review of the effect of peer tutoring on students with mild disabilities in secondary settings. *Exceptional Children, 74*(1), 8–30.

Townsend, M., & Hassall, J. (2007). Mainstream students' attitudes to possible inclusion in unified sports with students who have an intellectual disability. *Journal of Applied Research in Intellectual Disabilities, 20*, 265–273.

Underwood, M. K. (2004). Gender and peer relations: Are the two gender cultures really that different? In J. B. Kupersmidt & K. A. Dodge (Eds.), *Children's peer relations: From development to intervention* (pp. 21–37). Washington, DC: American Psychological Association.

Vaughn, S., Elbaum, B. E., & Schumm, J. S. (1996). The effects of inclusion on the social functioning of students with learning disabilities. *Journal of Learning Disabilities, 29*, 598–608.

ALAN L. EDMUNDS

9. THE PRINCIPAL'S ROLE IN THE ASSESSMENT AND IEP PROCESS

INTRODUCTION

By definition, students with exceptionalities do not learn easily or efficiently (except those categorized as gifted and talented) and, therefore, they do not usually benefit from typical instructional methods (and/or from exposure to the regular curriculum).

> Special education is a particular type of schooling that is constructed and delivered to suit the specific strengths and needs of students with exceptionalities ... special education is not something that should be viewed as being highly complex, secretive or mystical, nor should it be perceived as something that can only be practiced by a select few teachers ... special education is best viewed as nothing more than exemplary teaching practices that all teachers can easily implement or make adjustments to with some experience, wherein these teaching practices are designed and implemented based on specific types of information (Edmunds & Edmunds, 2007; pp. 20–21).

While the instructional responsibility for students with exceptionalities lies predominantly with teachers, the administrative responsibility for the processes that enable the design and development of such instruction lies with principals, vice-principals, and school board administrators. This chapter outlines the detailed inner workings of the entire assessment and IEP process and along the way provides administrators with a series of related recommendations that can be implemented to make the process more efficient and effective for their teachers. Many of the recommendations can be presented/discussed at staff meetings or delivered as part of an ongoing professional development program. The recommendations are an attempt to cover all of the important aspects of the assessment and IEP process and to address the major concerns that regularly arise for regular classroom teachers. While some of the recommendations may appear pedantic or trivial in the larger scheme of things, it is amazing how often they crop up when teachers are asked to present their pet peeves about this supposedly straightforward process. After reading this chapter and hopefully sharing it with your teachers, it is quite likely that you and your teaching staff will use its contents to formulate further recommendations to suit the specific needs of your school.

A. L. Edmunds and R. B. Macmillan (eds.), Leadership for Inclusion: A Practical Guide, 93–102.
© *2010 Sense Publishers. All Rights Reserved.*

THE ASSESSMENT AND IEP PROCESS

In the majority of cases, the formal psycho-educational assessment process and the resulting IEP provide educators with the specific types of information they need to make educational programming decisions about students with exceptionalities. The formal assessment involves a battery of diagnostic evaluations that typically examine *what a student knows* and *the cognitive processes he/she uses to learn or to demonstrate learning*. These and other specific pieces of information are collectively used to make decisions about the design and development of a student's IEP (Individualized Education Program). The IEP is an official and legal document that clearly portrays the instructional interventions that need to be implemented (or avoided) so that the student in question can achieve his or her academic potential (Council for Exceptional Children, 2004; IDEA: U.S. Department of Education, 2000). In some cases, the IEP also delineates the curricula to be taught, especially if it is considerably different from what the student would normally encounter in their age-appropriate grade or classroom.

The overall process of facilitating the psycho-educational assessment and developing a student's IEP is the *sine qua non* of inclusion. This proven, reliable and consistent process enables students with exceptionalities to remain in their regular classes, in their community schools, and to learn and associate with their peers, yet still benefit from differentiated instructional techniques that are individualized to suit to their personal strengths and needs. However, without a assessment or an IEP, educators are merely guessing about what needs to be done differently for students with exceptionalities and in these instances, educators are likely to make inappropriate educational decisions, if they make any decisions at all. Teachers and administrators are so well versed in their instructive and administrational disciplines that they can easily adapt to any student's *known* situation; however, no educator can adapt to even a single student's *unknown* situation.

The Six Phases of the Assessment and IEP Process

The assessment and IEP process described below is the most common approach found throughout the inclusion literature. According to Edmunds & Edmunds (2007), there are six fundamental phases: 1) identification; 2) diagnostic instruction; 3) referral; 4) assessment/IEP formulation; 5) educational intervention; and, 6) evaluation of student progress (p. 22).

Phase One: Identification

It does not take long for an experienced and/or conscientious teacher to figure out that a particular student is not learning as rapidly or as well as their peers, or that a student is demonstrating inconsistent abilities. This is especially true of elementary teachers because they spend more time with students on a daily basis than secondary teachers.

Recommendation #1. Encourage your teachers, especially elementary teachers, to trust their intuition that something is amiss and to act as early as possible. According to Lerner, Mardell-Czudnowski, & Goldenberg (1981), nearly 20% of legitimate special education referrals result from such observations.

Recommendation #2. Provide your special education teachers (or other specialists) with access to readily available commercial screening tests and make it a policy that they will have the time to implement and interpret these tests at the beginning of every year for all new students. These instruments account for the other 80% of legitimate special education referrals.

The inclusion literature is replete with evidence that an early identification process is exponentially beneficial for students' learning potentials (Shonkoff & Meisels, 2000). Additionally, the broad application of screening tests is multiply beneficial;
1) they are very cost efficient;
2) they quickly identify minor problems that can easily be rectified by proper instruction (or review), thereby reducing false-positive referrals;
3) they reduce the identification workload of regular classroom teachers;
4) the results are used to confirm teacher referrals.

Recommendation #3. Provide professional development for your teachers that specifically outlines the warning signs of students with learning problems so they can be confident in their knowledge and react quickly.

Phase Two: Diagnostic Instruction

Diagnostic instruction is the second step in the assessment process. This simply means that teachers are required to make minor or intricate instructional adjustments to their normal teaching methods (such as using manipulatives instead of lectures) and then document whether those adjustments alleviate the student's learning difficulty. This requirement improves and expands teachers' instruction, it prevents teachers from making unnecessary referrals, and it alerts teachers to the possibility that particular instructional approaches, despite their effectiveness for other students, can actually worsen a student's difficulties.

Recommendation #4. Provide professional development for your teachers that specifically outlines straightforward and quickly-made instructional modifications that teachers can make. This can easily be paired with the PD referred to in Recommendation #3 above.

It is important to note that this documentation of the attempted instructional changes and their effectiveness is crucial to all of the subsequent steps in the overall assessment and IEP process; it provides much needed information to the school-based team and to the student's other teachers and it provides insights as to how all required educational interventions need to be designed (or not designed).

Recommendation #5. Provide teachers with an example case study that outlines the successful use of Diagnostic Instruction as described above. It is often easier to emulate and/or modify the work of others than to create something from scratch, especially for new teachers.

Many teachers' intuitions about the significance of student learning problems are usually correct but often, and despite valid instructional adjustments, these problems persist. Nonetheless, with the results of the diagnostic instruction in hand, the teacher is well prepared to make a referral for further assessment.

Recommendation #6. Make sure that all school personnel are fully aware of the referral process and all the required paperwork. Particular attention must be paid to clearly announcing the individual responsible for receiving and acting on teacher or parent referrals. Nothing bogs the assessment and IEP process down more, or more often, than an inexact chain of procedure.

Responsiveness to intervention (RTI) is an assessment/instructional approach that is similar in conceptualization to Diagnostic Instruction except RTI is primarily designed for identifying students with learning disabilities and it is still in its early stages of validation. The US Department of Education in 2004 passed Public Law 108–446, the Individuals With Disabilities Education Improvement Act (IDEA, 2004), to change the assessment emphasis for students with learning disabilities from the discrepancy model to a model that emphasized instructional effectiveness. Many researchers and educators involved in learning disabilities were dissatisfied that under the discrepancy model, students with learning disabilities had to endure two or three years of failure before being eligible for the assessment process and supportive educational services. The IDEA statute reads as follows:

> In determining whether a child has a specific learning disability, a local educational agency may use a process that determines if the child responds to scientific, research-based interventions as a part of the evaluation procedures... a local educational agency shall not be required to take into consideration whether a child has a severe discrepancy between achievement and intellectual ability (Section 614 (b)(6)(B).

In addition to eliminating the previously required wait time before referring a student, RTI is founded on the notion of providing research-based interventions so that students are not being referred for assessments and/or special education services simply because they did not receive proper instruction.

It would appear that RTI's guiding principles of evidence-based practice as preventative instruction would benefit teacher's implementation of diagnostic instructional concepts. This author is in favor of its dynamic and recursive elements that emphasizes empirically proven instructional methods. It should be noted, however, that RTI is in its infancy and "...in order for RTI to gain appropriate validation, it must be put to careful and rigorous research. (Kame'enui, 2007). Peck and Scarpati (2007) further suggested that the existing guidelines for implementing RTI would change and evolve as new research investigated instructional and assessment practices.

Phase Three: Referral

Making a referral usually requires the completion of a referral form that outlines what the student's problems are perceived to be and the attempts made by teachers to correct those problems and the outcomes of these attempts. This document is usually accompanied by examples of the student's work, indications of the student's academic performance to date, and any other pertinent information that teachers feel may help the process (i.e.: attendance records and/or behavioral concerns).

Recommendation #8. Keep the referral form to one page and the information required on the form to a minimum.

Recommendation #9. Provide teachers with an example that delineates a minimal but effective list of pertinent information.

Completed referrals are presented to the school-based team (SBT) which has the responsibility of carefully examining all the presented referral information and deciding on a course of action. The SBT is usually comprised of the special education teacher, the referring teacher, the student's other teachers, and the principal or vice-principal (and sometimes parents). School-based teams usually select one of the following courses of action:
a) suggesting the trial use of not-yet-implemented instructional methods (teacher implements, evaluates, and reports back to the team);
b) referring the student for informal assessment testing by special education teacher;
c) referring the student for a formal psycho-educational assessment by a school psychologist.

Recommendation #10. Make sure that: 1) all members of the team have copies of the referral, 2) the person responsible for all the student's school files has them at the meeting, 3) the procedure by which the school based team operates is specific and formalized, and 4) the outcome decision is decided by majority vote. This will keep the meeting focused and meaningful.

Recommendation #11a. If the school-based team refers the student for a psycho-educational assessment, make it a school-wide policy that while waiting for the assessment to be completed, the student is to continue to engage in school activities as long as there is a reasonable assumption of success. It is inappropriate that educators allow the child to stagnate pending the outcome of the assessment results.

Recommendation #11b. If the work a student is required to do is considerably beyond their capabilities, allow your special education personnel, in consultation with the student's parents, to assign work that has the potential for success so the student do not become disheartened.

Recommendation #11c. Not all of the tests used in psycho-educational assessments have to be administered and interpreted by psychologists. Make it a policy that the psychologist provides your special education teachers with suitable assessment tools which can be used, after consultation with the psychologist by phone, to expedite some educational interventions.

Phase Four: Assessment/IEP

The psychologist's report contains the results of the psycho-educational assessment and can also include supplementary reports from other professionals (i.e.: speech and language pathologists, physical and occupational therapists, psychiatrists, social workers). The results are interpreted and transformed into recommendations for a variety of educational interventions and this information is presented to the school based team.

Recommendation #12. Respectfully but firmly require that the psychologist illustrate concrete examples of what teachers and other educators should do to help the student in question. Nothing aggravates teachers more than having to interpret the results and design teaching strategies without any input from the diagnostician. This is not teachers' expertise and it will only add to their feelings of being overwhelmed.

Based on discussions with the psychologist/diagnostician, the SBT describes the specific ways a student's special educational needs are going to be met and documents this information in the student's IEP. While many parts of this chapter deserve any administrator's full attention, the following section regarding the design and maintenance of the IEP warrants particular scrutiny because the principal is the person legally responsible for its proper implementation.

Recommendation #13a. Make it a school policy that your *working IEP document* be no longer than one page and that all other relevant information remain in the student's school file (see Edmunds & Edmunds, 2007 for an exaple of a comprehensive one-page IEP). There is considerable evidence that IEPs are too long, take too long to work through or change, create excessive paperwork for teachers, and cause special educators to leave the profession (Edgar & Pair, 2005; Whitaker, 2003).

Recommendation #13b. Make it a school policy that all descriptions contained in the IEP will be outlined in plain language and that the IEP will contain at least one specific instructional or curricular example for each of the suggested recommendations. This is especially important for the short term objectives that will dominate the student's immediate schooling and will guide teachers' instructional activities. Werts, Mamlin & Pogoloff (2002) reported that teachers need more and better types of this kind of information within IEPs.

Recommendation #13c. Make it a school policy that all IEP long-term and short-term goals will be measurable and will be systematically evaluated to periodically indicate a student's progress. Far too many IEPs contain a variety of goals that are either not useful, not implemented, or not remarked upon, or all three.

Recommendation #13d. Make it a school policy that all special education and related services are feasible within your school. Most IEPs allude to services that are not available or practicable in many schools.

Recommendation #13e. To be consistent with the fundamental tenets of inclusion, make it a school policy that the regular classroom will be the first instructional placement option, but not the only placement option, for all students with exceptionalities.

Recommendation #13f. Make it a school policy that all IEPs will contain very specific language that details how and when: a) the student's progress will be evaluated and reported, and b) the entire IEP will be re-evaluated and/or re-designed.

Recommendation #13g. Make it a school policy that wherever possible and practicable, the student and his/her parents will be consulted in the IEP development process.

For those of you who are new to the domain of inclusion, it should now be clear how important the assessment process is to the overall academic success of students with exceptionalities. Edmunds & Edmunds (2007) clearly described this vital interrelationship, "Without proper assessment there can be no IEPs, without IEPs we do not have an individualization of the learning process, and without individualization we lose the very essence of special education (p. 25)"

Phase Five: Educational Intervention

The additions, deletions, adaptations and modifications that educators make to instruction or curricula according to the IEP are called *educational interventions*. Just as educators must design educational outcomes and objectives for non-exceptional students based on particular curricular milestones and goals, so too must educational interventions be constructed for students with exceptionalities. However, if these interventions are not derived from the appropriate curriculum, educators will have a difficult time determining whether a student has progressed academically.

Recommendation #14a. Make it a school policy that all IEPs will contain educational interventions that are specifically designed to suit the strengths and needs of each particular student.

Recommendation #14b. Do not allow IEP writers to use generic descriptions or phrases as these do nothing to facilitate instruction. They do, however, cause reporting problems because they cannot clearly indicate standards of academic progress. Hint: A clearly and properly worded educational intervention should reveal the benefit the student will receive by its use and the academic progress he/she can expect.

Once the IEP has been designed and approved by the respective educators and parents, it is the responsibility of all educators to dutifully and conscientiously implement the IEP and all its related elements to the best of their abilities. The success of an IEP is not necessarily found in the academic progress of a student, although that is most certainly the most desirable outcome. Rather, the success of an IEP is in its proper design, evaluation and re-implementation in the face of less-than-desirable learning or behavioural outcomes for the student. Educators may not be able to guarantee academic progress for students with exceptionalities, but educators can guarantee the faithful and professional execution of their IEPS.

Phase Six: Evaluation of Student Progress

There is no question that one of the main complaints that teachers have about educating students with exceptionalities is the problem of knowing how to properly evaluate and report the progress of a student who is on an IEP. This writer suggests that the preponderance of these problems emanate from less-than-adequate assessment procedures, improperly designed and poorly worded IEPs, and from generically structured educational interventions that are not based on clear learning objectives.

Recommendation #15. Provide professional development for your teachers that specifically outlines the importance of the distinct curricular relationships that have to be upheld between and amongst assessment results, educational interventions, and the CBA approach (see below) to evaluating student progress.

Curriculum-based assessment (CBA) is a teacher's assessment of a student's academic progress (McLoughlin & Lewis, 2005) which compares that progress with either the curricular standards outlined in their IEP and/or the progress of their classmates. CBA utilizes brief and frequent evaluations of a student's mastery of academic domains (Overton, 1996) based on the long- and short-term objectives of the IEP. Curriculum-based assessment is preferred over standardized curricular tests which do little to properly indicate the educational abilities of students with exceptionalities (Gregory, 2000), especially given the systemic and curricular disconnect that naturally exists between standardized tests and classroom instruction. Unlike standardized measures which are static, CBA measures are constantly evolving to suit each specific student's ongoing progress. For these reasons, CBA has been found to be very effective in evaluating and monitoring the progress of students with exceptionalities (Fuchs and Fuchs, 1996; King-Sears, Burges, & Lawson, 1999) and it is a useful approach for determining whether teachers are on the right instructional track.

Recommendation #16. Strike and chair a select committee of two or three school board officials, three or four of your regular classroom teachers, and all your other special education personnel. The purpose of the committee is to establish how academic progress will be documented for each reporting period using the CBA approach.

In summary, CBA allows teachers to readily, consistently, and constantly monitor the progress of students with exceptionalities and enables them to provide clear and precise academic achievement reports to parents, administrators, and school-based teams. This information is then used to further modify the student's IEP, if needed. The overall approach described above will go a long way towards quelling the many fears and frustrations that most teachers have about evaluating and reporting the progress of students with exceptionalities (see Chapter 10 by Renihan & Noonan for further details).

CONCLUSION

The overarching assessment and IEP process outlined here is found in nearly all educational jurisdictions across Canada and the United States. Unfortunately, so too, are the problems and concerns that teachers in both countries face when trying to make the best use of the information that assessments and IEPs provide. One of the most difficult and enduring problems, however, is the teacher's responsibility to transform assessment and IEP information into effective instructional practices that can truly enhance student achievement. It makes sense, therefore, for principals and administrators to make the entire process as functionally efficient as possible. As the instructional leader of your school it behooves you avail yourself of straightforward but effective ways to assist all of your teachers in this endeavor. Being an effective educational leader requires both an understanding of the critical issues and developing insights into effective solutions. To this end, this chapter has outlined the detailed inner workings of the complete process and it has presented 16 clear and concise recommendations for principals to follow. Some of these recommendations are probably already in place, but based on this writer's experiences in numerous schools, some of the recommendations will need to be added and still others will need to be altered based on the options presented above. In any event, both your knowledge and solution repertoires about inclusion and the issues facing teachers have been expanded by reading this chapter, therefore, your potential for designing specific solutions that fit your school beyond those mentioned here has also increased.

REFERENCES

Council for Exceptional Children. (2004). *Analysis for IDEA Conference: CEC recommendations H.R. 1350 and S. 1248.* Arlington, VA: Author.

Edgar, E., & Pair, A. (2005). Special education teacher attrition: It all depends on where you are standing. *Teacher Education & Special Education, 28*(3/4), 163–170.

Edmunds, A. L., & Edmunds, G. A. (2007). *Special education in Canada.* Toronto, ON: McGraw-Hill.

Fuchs, L., & Fuchs, D. (1996). Linking assessment to instructional interventions: An overview. *School Psychology Review, 15*(3), 318–324.

Gregory, R. J. (2000). *Psychological testing: History, principles, and applications* (3rd ed.). Toronto, ON: Allyn and Bacon.

Individuals With Disabilities Education Improvement Act of 2004 (IDEA), Pub. L. No. 108–446, 20 U.S.C. 1400 (2004).

Kame'enui, E. J. (2007). A new paradigm: Responsiveness to intervention. *Teaching Exceptional Children, 39*(5), 6–7.

King-Sears, M. E., Burges, M., & Lawson, T. L. (1999). Applying curriculum-based assessment in inclusive settings. *Teaching Exceptional Children, September/October*, 30–38.

Lerner, J., Mardell-Czudnowski, C., & Goldenberg, D. (1981). *Special education for the early childhood years.* Englewood Cliffs, NJ: Prentice-Hall.

McLoughlin, J. A., & Lewis, R. B. (2005). *Assessing students with special needs* (6th ed.). Columbus, OH: Pearson/Allyn Bacon.

Overton, T. (1996). *Assessment in special education: An applied process* (2nd ed.). Columbus, OH: Merrill.

Peck, A., & Scarpati, S. (2007). Special issue: Responsiveness to intervention. *Teaching Exceptional Children, 39*(5), 4.

Shonkoff, J., & Meisels, S. (2000). *Handbook of early childhood intervention* (2nd ed.). New York: Cambridge University Press.

U.S. Department of Education. (2000). *A guide to the individualized education program.* Washington, DC: Office of Special Education and Rehabilitative Services.

Werts, M. G., Mamlin, N., & Pogoloff, S. M. (2002). Knowing what to expect: Introducing preservice teachers to IEP meetings. *Teacher Education & Special Education, 25*(4), 413–418.

Whitaker, S. D. (2003). Needs of beginning special education teachers: Implications for teacher education. *Teacher Education & Special Education, 26*(2), 106–117.

PAT RENIHAN AND BRIAN NOONAN

10. STUDENT ASSESSMENT PRACTICES IN INCLUSIVE SETTINGS

INTRODUCTION

This chapter addresses the school-based practical component of student assessment in inclusive settings from three perspectives. Part One provides an overview of assessment reform and the factors that can affect contemporary classroom assessment in providing meaningful programs of evaluation. This chapter is complementary to Chapter 9 which addresses the principal's role in the assessment and IEP process. Part Two explains how school personnel, and especially instructional leaders, can facilitate and support assessment programs for students with exceptionalities. Finally, Part Three presents a comprehensive overview of the nature and appropriateness of generally accepted classroom assessment procedures for students in inclusive settings.

PART ONE: OVERVIEW OF ASSESSMENT

School personnel (teachers, support staff, school-based leaders, principals) are all aware of the need to provide useful and meaningful information on the academic, social, and personal progress of all students. Various forms of student assessment such as quizzes, tests, and performance assessment have been common in elementary and high schools for many generations. Other forms of student assessment such as portfolios, peer assessment and/or self-assessment are relatively new to classrooms, the product of what has been labelled 'assessment reform'. Hence, we provide a brief overview of the assessment reform movement and its potential influences on classroom assessment as well as a description of the principles related to assessment in an inclusive settings. We accomplish this via a three-part framework that explains and describes the reasons for, and the value of, assessment practices designed for students in inclusive settings: 1) the effects of assessment reform; 2) re-thinking classroom assessment; and 3) the principles of inclusive assessment and accountability.

Assessment Reform

The assessment reform movement of the past decade or more has had a profound effect on the assessment and student evaluation activities of classroom teachers. Assessment reform has been a major component of the broadly overarching school reform movement of the past two decades or more. Much of the focus of

A. L. Edmunds and R. B. Macmillan (eds.), Leadership for Inclusion: A Practical Guide, 103–115.

reform has been on teacher accountability for student learning as well as an expectation that teachers will incorporate a wide range of grading and assessment processes. It is safe to say that measuring student achievement and using the results to improve learning has been a widely discussed issue in contemporary North American education. One element of assessment reform that has not been well documented or discussed, however, is the place of students with exceptionalities within assessment policies, procedures, and practices in K-12 schools.

Rethinking Classroom Assessment

It is recognized that education in general and student learning in particular, has become more globalized. The implementation of large-scale international student testing programs such as TIMSS (Third International Mathematics and Science Study) and more recently, PISA (Programme for International Student Assessment), is an indicator of interest and concern over student assessment, achievement and accountability world-wide. Although there is interest in the role and use of large-scale assessments, it is somewhat difficult to ascertain how the results of such programs can assist teachers or other school personnel in improving student learning. Thus, although large-scale assessment is of interest, it is *classroom-based assessment* guided by school-based professional personnel that will more effect educational change and encourage notable improvements in instruction and student learning. If such change is to occur, school-based personnel such as teachers, support staff, leaders, principals have to be responsible and accountable for developing and conducting assessment and grading practices that facilitate meaningful improvements in student learning. While this focus has been recognized to some extent, it has not led to establishing assessment and grading principles, procedures and practices for students with exceptionalities. The following provides guidance for implementing those practices.

Principles of Inclusive Assessment and Accountability

It is generally recognized that there is a need to incorporate principles of assessment and accountability in inclusive education. Traditionally, the vast majority of students with exceptionalities have not been included in a typical teacher's grading and assessment practices. It stands to reason, therefore, that a meaningful framework to assess students with exceptionalities has only recently been developed. In 2001, the National Centre on Educational Outcomes (NCEO) developed an assessment framework that presented six core principles of inclusive assessment and accountability which specifically apply to students with exceptionalities. These principles are based on a decade of NCEO's documentation of assessment and accountability systems and on review and comment from multiple stakeholders who share the common goal of improving outcomes for all students. This report presents six core principles to guide the inclusive assessment and accountability systems with a brief rationale and the specific characteristics that reflect each principle. While we address the principles here as they apply to students with disabilities, we suspect that with slight modification they apply also to students with limited English proficiency. The principles are:

Principle 1. All students with disabilities are included in the assessment system.

Principle 2. Decisions about how students with disabilities participate in the assessment system are the result of clearly articulated participation, accommodations, and alternate assessment decision-making processes.

Principle 3. All students with disabilities are included when student scores are publicly reported, in the same frequency and format as all other students, whether they participate with or without accommodations, or in an alternate assessment.

Principle 4. The assessment performance of students with disabilities has the same impact on the final accountability index as the performance of other students, regardless of how the students participate in the assessment system (i.e., with or without accommodations, or in an alternate assessment).

Principle 5. There is improvement of both the assessment system and the accountability system over time, through the processes of formal monitoring, ongoing evaluation, and systematic training in the context of emerging research and best practice.

Principle 6. Every policy and practice reflects the belief that *all students* must be included in state and district assessment and accountability systems (Thurlow, Quenemoen, Thompson, & Lehr, 2001).

Although these principles may seem quite general, the language of the report clearly establishes an expectation that students with exceptionalities deserve to be assessed in the same way and to the same extent as all other students. Principals and teachers are therefore challenged to develop and implement grading and assessment practices for students with exceptionalities on the same basis as non-exceptional students. The implications of the NCEO principles for all educators include, but are not limited to the following requirements:

– the progress of every student with disabilities will be assessed in a similar way.
– alternative forms of assessment or exemptions from assessment should be the same for students with disabilities as for other students.
– students with disabilities should be included in reports of student scores.
– information on the participation of students with disabilities should be used to improve the assessment policies and practices of schools and school jurisdictions.
– assessment of culturally or linguistically different students should be considered in an inclusive education environment.

As the NCEO framework emphasizes, students with exceptionalities who are educated in inclusive settings must be respected if there is to be a meaningful implementation of classroom assessment.

PART TWO: THE ROLE OF SCHOOL LEADERS IN THE ASSESSMENT OF
STUDENTS WITH DISABILITIES

One of the key findings in Stronge's (2002) comprehensive examination of studies relating to teacher effectiveness was that effective teachers know and understand their students as individuals in terms of their abilities, achievement, learning styles and needs, and that they can demonstrate effectiveness with the full range of student abilities. The important question is, then - How can principals give leadership to the development of these qualities? More specifically, how can they facilitate and support a program of assessment for students with special educational needs? Elsewhere (Noonan & Renihan, 2006) we have devoted considerable attention to examining how the principles of assessment should find expression in the instructional leadership role of principals. We have also examined the perceptions of high school principals regarding their experiences of the issues and tensions associated with the nurturance of an assessment culture within their schools. (Noonan & Renihan, 2008). Following her large-scale review of the literature on principals' roles in creating inclusive schools, Riehl (2000) concluded that principals need to attend to three broad tasks: a) fostering new meanings about diversity; b) promoting inclusive practices in the school; and c) building connections between schools and communities. Drawing from these diverse but complementary perspectives on leadership, we examine the sets of knowledge, appreciations and skills that can assist principals in integrating strategies for inclusion within the overall *assessment culture* within their school.

Leading Inclusive Assessment: Knowledge

Inclusion and assessment work best when educators have sound knowledge about their students. Effective principals can anticipate better than most the needs of their diverse student clientele. While this does not mean that principals, particularly those in large school contexts, must have a detailed grasp of the nature and educational needs of each and every student, they should be able to mobilize the planning systems and the intelligence of key personnel to fully understand present and incoming student populations in order to effectively plan for the promotion of inclusive practices. In addition, leadership knowledge about assessment within inclusion also includes a basic familiarity with the latest perspectives on teaching and inclusion in contexts of diversity, and their implications for authentic assessment. In short, instructional leaders should know enough about such developments so that they can: a) foster professional dialogue; and, b) effectively guide teachers in conducting relevant, student-centred assessment. Knowledge of the sources of information and related professional development opportunities that can keep teachers up-to-date regarding inclusion and assessment strategies is also an important leadership knowledge requirement. Finally, we are convinced that teaching and assessment conducted within inclusive contexts are both more powerful and more relevant when the perspectives of parents are understood and purposefully engaged. While cultural, socioeconomic, attitudinal, experiential factors often act as barriers to meaningful parental engagement, efforts to connect with parents in these contexts have been found to be well worth the effort in the form of improved student achievement. Such efforts are maximized when instructional leaders have knowledge of those socioeconomic, attitudinal and experiential circumstances of their parent groups.

Leading Inclusive Assessment: Appreciations

With regard to *appreciations*, a logical starting point is Salisbury & McGregor's (2005) underlying belief that every student needs to belongs to, and should feel membership in, the school community. How can principals foster new meanings about diversity? On the basis of this mindset, the term "inclusion" can itself instil a perspective that is antithetical to the belief it is intended to engender. One principal regarded as highly successful in inclusive education (Snow, 2001) put it this way:

> You take a child where he is and give him what he needs in the most natural and informal ways possible. An inclusive school provides all kids with whatever they need to master the regular curriculum, which may include curriculum modifications supports, assistive technology, or other assistance. In my opinion, you don't call a student an 'inclusion student' or have 'inclusion classrooms (p. 2).

What appreciations can promote inclusive practices in the school? First, an appreciation based on a continuing need for focused teamwork (Snow, 2001) among school professionals is the foundation for cultures of inclusion within which teachers share best practice in an *interdependent* environment rather than in an *independent* setting. Second, a well-conceived platform or set of beliefs about inclusion is the necessary precondition for leadership and meaningful supervision of this area of activity. Some of the beliefs included in such a platform are:
1. encompassing priorities for the role of teacher aides;
2. the relationship between teachers and aides;
3. the most appropriate classroom arrangements to maximize learning;
4. student involvement in classroom interactions; and
5. the relative value of alternative approaches to assessment

Naturally, the principal's leadership role in inclusion necessarily encompasses the collaborative work of therapists, paraprofessionals and parents. Thus, the principal's appreciation and valuing of these specialized roles and perspectives in working together to meet children's special educational needs becomes a critical leadership requirement.

Leading Inclusive Assessment: Skills

Instructional leaders are in a powerful position to engender new meanings about diversity and to promote inclusive practices in their supervisory activities. Skills of observing inclusive teaching practices and, more importantly, the ability to ask

probing questions about assessment practices in inclusive classrooms are critical, as is the realization that the power of inclusive assessment practices cannot be weighed in isolation from broader classroom practices, such as:
- the quality of the interaction among teacher, paraprofessional and student;
- the support and role clarification provided to paraprofessionals;
- physical arrangements made for special needs students;
- the availability of materials to meet learning needs;
- the relationship among diverse groups of students.

Instructional supervision in the broader sense provides an opportunity to identify issues that require school-wide attention and which have significant implications for professional development. Similarly, observation and discussion of inclusion and assessment practices at the *classroom level* can be a valuable catalyst for *school-wide* discussion and development. In this regard, both the initiation of school and classroom action plans based upon student data, and the promotion of broader discussions of assessment practices for inclusion, represent opportunities upon which effective instructional leaders must capitalize. Finally, the importance of the parent-school partnership is arguably magnified in the context of inclusion. It follows that those school leaders who have the skills to relate with, connect, and seek the engagement of parents of students with exceptionalities are in a much stronger position to nurture the effective provision and assessment of diverse student learning. It also helps a great deal when parents and teachers know that the principal has the motivation and ability to elevate inclusion to a leadership priority within the school and school system.

Facilitating Leadership for Inclusive Assessment

In synthesizing the above discussion and in attempting to portray a forward-thinking perspective on inclusive assessment, we suggest that:

A. *Effective assessment leaders in inclusive settings know:*
- changing definitions and perspectives on diversity and inclusion, and their implications for authentic assessment;
- teacher and parent needs regarding such changes in perspective;
- emerging research into issues of inclusion and related patterns of assessment;
- the sources of information that can keep staff and community up-to-date on inclusion and related assessment 'best practices;'
- the mechanisms by which such information can be introduced to, and evaluated by, classroom professionals and paraprofessionals;
- the nature of the present and future student population to facilitate effective planning for the promotion of inclusive practices
- perspectives of parents regarding inclusion-related school strategies and assessment practices;
- alternative strategies for connecting to the parents of students in inclusive settings.

B. *Effective assessment leaders in inclusive settings appreciate:*
– that every student belongs and should feel membership in the school community;
– the deeper meaning of inclusion;
– the need for collaboration in developing inclusive practices and assessments;
– the value if interdependence among key actors in the school community;
– the importance of a clearly thought-out platform of inclusion and assessment;
– the value of the specific roles and perspectives of key actors.

C. *Effective assessment leaders in inclusive settings have skills of:*
– observing inclusive teaching;
– identifying questions to ask about assessment in inclusive classrooms;
– matchmaking teachers and students to new and available resources, ideas and strategies for assessment;
– engendering attitudes of flexibility and flexibility among teachers, special educators and paraprofessionals;
– collaboration with key actors;
– elevating inclusion as a leadership priority in the school and system;
– removing roadblocks to relevant, student-centred assessment.

How the above qualities can be realized is largely a matter of excellence in leadership preparation. The senior leadership within school systems can provide the needed support structures that can bring much of this forward-thinking to reality. In much the same manner as previously described, senior leaders must fully understand their constituency – principals – and they must fully appreciate principals' desire to professionally enact inclusion. Therefore, in priority fashion, senior leaders must provide principals with meaningful opportunities to enhance their knowledge and skills with regards to inclusion. While we point out that this set of qualities is by no means all-inclusive, we suggest that it constitutes a useful starting point for those committed to putting in place a viable leadership infrastructure for inclusion-focused assessment.

PART THREE: CONTEMPORARY CLASSROOM ASSESSMENT IN INCLUSIVE SETTINGS

Classroom assessment is not a new idea; teachers for generations have constructed and used various forms of tests for students at all levels. However, alternative methods such as portfolios, peer/self assessments, and/or performance assessments have more recently become common in classrooms at all grade levels. The following is an overview of contemporary classroom assessment principles and practices and a description of how they can best serve students in inclusive settings.

Student-Oriented Assessment

One of the primary principles of assessment reform is to emphasize the focus on individual student learning whereby whatever type of assessment practice or grading strategy is involved, it should be indicative of individual student performance or improvement. Thus, student assessment in inclusive settings is guided by several basic assumptions. It should be emphasized that these assumptions are not unique to schools with inclusive environments and that they are the responsibility of the principals and staff to implement and manage. The point here is that exemplary assessment applies universally for all students and needs to be universally applied by all educators.

First, and most importantly, assessment in inclusive settings requires a number of *adaptations* by teachers, support staff, and principals: adaptations to students' physical, interpersonal, and academic environments. Thus, schools must be prepared to provide additional equipment (i.e., computer technology, audio/visual support) and spaces that are safe for students with exceptionalities. As well, staff and students must ensure that these students have ample opportunities for positive interpersonal relationships (i.e., buddies, role models, cooperative learning groups, participation in mainstream school activities, etc.). Required academic adaptations typically include but are not limited to: reorganized or reduced curriculum content; teaching strategies such as the use of question wait time or carefully presented instructions (oral or verbal); and cooperative learning or computer-assisted instruction. Perhaps most important, however, is the use of assessment adaptations or accommodations made by teachers. In this way, when students with exceptionalities are being assessed or tested, the teacher, support staff or principal should use strategies such as reduced reading level, alternative formats/numbers of questions, extended time or separated blocks of time, take home or open book tests or other related adaptations as needed. The fundamental belief is that accommodations provide students with exceptionalities with opportunities to demonstrate what they have learned; accommodations do not any sort of academic advantage.

The second assumption of student-oriented assessment is to emphasize a *criterion-referenced* approach rather than a norm-referenced approach. In doing so, students are assessed based on the extent to which they have achieved or mastered the intended learning outcomes of particular unit of study. Such measures are generally not standardized and are *curriculum-based* assessments. Thus, students are assessed on the extent to which they have achieved curricular goals established in their IEP. As such, students with exceptionalities are not assessed in comparison with other students or classmates, they are assessed in comparison with their own individualized standards of progress and achievement. This does not, however, eliminate the use of some standardized tests by teachers or educational experts to determine student progress or current functional status for particular skill sets (i.e., math achievement, behaviour, language abilities, etc.).

Another important facet of student assessment in inclusive settings is an adherence to the principle of the *full scope of learning*. Though classroom assessment practices continue to focus on traditional measures of academic achievement (literacy, numeracy, etc.) contemporary educators should expect to utilize a broader range of indicators of student learning. This is particularly important for students with exceptionalities in inclusive settings because, more often than not, their IEPs delineate that they need to acquire 'non-academic' skills and knowledge – such as social and personal skills and values, technology and information skills, and independent learning and living skills, and proficiencies in other curriculum-related knowledge, skills, and attitudes. Thus, educators who are committed to this broader concept of learning are more likely to develop and use assessment strategies that provide information on their students' learning and on how their performance is improving.

A third important assumption of assessment in inclusive settings is to consider the *roles of other adults* in student learning. The role of parents should be clarified as should the role of instructional assistants or other paraprofessionals who are involved directly with students with exceptionalities. As well, a very important role that is often overlooked or not emphasized is the role of the principal. This chapter has sought to rectify, at least partially, this oversight.

Therefore, although classroom assessment in inclusive settings is quite similar to mainstream assessment practices, it is important to recognize that mindful adaptations and accommodations are required and must be considered part of the curricular and instructional expectations for teachers, school staff, and principals. As outlined in the next section, this is an obligation that schools have for students with exceptionalities.

FORMAL AND INFORMAL STRATEGIES

The instructional and assessment strategies and practices used by teachers in inclusive settings are, in principle, exactly the same as those used by all good teachers. However, as we have pointed out, trained professionals (teachers, support staff, consultants, principals) have to provide, where appropriate, adaptations to current assessment practices that make the measuring and reporting of student performance meaningful to first, the student, and second, to all others who have a vested interest in the child's educational progress and well being. Following is an overview of current classroom assessment practices that, in the context of assessment reform, provide assessment *as* learning, *for* learning, and *of* learning. It should be emphasized, however, that for students with exceptionalities, adaptive assessment is a principle that can help guide decision-making regarding student progress. The classroom practices outlined here are categorized as formal and informal based on the way the assessment strategy is designed and how it is used.

Formal Assessment Strategies

Although there an increasing number of different classroom assessment techniques used by teachers, the following are typical of those used by teachers in both regular and inclusive classrooms. Following is a description of how generally accepted formal assessment strategies can be adapted for inclusive settings.

Classroom tests and quizzes. Tests and quizzes are the most recognized and most common assessment practices in education. In the case of inclusive education, such tests help provide information about student progress in knowledge, skills or attitudes. Typically these assessments are designed by classroom teachers, are focussed on particular curricular content, and are often 'adapted' to better address the skill/ability of students with exceptionalities. Teachers use a table of specifications to identify the knowledge or skills that are appropriate for students with exceptionalities. Bloom's Taxonomy is often used to construct a table of specifications to ensure that the intended learning objectives are being measured in the teacher-made test or quiz. Teachers using these strategies with students with special needs should ". . . consider (students') academic skill demands. Students must be able to read quiz questions. . ." (McLaughlin & Lewis, 2008; p. 123). There is of course, a wide range of types of quizzes and tests that teachers can consider for inclusive settings such as matching questions, multiple choice, short answer, completion or true-false items. The format chosen by the teacher will be partially dependent on the skill levels of the student with special needs. As well, the teacher will need probably need to adapt the manner of administering the test – i.e. using readers to facilitate student participation, employing assistive technology as per a student's IEP, and adapting the assessment to ensure fairness and accuracy. This is particularly true of older special needs students who may be preparing for work or work education programs.

Checklists and rating scales. Teachers frequently develop and use a variety of checklists and rating scales, some of which may be formal instruments created by publishers or curriculum developers. Checklists typically use a yes-no (or similar scale) to measure the extent to which a student has achieved knowledge, skills or attitudes that are observed by teachers or teacher assistants. To ensure assessment validity, teachers should make all checklist statements clear, concise, and directly related to important behaviours or student characteristics that help the teacher assess student performance.

Rating scales serve purposes similar to checklists but typically use Likert-type scales with verbal or numeric scores (i.e., 1 = Strongly Disagree to 5 = Strongly Agree). Such scales are most useful when teachers want to determine varying levels of knowledge, skills, or attitudes. As with checklists, rating scales must be designed carefully to ensure meaningful interpretations by teachers, parents, or other persons involved in assessing student ability or performance. Rating scales can also be used by students when teachers are seeking opinions of others. In some cases ranking scales may also be appropriate, however, the ranking of student performances may be difficult to interpret, may not add meaning to measuring student performance, and probably will not help modify or change instruction.

Goal attainment scaling. A relatively simple method of measuring individual knowledge, skills, or attitudes is found in a formal measurement process called Goal Attainment Scaling (Kiresuik, Smith, & Cardillo, 1994). GAS, developed in the 1950s for mental-health and medical assessments (i.e., gerontology) uses a five-point scale (-2, -1, 0, 1, 2) to measure an individual's performance in a number of areas of some attribute. After assessing the individual on a number of areas, a total score is produced and compared to previous levels of performance. The score(s) can be either norm-referenced or criterion-referenced and is interpreted by experts to determine an individual's ability or performance. Although not a new idea, GAS still has potential for use in inclusive classrooms where such information can assist teachers or others in determining student performances relative to a standard or expectation.

Large-scale assessment is the final form of assessment common in today's schools. In the past, students with exceptionalities were not required to write standardized achievement tests or large scale assessments. Today, however, it is common for students with exceptionalities be required or asked to take those tests because school administrators and teachers have become more accountable for student learning and achievement. Depending on the jurisdiction, student participation may or may not be mandatory. In general, there does not seem to be any conclusive opinion as to how large-scale assessments can best be used (if at all) in inclusive settings.

Informal Assessment Instruments and Processes

The formal assessment instruments described above are most useful when some level of 'high stakes' decision is required for student performance (i.e., referral to a program, information to parents or specialists, grade placement, etc...) However, it is recognized that teachers working in inclusive settings are frequently required to provide information or opinions on day-to-day student behaviours, academic performance, or on particular learning tasks/opportunities. In these cases, the more informal assessment strategies that follow should be implemented:

Questionnaires. Written questionnaires and surveys are typically more general or less structured than rating scales and are used to obtain information on relevant policies or procedures. Referrals to inclusive programs often involve the referee completing a questionnaire to help guide decision makers.

Observation and task analysis. The observation of students is part of everyday instruction/learning process and the results of observations provide context for meaningful assessments in inclusive settings. Observations may be made independent of other forms of assessment or in some cases as part of the formal assessment process (e.g., GAS is often observation intensive). Such informal observations may or may not be recorded and may be most useful as feedback and information for teachers, teacher assistants, or other decision makers. For example, an observer may watch an over-active student intensively for 30 minutes recording his/her actions every two to five minutes to record the frequency of hyperactive behaviours. In more formal settings, such forms of observation and analysis are called *task analysis*. Although task analysis usually focuses on a student's behaviour or performance, it is often useful as a form of curriculum assessment. In that sense, the observer (teacher or specialist) is using the observed data to determine the relevance of particular curriculum-based intended learning outcome for a student or group of students.

Inventories and interviews. As has been pointed out, teachers have access to an array of assessment strategies that provide formative evaluations for the purpose of determining student performance or for providing information about curriculum relevance. Informal *inventories*, similar to rating scales and checklists, can also be used as formal classroom assessments (i.e. quizzes). The important and vital difference is that the inventories may also be used to plan appropriate teaching/learning strategies rather than to simply assess student performance. *Interviews* provide similar information to questionnaires but allow for more breadth and depth of analysis. Being able to probe student or parent responses helps provide more meaningful interpretations that can guide teacher planning and/or assessment. It should be emphasized that although interviews can be a very useful assessment practice, they can also be intimidating to respondents unless conducted in a professional, subject-sensitive manner.

Portfolio assessment is one of the most beneficial outcomes of assessment reform described earlier. Portfolios involve the collection of first hand evidence of student learning organized around themes that indicate growth in knowledge, skills, and attitudes. These collections typically include samples of student work that illustrate achievement of intended learning outcomes. In addition to providing data for teachers, portfolios are often considered a focus for student self-evaluation or in some cases peer evaluation. Although portfolio assessment is strongly supported by experts in classroom assessment and experts in special education, its full application in inclusive settings hinges on the proper use of individualized learning outcomes as prescribed in each students' IEP. More research is needed to better determine how portfolio assessment can contribute to student learning in inclusive settings.

Grading Practices

With the incorporation of student with exceptionalities into regular classrooms and school programs, and with the commitment by teachers to use proven assessment strategies, it is predictable that schools will try to ensure that students are graded in much the same way as students without exceptionalities. Until more recent times, teachers would typically use generally accepted grading forms such as letter grades, pass/fail or credit/no credit grades depending on the student's age, grade or subject being considered. Research on inclusive settings has expanded upon the grading process in that it is seen as more than just symbolizing student performance. For example, Salend & Duhaney (2002) have suggested that the grading system in inclusive settings should depend on the purpose of the grade. Does a particular grade show mastery, progress, effort, feedback for parents, post-school planning, or graduation/promotion? Once the rationale and meaning of the grade is established, the student is graded using one of the conventional approaches. The options available include not only the typical checklists, scales, letter grades, etc but also some of the more collaborative practices such as mastery-level grades, progressive improvement, multiple grades, level grades, etc...

(Salend & Duhaney, 2002; p. 11). Thus, it seems clear that teachers and other staff in inclusive settings have shown that not only are well-known assessment practices used in inclusive settings but so too are grading practices.

SUMMARY

The current emphasis on a *culture of inclusion* facilitates the accommodation of students with exceptionalities in many ways including assessment and grading principles, policies and practices. Typically, classroom teachers and special education support staff are responsible for conducting adaptive assessments or providing accommodations for students with exceptionalities. Understanding how traditional testing programs or more contemporary types of assessment such as portfolio, observation, performance-based or peer assessments can be used with special needs students is part responsibilities to students in inclusive settings. The social and interpersonal communication aspects of inclusion are basic to successful inclusive education, however, principals also have an obligation to understand, support, and facilitate how student assessment is incorporated into this inclusive setting. The principal's role in supporting teachers' assessment responsibilities such as planning appropriate assessment strategies, grading practices and reporting processes for classroom teachers is central to the successful implementation of adaptive assessment for students with disabilities in inclusive settings.

REFERENCES

Kiresuik, T. J., Smith, A., & Cardillo, J. E. (1994). *Goal attainment ccaling, applications theory and measurement.* Hillsdale, New Jersey: Lawrence Erlbaum & Associates Publishers.

McLoughlin, J. A., & Lewis, R. B. (2008). *Assessing students with special needs* (7th ed.). Upper Saddle River, New Jersey: Pearson Prentice Hall.

Noonan, B., & Renihan, P. (2006, November 4). Demystifying assessment leadership. *Canadian Journal of Educational Administration and Policy,* (56).

Noonan, B., & Renihan, P. (2008). Building assessment literacy: Perceptions of high school principals. *International Journal for Leadership in Learning.* 2009 (In Press).

Reihl, C. (2000). The principal's role in creating inclusive schools for diverse students. *Review of educational research, 70*(1), 55–81.

Salisbury, C., & McGregor, G. (2005, November). *Principals of inclusive schools.* On Point Series. National Institute for Urban School Improvement, Arizona State University.

Salend, S. J., & Duhaney, L. M. G. (2002). Grading Students in Inclusive Settings. *Teaching Exceptional Children.* Council for Exceptional Children, *34*(3), 8–15.

Snow, K. (2007). *Inclusive education: A principal's perspective.* Retrieved from http://www. disabilityisnatural.com/images/PDF/incledprin.pdf

Stronge, J. H. (2002). *Qualities of effective teachers.* Alexandria, Virginia: Association for Supervision and Curriculum Development.

Thurlow, M., Quenemoen, R., Thompson, S., & Lehr, C. (2001). *Principles and characteristics of inclusive assessment and accountability systems* (Synthesis Report 40). Minneapolis, MN: University of Minnesota, National Center on Educational Outcomes. Retrieved [December 31, 2007], from the World Wide Web: http://education.umn.edu/NCEO/OnlinePubs/Synthesis40.html.

KENNETH A. PUDLAS

11. LEADING TEACHERS IN PROFESSIONAL DEVELOPMENT FOR INCLUSION

INTRODUCTION

Full Inclusion is a widely accepted paradigm for the placement of students with special needs in American and Canadian public education (Edmunds, 2003). This chapter explores the vital role played by administrators in establishing an inclusive ethos for the school and classroom. The nature of each school community will vary and concomitantly so will the professional development needs of that community. Thus this chapter cannot be prescriptive of what must be done but rather it presents a descriptive overview of what might be done, and why. The chapter explores a theoretical basis for professional development, presents an overview of possible contributions from the concept of invitational education, and concludes with several simple applications of professional development strategies for promoting inclusive school communities.

A VISION FOR PROFESSIONAL DEVELOPMENT

At the outset it is worthwhile to re-vision what professional development is. Professional development is as much the process of holistic development of the person who is the professional as it is a particular programme or set of workshops or other learning opportunities. When addressing professional development it is imperative that all of the learning domains be considered. It might be suggested that professional development needs to address the head, and the hands and the heart of educators (see Figure 1). Thus it is important to consider knowledge and skills and attitudes together. The latter, the affective portion or heart or attitude, as pertaining in particular to individual and collective attitudes towards students with special learning needs will be shown to be an important factor. It has been suggested that "even our most impulsive and habitual actions reveal our underlying convictions, and implicit theories – in other words our beliefs" (Lefrancois, 2000, p. 5).

If teaching is to be done well it must be based on sound psychological principles, but that is not enough. Those sound principles must be applied with enthusiasm, and that still is not enough. To be truly effective, the foregoing must be infused with a love of teaching and a love of children. While that may sound somewhat ethereal, consider the implications. To love someone or something is to be devoted to it and to seek the best for that person or thing. To love teaching goes beyond enjoyment to a desire to continually hone the craft of teaching; to love

A. L. Edmunds and R. B. Macmillan (eds.), Leadership for Inclusion: A Practical Guide, 117–130.
© 2010 Sense Publishers. All Rights Reserved.

Head

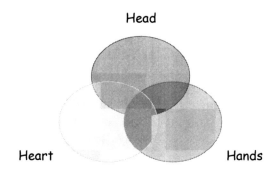

Heart   Hands

Figure 1. Confluence of head and heart and hands toward development of inclusive professionals.

students is to seek their best interests, to know what they need to be successful, and to empower them toward that success. These principles certainly pertain to a paradigm of professional development.

Congruent with the search for and application of those aforementioned sound psychological principles is the metaphor of teacher as researcher. Noddings (2008) suggests that teachers should be willing to think critically about education theory and about what might be called "propaganda" (p. 13). By propaganda we might consider such potentially contentious issues as No Child Left Behind and, yes, even Full Inclusion. Thus a part of professional development, developing teachers as professionals, involves critical analysis, self-reflection and other forms of inquiry into attitudes and into best practices as they apply to full inclusion. All of which can be encouraged in the school community by supportive principals.

These issues pertaining to good teaching, particularly within inclusive environments, are related to *praxis*, defined here as *the exercise or practice of an art, science, or skill,* and; *customary practice or conduct.* What is it that teachers need to do as a part of their customary conduct that will help establish inclusive communities and how can principals best fulfil their critically important supportive role?

Many factors contribute to the successful inclusive experience of students with special or diverse learning needs. Germane to the discussion here are the *school ethos* and *educators' characteristics*, and how they influence and are influenced by enabling conditions. Figure 2 offers a schematic for examining the various interrelated aspects of a merger of special education with regular education. The figure clearly illustrates the pivotal role that school administrators can play in establishing an inclusive school community. What the figure illustrates is that there is a cause and effect relationship between the achievement of desired educational outcomes, such as various social and academic competencies and a sense of community, and the nature and character of teachers.

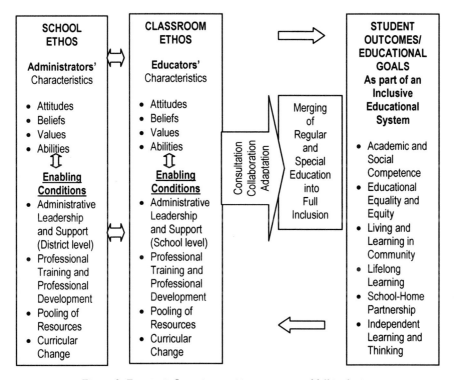

Figure 2. Factors influencing positive outcomes of full inclusion.

(adapted from: Andrews, J. & Lupart, J. (2000). *The inclusive classroom: Educating exceptional children*. Scarborough ON: Nelson).

Thus one of the purposes of professional development is to cause practicing teachers to become explicitly aware of their existing attitudes and dispositions, those underlying factors that motivate their behaviours in the heat of the battle. And, should those attitudes prove less than inviting or positive, to present new ones that can be learned and internalized as part of the motivation for their interaction with students.

Thus it follows that if teachers are to provide a classroom ethos that is inclusive and inviting – and they are, as will be further elaborated - then those teachers must be both professionally and personally *inviting* and well-grounded. The idea of *invitational education* has been posited by Purkey and Novak (1996) and its usefulness in addressing full inclusion and professional development appears to be supported by research. This chapter lays a framework for understanding invitational education, for understanding the significance of these factors applied to professional development, and presents a number of practical ideas for teachers' personal and professional growth and development toward becoming inviting inclusive educators.

In considering the various interconnected factors leading to an inclusive and inviting school community as illustrated in Figure 2 it may also be useful to consider teachers' perceptions of their professional efficacy and how those perceptions influence their response to students with special learning needs. That is, one of the goals of inclusion is that all students perceive themselves as part of the community and to that end teachers must provide a safe and inviting environment. If teachers perceive students with special needs as a threat to their professional efficacy they are far less likely to model inclusive and inviting behaviours. This is illustrated in a self-efficacy index in which the numerator is success and the denominator is aspirations (see Figure 3). For the efficacy side of the equation to be 100 percent, there must, of course, be equality between the numerator and the denominator on the other side of the equation. The common aspirations include such factors as: power, the ability to control the environment in appropriate ways; significance, a sense of being valued for being alive; competence, the ability to perform competently in areas that are important to the individual and to society, and; worth, the ability to live according to the rules of society and to do so flexibly. Teachers, long successful in their careers, may not have had sufficient experience or education to give them a sense of competence regarding the inclusion of students with special needs. They may feel disempowered because they were not consulted about their classroom composition. Pre-service teachers' may similarly be fearful about their abilities successfully to include all students in their classrooms. In all of these situations, once pre-service teachers enter the profession, school administrators, who until recently were considered to be the master teachers in the school building, hold the key to the in-service professional development requisite for the successful promulgation of inclusive school communities.

Teachers generally concur that full inclusion is a worthy ideology but they are concerned about their abilities to meet effectively the wide range of needs that exceptional students bring to the classroom (Bunch, 1993; Pudlas, 2003; Weisel & Dror, 2006).Teachers also indicate they do not always perceive that their principals give them adequate support in making inclusion work (Pudlas, 2005). This perception, which admittedly may not accurately reflect reality, nevertheless needs to be addressed.

Self Efficacy = $\dfrac{\text{Success}}{\text{Aspirations}}$

Aspirations include:
- Power
- Significance
- Competence
- Worth

Figure 3. Factors influencing self-efficacy.

Ethos of the Inclusive School/Classroom Community

As illustrated in Figure 2, there are both a school ethos and an individual classroom ethos. These are determined by a reciprocal interaction between a set of educators' characteristics and enabling conditions and a set of administrators' characteristics and enabling conditions. Educators' characteristics are also inextricably interwoven with administrators' characteristics. From the list of enabling conditions, professional training and development and administrative leadership and support are of primary concern in the context of this chapter. If the ethos of the school is to flourish and the development of an inclusive community is a definite and necessary goal, competent and supportive administrative leadership is a necessity.

According to Duff, Keefe and Moore (2006) administrators must "make a constant effort to provide resources, personnel, equipment, and time, highly specialized programs, actively seek out resources from the district, state and university, be flexible because the program changes as the students and their needs change, live with uncertainty with the goal of inclusion clearly in mind, have an awareness program on the school's inclusion philosophy, which is introduced to the staff and printed in a parent handbook" (pp. 175,176). To move towards the desired result of an inclusive school community, professional development must be both encouraged and provided by the administration at all levels.

The question of whether inclusion is an administrative headache or an opportunity is posited by Rieck and Wadsworth (2000). An honest affirmative response to the question, that inclusion is an opportunity, can be the catalyst that propels administrators to provide and encourage professional development that empowers teachers to have inclusive classrooms. In order for administrators to take seriously their role in promoting professional development there are numerous factors which must be considered.

The experience and confidence of principals in meeting the needs of special students is an important factor and has been investigated by Lasky and Karge (2006). They examined the formal training of several hundred principals in southern California and as a result of their analysis suggested at least four requisite competencies. These competencies include first, the display of knowledge and skills in effective instruction, assessment, and discipline to provide support and feedback to teachers. Second, principals must acquire skills in establishing and supporting instructional teams. A third identified competency is that principals demonstrate the willingness to support collaborative group interactions. And a final requisite competency is that principals have a clear vision that results in a commitment from the school and community (p. 20).

Secondary school administrators' knowledge of the current issues in Special Education was investigated by Wakeman, Browder, Flowers, and Ahlgrim-Delzell. (2006). While this chapter focuses primarily on principals' responsibilities for being professional development leaders and providers, Wakeman et al. suggest that the need for professional development in special education for principals themselves has been well established (2006, p. 154). Further they report that it is also well-demonstrated that principals themselves are receiving little or no pre-service or in-service in special education. This is problematic if, as has been suggested above, principals are to be the leaders in providing further special education in-service to their school-based staff. Perhaps the mutual need for professional development can be a catalyst that brings together teachers and administrators as learners in community.

Similarly, but at the elementary level, Praisner (2003) investigated the attitudes of administrators toward inclusion. She suggests that, "… for inclusion to be successful, first and foremost, the school administrator must display a positive attitude and commitment to inclusion" (p. 136). These findings further emphasize the importance of principals' attitudes, the heart aspect, toward the inclusion of students with disabilities. Three related areas are highlighted by Praisner's research as worthy of further study. First, factors related to placement perceptions; second, the role of experience with students with disabilities, and; third, types of training in inclusive practices. All three of these, but the latter in particular, speak to the importance of pre and in-service opportunities.

The consideration and outcomes of the factors listed above will influence how administrators approach the professional development of their teachers. That is, how principals will empower teachers to be personally and professionally inviting and inclusive of learners with diverse needs. That consideration and some suggestions for praxis follow.

Professional Development: What is it and Why is it Important?

Learning to teach well is a lifelong process. Good teachers have many years of experience, as opposed to one year of experience many times. Arends (1994) suggested this process includes developing habits of reflection, finding ways to keep abreast of current research on teaching and learning, and keeping up-to-date in one's subject (p. 460). Similarly, Parkay, Stanford, Vaillancourt, and Stephens (2005) describe a variety of opportunities for continuing professional development including: *self-assessment* (reflection), *teacher workshops*, *teacher centres*, *supervision and mentoring of student teachers*, *graduate study*, and *study on the internet*. Each of these opportunities can be endorsed and enhanced by innovative and flexible administrators and applied to the unique needs of teachers in their schools.

The most effective in-service programmes tend to be the ones that teachers request and often design and conduct (Parkay et. al., 2005). What role then do principals play? One commonly stated goal of full inclusion is that of *community*. Clearly, as previously articulated by Lasky and Karge (2006), school administrators have a key part in fostering that sense of community; that is, of common purpose and of being equipped to meet common goals and meet common challenges. Administrative leadership in this instance may paradoxically best be demonstrated by principals who take on a servant role. That is principals can encourage teachers to reflect and determine what their professional development needs are and then provide the means to have those needs met.

Efficacy of In-service: What is Extant and Is It Working?

It has already been noted that the most effective in-service programmes tend to be the ones requested, designed and conducted by teachers (Parkay et. al., 2005). This is often evidenced in the Professional Development Programs conducted by the Teachers Associations across the country. Groups of teachers determine the needs of the district, design the program, and then arrange for the speakers, who are often practitioners from the school system. This workshop paradigm is only one model which can be utilized to promote inclusive communities. However, the promotion usually occurs, effectively, at the individual classroom level but may not carry over to the overall school community. Supportive and encouraging administrators who place a focus on Professional Development for inclusive communities will transform schools from individual inclusive classrooms into whole-school, inclusive communities. What proactive steps can principals take?

Salisbury and McGregor (2002) investigated the administrative climate and context of five elementary schools committed to inclusive practice in the United States. The authors suggest that successful change toward inclusive practice can be incremental. That is, surface changes can be made with relatively small expenditures of resources and time (p. 270). This certainly should provide hope for administrators who need to be good stewards of limited resources both of time and of finances. Their study revealed commonalities in leadership practices and core principles across the schools, consistent patterns in measured climate indices, and a range of administrative strategies to promote inclusive practice. Notably one of the criteria for inclusion in the study was the principal's willingness to commit to involvement in action research for at least a two year period. Thus with limited resources but commitment to building community principals can make a significant difference.

Models for Successful Professional Development

Following from the aforementioned study six characteristics of inclusive administrators seemed to emerge. These characteristics included: self-directed, risk taker; invested in relationships; accessible; reflective; collative, and; intentional (Salisbury & McGregor, 2002, p. 268). In demonstrating these personal characteristics, based on Salisbury and McGregor's (2002, p.270) work, five different types of supportive administrator practices are summarized here as:
- Instructional support: enabling team teaching between special and general educators.
- Using adult mentors in classrooms: connecting various initiatives to a school improvement plan.
- Deploying special education staff to grade-level teams: that is, allowing flexible grouping and re-grouping thereby evidencing a big-picture school-based vision of a quality inclusive school.

– Providing regular blended staff development opportunities. For example, in the aforementioned study, prevention-oriented reading initiatives were implemented in the early grades.
– Principals leveraging resources to support inclusive practices: principals modelling inclusive attitudes and expectations *and* encouraging regular dialogue involving reflection on the core values.

Evidence would suggest then that the promotion of inclusive communities will be dependent upon successful Professional Development. Although the workshop model of professional development has been effectively used for individual classrooms, it is proposed here that district and school administrators become proactive in the provision of a variety of professional development models that will motivate all school personnel to strive towards inclusive schools.

A variety of professional development models are available to today's educators. These models can be classroom-based, school-based, and/or off-site-based (Roberts & Pruitt 2003). The vehicles within any site-based professional development are also varied. These include, but are not limited to, the, Professional Inquiry Process (Minnesota Arts Best Practice Network, 2002), Shared Leadership, Teamwork Model, Study Groups, Collaborative Model, and Use of Portfolios (Roberts & Pruitt 2003), and the Community Partnership Model of Professional Development (Sanders 2006). It is the mandate of each administrator to match one or more of the professional development models to the needs of the teachers in his/her school to achieve an inclusive school community.

Administrative leadership can take many forms. Inclusive classrooms need to exist in inclusive school communities and achieving such communities may require re-visioning of how students learn and how instruction is organized. The building administrator, more than any other single individual, must be committed to inclusion efforts and needs to show leadership toward that end.

Praxis: How to Equip Your Teachers to be Inclusive

This sub-section might be called, "What can I do in September (or on Monday morning)?" Or, better yet, "What can I do in May in preparation for next Fall?" As an initial response: reflection or self-assessment is a necessary first step in pursuing professional growth (Parkay et al., 2005, p. 63). Teachers and principals both know however that once the school term begins in earnest, despite tacit assent to the importance of reflection, the realities of day to day classroom and school management make it difficult, unless it is purposely built into the school schedule. For the purposes of professional development toward inclusion, reflection could simply be the act of asking the right questions, and one such set of questions might pertain to how students with special needs are experiencing their education. It follows then that one means of spurring effective reflection would be to allow opportunities for teachers and administrators to engage in simulation exercises. For example, by trying to understand the barriers that students with various exceptional learning needs face, teachers will be able to empathize with those students and may be better motivated to plan means to overcome those barriers.

Attitudinal shifts. One theme emerging from the literature cited above is that principals' attitudes are an important factor as they seek to nurture an inviting and inclusive community. One factor influencing attitude is experience and knowledge. Often that which is unknown is feared and thus knowledge and experience can break down attitudinal barriers. The positive influence of even a modicum of knowledge and experience was demonstrated by Pudlas (2005) in a study that suggests that teacher attitudes can be positively influenced through pre-service education. In that research students' attitudes toward the inclusion of students with special needs were assessed pre and post an introductory course on educating students with special needs. The results indicated a significantly less negative attitude toward full inclusion after the completion of the course. One of the hallmarks of the course is an emphasis on affective outcomes. Through a series of simulations, biographies, and videos, students are introduced at a personal level to students with special learning needs and to their families. For example pre-service education students engage in an *Unfair hearing test* in which they attempt a spelling test while experiencing a mild high frequency hearing loss; they participate in a *Blind walk* in which they experience first hand the realities of orientation and mobility; they undertake several learning exercises with imposed "learning disabilities" to experience the frustration and anxiety experienced by students with identified L.D; and they attempt numerous simple tasks while simulating fine-motor-skill disabilities. Once they have experienced examples of some of the educational barriers encountered by students with exceptional learning needs the pre-professional education students learn basic strategies for overcoming those barriers. They also learn of potential professional partners in working toward meeting those needs. Thus when the pre-professional teachers eventually do encounter such students in their own classrooms they can recall their own experiences of frustration and failure and hopefully take a disability perspective in which they have empathy for their students rather than seeing them as a threat to their professional efficacy. They also have an understanding that they are not alone in helping their students to overcome barriers to learning and providing educational and related services.

Principals can certainly avail themselves of such simulations for professional development opportunities for their staff. Better yet, principals can invite school district specialists in various areas of exceptionality to facilitate professional development workshops as part of regular staff meetings or as Professional Development days. Principals can include other specialists in those in-services. As one example of sources of information, the Council for Exceptional Children (CEC) provides numerous resources for professional development (http://www.cec.sped. org/AM/Template.cfm?Section=Professional_Development). It would be worthwhile for teachers to join the Council for Exceptional children and at the very least the school could subscribe to the various publications the membership affords, such as the journals *Exceptional Children* (a more research-oriented journal) and *Teaching Exceptional Children* (focused more on praxis). Other journal sources in specific disability areas are available and *Exceptionality Education Canada* offers up to date research. Or perhaps principals have a pool of untapped professional resources in-house; how might those resources be utilized?

Not how smart are my teachers – but how are my teachers smart?. The widespread interest in multiple intelligences can provide some perspective on the wide range of professional abilities that may already be extant in any school. Resulting from Howard Gardner's (2006) work has been an attitudinal shift from "How smart are kids?" to "How are kids smart?" Principals would do well to ask a similar question; to see in their teaching staff a group of people who are smart in various ways, and who collectively possess abilities greater than the sum of the individual parts. Among the teaching staff will be some who are more familiar (or more comfortable?) dealing with students who have special needs. Those teachers may be the resource persons who can be empowered with leading professional development seminars and simulations. The literature has amply demonstrated the critical importance of principals who are willing to facilitate a collaborative approach to meeting special needs. Thus professional development might occur simply and naturally through pooling of extant resources, and all that would be required would be an administrator's willingness to provide flexibility in scheduling.

Educator Assistance Teams (EATs) may be one simple example of how school administrators can simply and cost-effectively facilitate positive inclusive practice. EATs do not serve the same function as Individualized Education Plan (IEP) teams. Rather they are an informal in-house network of educators who come together to brainstorm and attempt to find solutions that will enable particularly problematic students to overcome their learning barriers. The characteristics and functions of EATs are summarized in point form:
- Students' problems with learning, behaviour, and performance can be a source of professional frustration and a *threat to professional efficacy.*
- Educators individually and collectively possess considerable knowledge and talent and learn best by actively working to solve problems.
- Educators can solve many more problems when cooperatively working together rather than by working alone.
- These assumptions point to the importance of an educator support system within which the responsibility for decision-making and communication rests with the teachers themselves.
- Educator Assistance Teams (EATs) can be a foundational basis for empowerment and control, educator initiative, teacher initiated actions, professionalism, and accountability.
- EATs are not synonymous with IEP Teams and need not be as formal.

As one example, an EAT may be constituted of a special needs student's current teacher, last year's teacher and one or two others. That small group of teachers may meet to identify the nature of the student's current learning barriers and the antecedents, and to explore possible in-house solutions. This might involve discussing possible enrichment opportunities for a student who is gifted or devising alternate reading or writing strategies for students with learning disabilities in those areas. The key, however, is that these teachers are able to find time meet. Such meetings require the supportive intervention of the principal who is committed to the collaborative process and who finds creative ways to free up meeting times.

INVITATIONAL INVITING EDUCATION

Principals set the tone for the school community. And community – in the full sense of the word - is one of the goals of full inclusion. To that end, bringing principles of invitational education to professional development can contribute to more inclusive communities. As defined by Purkey and Novak (1996, p. 3) *invitational education* centres on five basic principles:

1. People are able, valuable, and responsible and should be treated accordingly.
2. Educating should be a collaborative, cooperative activity.
3. The process is the product in the making.
4. People possess untapped potential in all areas of worthwhile human endeavour.
5. This potential can best be realized by places, policies, programmes, and processes specifically designed to invite development and by people who are intentionally inviting with themselves and others personally and professionally.

As such it is in keeping with the current focus in education on differentiated instruction; the systematic approach to helping teachers ensure that every student is learning, regardless of interests, learning styles, or readiness for school. This, in turn, is in keeping with the work of Howard Gardner (2006) on multiple intelligences and of Daniel Goleman (1995) on emotional intelligence (a full discussion of which is beyond the scope of this chapter). The foregoing reflects a focus on the uniqueness and worth of the individual student.

This chapter, however, is focused primarily on teachers and administrators and specifically on the importance of their attitudes. So the emphasis is on the concepts surrounding invitational education, which centers on four guiding principles: respect, trust, optimism, and intentionality. To elaborate briefly on each of those principles:

1. *Respect*: Everyone in the school is able, valuable, and responsible and is to be treated accordingly.
2. *Trust*: Education is a cooperative, collaborative activity where process is as important as product.
3. *Optimism*: People possess relatively untapped potential in all areas of worthwhile human endeavor.
4. *Intentionality*: Safe schools are best realized by creating and maintaining inviting places, policies, processes, and programs and by people who are intentionally inviting with themselves and others, personally and professionally.

By centering itself on respect, trust, optimism, and intentionality *Invitational Education* provides a common language of transformation and a consistent theory of practice (Purkey, 1999). Further, Purkey and Novak suggest that, "Any approach to education is based on certain assumptions about what people are like and what they might become" (1996, p.19). This relates directly to the previous research that indicated the importance of principals communicating with their teachers and mutually working toward shared values and goals. Principals can model for their teachers the kind of inviting attitudes and behaviors that when adopted by those teachers are likely to lead students to perceive they are included.

Being Professionally Inviting

John Dewey in the last millennium, suggested that, "Everything the teacher does as well as the manner in which he does it incites the child to respond in some way or another and each response tends to set the child's attitude in some way or another" (1933. p. 59). More recently Guy Lefrancois (2000) in his widely used text for educational psychology set a foundational tone by initiating the first chapter with a discussion entitled, "Teaching and your beliefs" (p. 5). He suggests that beliefs are reflected in attitudes, prejudices, judgments and opinions (p. 5), and that they guide our thinking and our actions. Thus in the diverse climate in which teachers teach, it is increasingly important that their beliefs be examined and that they lead to invitational classrooms and experiences for all students. Prejudicial or inaccurate beliefs need to be "stamped out" to use a term popularized by Thorndike. That is one of the reasons for the previous study (Pudlas, 2005) that examined the effect of providing new knowledge to replace the ignorance and fear held towards students with diverse learning needs.

Being an Inviting Educator

Two assumptions of invitational education need to be addressed here. First, is that inviting and disinviting messages primarily result from perceptions, and second, that these messages significantly affect students self-concepts, their attitudes toward school, the relationships they form at school, and their school achievement (Purkey & Novak, 1996). Teachers who want to be a positive influence in the lives of their students need to see those students as able, valuable and responsible. Equally, if not more, important educators need to see *themselves* and education in positive and favourable ways. Having a positive and realistic view of oneself is an important aspect of invitational education (as per Figure 3). Principals need to ask themselves how, in their unique learning community, can such positive perceptions be fostered?

The invitational constructs, *able, valuable*, and *responsible,* to be applied by teachers to their students must also be applied to themselves. So, in that vein, Purkey and Novak (1996) discuss what they refer to as teacher stance, and suggest that teacher stance is built around four assumptions or invitational values: trust, respect, optimism, and intentionality. Teachers may, almost by accident, be inviting. But the aforementioned values must be consciously and intentionally applied. A possible framework for self-assessment of one's professional conduct is reproduced as Table 1. By intentionally modelling trust and trustworthiness, being respectful and worthy of respect, and encouraging self-efficacy through optimism about students' abilities, teachers engender an inviting ethos. It might be an interesting exercise to utilize Table 1 and have professional peers chart behaviours over a period of time. Each example noted would receive the score of that quadrant, with the higher score indicating a higher level of invitational behaviour.

Table 1. Inviting and disinviting behaviours with numeral indicating degree of intentionality

Negative Behaviours	Positive Behaviours
1. Intentionally disinviting E.g. *You never think!*	3. Unintentionally inviting May be effective; but can't say why.
2. Unintentionally disinviting E.g. *This is easy, anyone can do it.*	4. Intentionally inviting Have made inviting teaching part of their praxis.

SUMMARY: RE-VISIONING THE INCLUSIVE SCHOOL

Returning to Figure 2, the right side indicates the desired outcomes of an Inclusive Educational System. This chapter has been descriptive of some of the factors to be considered in the development of professionals who are professionally and personally inviting and who thereby contribute to an inclusive ethos in their classrooms and their school communities. Administrators will know that they have fostered an inclusive school community via successful professional development when as per the figure, all students are "Living and Learning in Community" and when "Lifelong Learning" is promoted for all students. As this occurs, there will be a re-visioning (renewed vision) for the Inclusive School Community.

Sample Resources for Professional Development

Publications
Jorgensen, C, & Schuh, M. (2005). *The inclusion facilitators guide.* Baltimore, MD: Brookes Publishing Company.
Moore, V., & Duff, F. (Eds.) (2006). *Listening to the experts: Students with disabilities speak out.* Baltimore, MD: Brookes Publishing Company.

Governmental Organizations
British Columbia Ministry of Education: Special Education
http://www.bced.gov.bc.ca/specialed/sped_res_docs.htm.

Non-Governmental Organizations
Council for Exceptional Children. Arlington, VA. [http://www.cec.sped.org/]
http://www.cec.sped.org/AM/Template.cfm?Section=Professional_Development

REFERENCES

Andrews, J., & Lupart, J. (2000). *The inclusive classroom: Educating exceptional children.* Scarborough, ON: Nelson.
Arends, R. (1994). *Learning to teach.* New York: McGraw-Hill Inc.
Bunch, G. (1993). *Educator opinion questionnaire.* ON: Inclusion Press.
Dewey, J. (1933). *How we think.* Lexington, MA: DC Heath.
Duff, F. R., Keefe, E. B., & Moore, V. M. (Eds.). (2006). *Listening to experts.* Maryland: Paul H. Brookes Publishing Co.

K. A. PUDLAS

Edmunds, A. L. (Ed.). (2003). Preparing Canadian teachers for inclusion. *Exceptionality Education Canada, 13*(1), 5–6.

Gardner, H. (2006). *Multiple Intelligences: New horizons.* New York: Basic Books.

Goleman, D. (1995). *Emotional intelligence.* Toronto, ON: Bantam Books.

Lasky, B., & Karge, B. D. (2006). Meeting the needs of students with disabilities: Experience and confidence of principals. *NASSP Bulletin, 90*(1), 19–36.

Lefrancois, G. (2000). *Psychology for teaching* (10th ed.). Toronto, ON: Wadsworth.

Minnesota Arts Best Practice Network. (2002). *Critical links: A professional inquiry process.* Minnesota: Perpich Center for Arts Education.

Noddings, N. (2008). All our students thinking. *Educational Leadership, 65*(5), 8–13.

Parkay, F., Stanford, B., Vaillancourt, J., & Stephens, H. (2005). *Becoming a teacher.* Toronto, ON: Pearson Education Canada.

Praisner, C. L. (2003). Attitudes of elementary school principals toward the inclusion of students with disabilities. *Exceptional Children, 69*(2), 135–145.

Pudlas, K. A. (2005, August). *Inviting inclusive education: Affective considerations.* Paper presented at the Inclusive and Supportive Education Conference, University of Strathclyde, Glasgow, Scotland.

Pudlas, K. A. (2003). Inclusive educational practice: Perceptions of students and teachers. *Exceptionality Education Canada, 13*(1), 49–64.

Purkey, W. (1999). Creating safe schools through invitational education. *ERIC Clearing House,* ED435946.

Purkey, W., & Novak, J. (1996). *Inviting school success: A self-concept approach to teaching learning, and democratic process* (3rd ed.). Toronto, ON: Wadsworth Publishing Company.

Rieck, W. A., & Wadsworth, D. E. (2000). Inclusion: Administrative headache or opportunity? *NASSP Bulletin, 84*(618), 56–62.

Roberts, S. M., & Pruitt, E. Z. (2003). *Schools as professional learning communities: Collaborative activities and strategies for professional development.* Thousand Oaks, CA: Corwin Press.

Salisbury, C. L., & McGregor, G. (2002). The administrative climate and context of inclusive elementary schools. *Exceptional Children, 68*(2), 259–274.

Sanders, M. G. (2006). *Building school-community partnerships: Collaboration for student success.* Thousand Oaks, CA: Corwin Press.

Wakeman, S. Y., Browder, D. M., Flowers, C., & Ahlgrim-Delzell, L. (2006). Principals' knowledge of fundamental and current issues in special education. *NASSP Bulletin, 90*(2), 153–174.

Weisel, A., & Dror, O. (2006). School climate, sense of efficacy and Israeli teachers' attitudes toward inclusion of students with special needs. *Education, Citizenship and Social Justice, 1*(2), 157–174.

TONY DIPETTA, VERA E. WOLOSHYN, TIFFANY GALLAGHER,
ANN-MARIE DIBIASE, MARILYN HYATT, DON DWORET
AND SHEILA BENNETT, (IN COLLABORATION WITH THE
DISTRICT SCHOOL BOARD OF NIAGARA)

12. RECOMMENDATIONS FOR IMPLEMENTING INCLUSIVE PRACTICES: LESSONS FROM THE FIELD

INTRODUCTION

In Lewis Carroll's, Alice in Wonderland, a scene is described where Alice comes to a fork in the road and asks "Which way should I take?" The Cheshire Cat, appearing nearby responds with the question, "Where do you want to go?" to which Alice answers, "I don't know. "Then", said the cat, "It doesn't matter."" The Cheshire Cat's remark to Alice can be seen as an allegorical response to many educational leaders who ask how they should plan for inclusive practices in their schools or boards. If the applications of inclusive practices are to be successful then leaders require a clear vision for inclusion. Administrative leadership as Edmunds and MacMillan argued in Chapter 1 indirectly influences or mediates the climate for inclusion within classrooms, schools and communities. In this chapter we examine the nature of that influence and present practical recommendations derived from the literature and the from experiences of a group of administrators involved in the implementation of a board-wide inclusive Intensive Support Program (ISP) in Southern Ontario, Canada.

In order for inclusion programs to be successful, the whole school community including administrators, teachers, staff, students, parents and volunteers must develop a "shared" vision of inclusion (Fredrickson, Simmonds, Evans & Soulsby, 2007; Meijer, 2001). Administrators play a vital role in the negotiation, implementtation and promotion of such a shared vision, in essence, fostering a culture of inclusion within which inclusive practices are seeded and grown (Kuglemas, 2003; Lambert, 2002, 2003; Riehl, 2000). The orientation to, and implementation of, inclusive practices has increased dramatically over the past two decades across North America. A U.S. Department of Education (2000) report notes that 70% of students with disabilities are provided with special education services in general education classrooms. The profile is similar in Canada (Bennett & Wynne, 2006; Edmonds & Edmonds, 2007). In a systematic review of the literature spanning two decades, Kalambouka, Farrell, Dyson and Kaplan (2007) concluded that the inclusion of students into regular classrooms was shown to have no detrimental academic impact on the achievement of students within those classes. Inclusive practices have also promoted positive attitudes towards individuals with exceptionalities among all students (Bunch & Valeo, 2004; McDougall, DeWitt, Kinga, Miller & Killip, 2004).

A. L. Edmunds and R. B. Macmillan (eds.), Leadership for Inclusion: A Practical Guide, 131–142.
© 2010 Sense Publishers. All Rights Reserved.

Despite these benefits, many educators' willingness to participate in inclusive programming is tempered by authentic concerns about lack of training and resources (Edmonds, 2003a; Luppert, 2001; Naylor, 2004; Slee, 2006; Woloshyn, Bennett & Berrill, 2003). Teachers indicate that they often feel under skilled and under resourced to provide what they would consider an optimal learning environment (Avarmidis & Norwich, 2002). Many teachers also hold lingering and unfounded concerns about the social acceptance of students with exceptionalities and the quality of academic programming in inclusive settings (Coleman, 2001; Winzer, 2005). In such contexts, administrators play an especially important role in the successful promotion, implementation and maintenance of inclusion programs (Kaffmann & Hallahan, 2005; Walther-Thomas, Korinek, McLaughlin, & Williams, 2000; Zollers, Ramanathan, & Yu, 1999).

We discuss the importance of this leadership role in the context of the ISP project, using this program as a focal point for discussion. We draw upon the voices and lived experiences of administrators, teachers, staff and students engaged in the implementtation of that inclusive program to form recommendations for educational leaders. Specifically, we used survey design (Creswell, 2005) to gather data examining and comparing stakeholders' (educators, parents, and students) perceptions of the ISP immediately before and after its first year of implementation. We supplement this information with interview data obtained from the participating principals and the chief administrator in charge of Special Education Services for the board (otherwise referred to as the Superintendent of Special Education).

THE INTENSIVE SUPPORT PROGRAM (ISP)

The Intensive Support Program presented here represents a 5-year effort on the part of one school board to implement board-wide inclusive programming for students with either learning disabilities (LD) or mild developmental disabilities (MID). Prior to the implementation of this program, most students identified with either of these exceptionalities received programming in a segregated classroom removed from their home school. In 2003–2006, the ISP was initiated as a pilot project in three rural schools. In 2006–2007 it was extended to 9 urban schools, rippling to another 15 schools within the year. In 2007–2008 the program was then extended to the remaining 25-plus schools within the board. The program evolved from a shared vision and language of inclusion developed and promoted by the ministry of education which in turn was embraced by senior school-board administrators. Guiding principles of this vision included the beliefs that *all students can learn* and that *all teachers can teach all students* (Ontario Ministry of Education, 2005). The recommendations presented below were informed by the insights and reflections of teachers, administrators and paraprofessionals involved with the implementation of the program.

Recommendation #1. *Develop and Promote a Shared Vision for Inclusion.* Inspired by these principles, the school-board completed a pilot project of the ISP in three small rural schools. Staff and administrators from the pilot schools became central personnel in the design and delivery of board-wide professional learning workshops and their classrooms were visited frequently by other administrators and ISP staff. These in-house experts or informal consultants provided continuity and guidance for the board-wide implementation of the ISP. They also added frontline credibility to the overall vision for inclusion and were a source of motivation for those unfamiliar with the proposed inclusive practices.

> *...we selected people who were known and respected by staff throughout the board and who had been involved in the pilot project to help facilitate and promote the program in other schools. Their background and experience meant that they understood the core values of the project and could talk about what those values would look like in practice. (Therese)*

Recommendation #2. *Provide Foundational Professional Learning.* Using the experiences of the pilot schools, school-board central staff and school administrators collaboratively designed a series of professional learning workshops that would promote the vision of inclusion at the core of the ISP, as well as prepare and sustain school staff throughout the board-wide implementation. As part of these workshops teachers, special education and learning resource teachers, administrators and central board staff were presented with information about the nature of learning disabilities (LD) and mild developmental disabilities (MID), the principles and practices of universal design, differentiated instruction, assistive technologies and effective instructional and assessment techniques for working with students with either LD or MID. The workshops were designed to provide all educators with the knowledge and classroom skills needed to enhance students' academic performance, social skills, and to encourage positive peer relationships between all students. These professional learning sessions were critical to the success of the ISP in that they ensured that all school staff shared a foundational knowledge base and skill set. A series of ongoing professional learning sessions was also seen as a means of overcoming resistance to change and insufficient or ineffective knowledge transfer associated with the use of one-time-only workshops for professional development (Sarama & DiBiase, 2004). Requiring administrators to attend these sessions with their staff was intended to solidify and promote the shared vision and demonstrate administrative commitment to inclusive practices.

> *It was the rollout that set the stage for what followed. The rollout provided the kind of preparation and training that everyone needed to help focus on meeting the ISP students needs in their classes...and it helped create the kind of school environment where the talk about inclusion reflected what we were actually doing. (Therese)*

School-board superintendents, special education consultants, school principals and the ISP staffing subcommittee also collaborated to allocate board-wide staffing and resources for the ISP. Schools were provided with a variety of implementation supports ranging from additional materials to the placement of a resource teacher assigned to work with students in the ISP and their teachers as determined by enrolment numbers and existing school resources.

Consistent with recommended leadership practices for inclusion (Senge, Cambron-McCabe, Kleiner, Dutton, & Smith, 2000; Timmons, 2006, Winzer, 1998), principals and their staff were then empowered to modify the implementation of the ISP at the school level to meet the unique needs of their constituents. While the essence of the ISP required that all students return to their home schools and receive inclusive programming, the nature of instruction varied across schools depending on student needs and school resources. In some schools, students were withdrawn for differentiated instruction in English and/or mathematics. In other schools, ISP staff team taught with homeroom teachers or provided them preparation time. In some instances, educational assistants and/or other para-professionals provided additional support in other content areas including history, science and French as required. All cases, instructional format was dynamic and changing, with school staff varying their instructional approaches as a function of students' changing needs.

Recommendation #3. *Place Students First*. The principals involved in the ISP project initially were challenged by the implementation demands of the ISP. There were a number of inherent scheduling and timetabling challenges associated with hosting the ISP so that students with either LD or MID would receive the intensive support that they required in language and mathematics.

> *It was a scheduling nightmare. We couldn't get it right until the first week of November. We were constantly trying to make it work for everybody and have the core, math and language not be interrupted. (Kelsey)*

It became apparent to the principals that in order for the ISP to be successful, students' needs would need to drive scheduling rather than teacher preferences. For some principals, therefore, scheduling became an issue of leadership and decision-making.

> *I think as much as I wanted to be respectful of the teachers and their autonomy and ability to plan a timetable, it really came down to me saying, 'Okay everybody, periods 1 and 2 are language, periods 3 and 4 are math.' I laid it out for them and I thought that it would not be well received, but it was exactly the opposite. (Marla).*

> *In the morning, all classroom teachers are instructing in language and math and that's all the way from grade 1 to 8. We have the uninterrupted literacy and numeracy blocks and there is no rotary in the morning. (Reanna).*

> *The big adjustment has been around flexibility because teachers are used to having control over their schedule. In the past if a teacher wanted to switch things around and have math here or switch other subjects he or she could do that. But you can't do that in the Intensive Support Program because kids go out for math. (Patti)*

Goleman (2000) recommends that leaders learn to use a variety of styles in order to successfully meet changing organizational or programmatic situations or needs.

From a leadership perspective, the proscriptive approach taken to scheduling by some of the principals can be viewed as a simple and direct solution to a logistical problem. However, the literature on teachers and teaching generally describes teachers as conservative in reaction to organizational change, focused on short-term rather than long- term planning and tending to value and demonstrate a high degree of independence in their classrooms (Darling-Hammond, 1999; Riehl, 2000). Fortunately, having these teachers participate in the board-wide professional learning workshops prior to the ISP implementation promoted the belief that inclusion and inclusive practices were in the interest of their students. Inadvertently, they helped foster a collaborative climate that prioritized students' learning needs and well being.

Recommendation #4. *Build and Sustain an Inclusive Team.* Leadership was key to establishing and maintaining school-based teams that acknowledged and respected the roles and contributions of all staff members and paraprofessionals working with students in the ISP. Traditionally, paraprofessionals provided behavioral support for students with special needs. In the context of the ISP project, these paraprofessionals were provided with the mandate to participate in the development and delivery of the academic program. Administrators' support and approval of the revised role of these paraprofessionals was critical in teachers' acceptance of these contributions.

> *The educational assistant is now there for academic support instead of being there for behavior support... so the educational assistant is far more involved in the programming and supporting the work that kids are completing. (Kelsey)*

> *A key component in the ISP is our educational assistants. Having them be a part of and in our classrooms assisting teachers with differentiated instruction and giving the teachers suggestions on how to differentiate, was something new for our teachers. (Charlette)*

The administrators understood and demonstrated the importance of establishing collaborative and cooperative relationships between and among professional and paraprofessional staff working in the ISP. Beyond the ability or willingness to manage the program, leadership involved the recognition of the need to build and sustain working relationships between and among various levels of staff, paraprofessionals, parents and other volunteers (Capper, Frattura, & Keyes, 2000; Meijer, 2001; Riehl, 2000).

Recommendation #5. *Promote Professional Learning Communities.* Within each of the participating schools, teachers formed school-based professional learning communities where issues and concerns associated with the implementation of the ISP were addressed and solutions for effective practice shared. These meetings were facilitated by the school administrator, with teams meeting once within a 10-day rotation. School staff were also provided with the opportunity to visit colleagues in other schools to develop inter-school collaborations. These meetings posed scheduling concerns for the principals, especially during the initial implementation phases, forcing some to resort to a directive leadership approach where they unilaterally scheduled meetings and mandated attendance.

We have meetings regularly. I try to have them once every 10 days in a cycle. It's not always perfect. The learning resource teachers and educational assistants both come and we meet at 8:00 a.m. and we review the kids and how they're doing. Then we have some time for professional development. (Marla)

Once scheduled, school staff reported that these sessions were beneficial and motivational. Educators were able to problem solve collectively around academic programming challenges and share their experiences using specific strategies associated with the delivery of differentiated instruction.

The Intensive Support Program teacher works on individualized programs for these kids but communicates on a regular basis with the classroom teacher on where the student is at and where we need to move the student. (Tom)

As the program implementation progressed and as teachers became more confident in their abilities to address programming challenges, teachers' support for the continuation of these meetings tended to lessen. School administrators on the other hand were reluctant to abandon these sessions. They acknowledged an ongoing need for school staff to monitor their understanding of inclusion and delivery of the ISP as well as their students' progress. Consistent with others (Biggs, & Wohlstetter, 2003; Booth, Ainscow, & Dyson, 2000; Winzer, 2005), these principals recognized that educators' understandings and expectations of inclusion differed and that ongoing professional discussion was critical with respect to moving individuals along this continuum.

We need professional learning community time. Once the school board gave us all this stuff (professional development workshops on inclusion, differentiated instruction, data walls, etc.) you need professional learning community opportunities for people to actually sit down, plan units and do it within their school. Ideally, the grade four through six teachers should be able to sit together and plan out a couple of the curriculum units. (Jo)

The growth area is not just with the kids - the growth area is also with the staff. The kids are doing fine, because they are with their friends and they are receiving what they need as far as language and math. The kids adjust quickly. It's the staff that require more time to adjust. (Patti)

Recommendation #6. *Provide Responsive Professional Learning.* When teachers were asked about their primary areas of concern prior to the ISP implementation, they questioned whether students in the program would be able to behave appropriately in their classrooms. Although these concerns were later demonstrated to be unfounded, they illustrated the importance of providing differentiated professional learning opportunities for teachers and staff. The initial board-wide professional learning workshops did not include management strategies for inclusive classrooms. Acknowledging teachers' concerns and providing opportunities for problem solving and sharing were critical for the success of the ISP at the school level and underscore the importance of administrators remaining "attuned" to the unanticipated or evolving concerns of their staff and extended school community (Capper, Frattura, & Keyes, 2000; Fullan, 1999; Kugelmass, 2003).

We knew there would be problems and things that would crop up that we didn't anticipate but we were prepared for that…we had resources in place and we kept everyone on alert for problems and they knew we were there to help them and would work with them to make things work. (Therese)

As teachers and school staff adopt inclusive practices as part of their everyday routines, administrators must provide professional learning opportunities that are responsive to teachers' developing skill sets and students' programming needs. That is, administrators must provide differentiated professional learning opportunities that recognize teachers' initial understandings and abilities and move them along a continuum of inclusive practice. In part, such movement may require distributed leadership whereby teachers assume greater responsibility for their professional learning (Portin, 2004).

Recommendation #7. *Communicate and Celebrate Success.* Consistent with the literature, all stakeholders acknowledged that all students benefitted socially and emotionally from their participation in the ISP (Hunt, 2000; Killoran, 2002; Kochhar, West, & Taymans, 2000; Salend, & Duhaney, 1999).

One mom is just over the moon about the program and wonders where this program has been for all these years. This is exactly what her son needed, to have him supported in the areas that he required it but to still be with a class and to feel that connection and inclusion in a group. (Tom)

Another mom, who has a son entering grade 8 next year, has been so happy with his behavior this year because he has not been suspended. (Reanna)

Somewhat surprisingly however, teachers did not recognize parallel academic gains. It was only when provided with data from performance indicators (i.e., report cards) did they recognize that such improvement did occur. Teachers' uncertainty about the effectiveness of their programming with respect to promoting academic gains suggests that formative feedback of student performance should be an integral part of ongoing school-based discussions. These conversations can be enhanced with the sharing of feedback from parents, students and other stakeholders.

They [students] have all shown improvement. When you look at their test scores, they're all moving ahead and they're gaining skills. (Marla)

Sabrina's [a grade 8 student] mom and dad called and said that they noticed an improvement in her academics this year and also in her self-esteem. That was very, very positive. (Reanna)

Teachers are most likely to adopt new practices or alter existing ones when they are able to see improvements in student achievement or behavior (Sindelar, Shearer, Yendel-Hoppey & Liebert, 2008; Stanovich & Jordan, 2004). Celebrating and building on the progressive success of students means that school leaders need to keep sight of the larger picture of inclusion in their schools. In the ISP, teachers working with ISP students were so fully engaged in their inclusive activities and planning for their students that they did not see the changes that were taking place in student academic attainment until assessment data indicated that such improvement did in fact occur in some areas.

Recommendation #8. *Conduct Formative Program Review, Visioning and Re-visioning.* Formative review is an essential component of the evolution of any program (Fullan, 1999; Riehl, 2000; Senge et al., 2000; Shadish, & Reichardt, 1987). As administrators encouraged their staff to vision for the future of the ISP, they also needed to monitor current practices associated with its delivery. This examination process ensured that programming adhered to the central beliefs of inclusion and warded against systemic and/or subliminal pressures to revert to non-inclusive practices. For example, resisting the well-intentioned temptation to have learning resource teachers deliver programming in segregated settings versus working with students and their teachers in the classroom.

> *People have to walk the walk as well as talk the talk when trying to be inclusive. That means that we have to stop thinking about regular classrooms and inclusive classrooms and move beyond that limitation to reach a new understanding of how to help all students learn and teachers teach all students. (Therese)*

Administrators' abilities to facilitate future planning were central to the forward momentum and evolution of the ISP. In part, such planning required careful and ongoing review of the current program as well as a visioning and re-visioning of the program's potential. For example, school staff comments about the importance of professional dialogues with their secondary school colleagues with respect to transition planning for students in the ISP program, inspired and revitalized ongoing dialogues within the board-based family of schools.

> *Curt is going to high school next year. We've talked to the high school to make sure that the supports are in place for him and that he has the resource opportunities. We are hoping that by talking with them that we will get that transition to happen more readily and ensure that his needs are met. It's just good communication to me - making sure everyone is on board and understands what is needed to ensure success for next year. (Reanna)*

When school staff contemplated whether all students should be provided with access to assistive technologies such as text readers and speech recognition software rather than restricting their use to students identified with learning exceptionalities, an assistive technologist position was incorporated as part of the school-based teams in the third year of the program implementation.

We are trying to bring the ISP in line with other programs and plans we have for helping students in our board. That means that if we see or learn about something that would help one group of students we look carefully to see if that same thing would benefit all students and then plan for how to ensure that everyone gets the same advantage or benefit. (Therese)

Recommendation #9. *Position and Leverage Inclusive Programs.* The philosophical underpinning of the ISP was based on a vision of inclusion that was accepted by a variety of educational stakeholders ranging from the ministry of education to the parent community. School-board administrators carefully positioned the ISP program in context of government and regional efforts that enabled them to advocate effectively for resources and supports.

You have to advocate for what you believe and that means that you have to take every opportunity to talk about the program at meetings and with stakeholder groups and use every bit of leverage you can get to build support for what you know will ultimately benefit the students in the board. (Therese)

In order to implement the inclusion program effectively, administrators need to contextualize their efforts with respect to broader educational initiatives (i.e., state or federal levels) while remaining sensitive to the realities and needs of local schools (Capper et al., 2000; Sailor, 2002). Administrators are encouraged to seek local resources to validate their programs. For example, school-board central staff invited faculty from their local university to conduct an independent review of the program. In turn, they were able to use the collected data advantageously to validate the program and advocate for its continuation.

CONCLUSION AND DISCUSSION

A new definition of school leadership is emerging that empowers school staff to become involved as leaders in inclusive programming. This form of leadership may be described as interactive, collective and invested in many as opposed to the few. Leadership is based on interactions between and among individuals for the common good of improved student learning and school improvement (Court, 2003; Lambert, 2002; Murphy, 2005). Further, leader mentorship requires fostering an environment for professionals to work and learn together to create a synergy greater than the sum of individual efforts (Bennett, Wise, Woods, & Harvey, 2003; Portin, 2004; Usdan, McCloud, & Podmostkop, 2001).

Teachers can serve as leaders in their classrooms, schools and broader educational communities. Such distributed leadership does not however, diminish the need for principals to be formal leaders who create the conditions for inclusive teaching and learning. In this chapter, we shared administrators' experiences to a board-wide implementation of an inclusion program designed for students in grades four through eight with either learning disabilities or mild intellectual disabilities. Inclusion programs like the ISP have blurred the distinction between classroom instruction and special education, with teachers increasingly required to program for students with a variety of exceptionalities (Edmonds & Edmonds, 2007;

McPhail & Freeman, 2005; McLeskey, & Waldron, 2002). Consistent with the findings of others (Edmonds, 2003b; Stanovich & Jordan, 2004), the success of the ISP program was a result of a combination of factors including administrative leadership, support and planning, professional learning and preparation, and collaboration and cooperation between and among stakeholders. Our work with the ISP, has led us to conclude that successful leadership requires administrators to engage in a shared vision of inclusion while maintaining sensitivity to local contexts and conditions. More importantly, we believe that the success of any inclusion program is contingent on adherence to the foundational principles of the ISP - *All students can learn* and *All teachers can teach all students.*

REFERENCES

Avramidis, E., & Norwich, B. (2002). Teachers' attitudes towards integration /inclusion: A review of the literature. *European Journal of Special Needs Education, 17*(2), 129–147.

Bennett, N., Wise, C., Woods, P., & Harvey, J. A. (2003). *Distributed leadership: Full report.* UK: National College for School Leadership.

Bennett, S., & Wynne, K. (2006). *Special education transformation: The report of the co-chairs with recommendations of the working table on special education.* Ministry of Education, Ontario. Retrieved from http://www.edu.gov.on.ca

Biggs, K. L., & Wohlstetter, P. (2003). Key elements of a successful school-based management strategy. *School Effectiveness and School Improvement, 14*, 351–372.

Booth, T., Ainscow, M., & Dyson, A. L. (2000). *Index for inclusion: Developing learning and participation in schools.* Bristol, England: Center for Studies on Inclusive Education.

Bunch, G., & Valeo, A. (2004). Student attitudes towards peers with disabilities in inclusive and special education schools. *Disability and Society, 1*(1), 61–78.

Capper, C. A., Frattura, E., & Keyes, M. W. (2000). *Meeting the needs of students of all abilities: How leaders go beyond inclusion.* Thousand Oaks, CA: Corwin Press.

Coleman, M. R. (2001). *Conditions of teaching children with exceptional learning needs: The bright futures Report.* ERIC Clearinghouse on Disabilities and Gifted Education Arlington VA. ERIC Identifier: ED455660.

Court, M. (2003). Towards democratic leadership. Co-principal initiatives. *International Journal of Leadership in Education, 6*, 161–183.

Creswell, J. (2005). *Educational research: Planning, conducting, and evaluating quantitative and qualitative research.* Upper Sadler River, NJ: Merrill Prentice Hall.

Darling-Hammond, L. (1999). Educating teachers: The Academy's greatest failure or its most important future? *Academe, 85*(1).

Edmonds, A. L. (2003a). The inclusive classroom – Can teachers keep up? A comparison of Nova Scotia and Newfoundland & Labrador teachers' perspectives. *Exceptionality Education Canada, 13*(1), 29–48.

Edmonds, A. L. (2003b). Preparing Canadian teachers for inclusion. *Exceptionality Education Canada, 13*(1), 5–6.

Edmonds, A. L., & Edmonds, G. A. (2007). *Special education in Canada.* Toronto, ON: McGraw-Hill Ryerson.

Frederickson, N., Simmonds, E., Evans, L., & Soulsby, C. (2007). Assessing the social and affective outcomes of inclusion. *British Journal of Special Education, 34*(2), 105–115.

Fullan, M. (1999). *Change forces: The sequel.* Philadelphia: Falmer Press.

Goleman, D. (2000). Leadership that gets results. *Harvard Business Review*, 78–90.

Hunt, P. (2000). 'Community' is what I think everyone is talking about. *Remedial and Special Education, 21*(5), 305.

Kaffman, J. M., & Hallahan, D. P. (2005). *Special education: What it is and why we need it.* Toronto, ON: Pearson.

Kalambouka, A., Farrell, P., Dyson, A., & Kaplan, I. (2007). The impact of placing students with special education needs in mainstream schools on the achievement of their peers. *Educational Researcher, 49*(4), 365–382.

Killoran, I. (2002). The road less travelled: Creating a community where each belongs. *Childhood Education, 78*, 45–62.

Kochhar, C. A., West, L. L., & Taymans, J. M. (2000). *Successful inclusion: Practical strategies shared responsibility.* Upper Saddle River, NJ: Prentice-Hall.

Kuglemass, J. W. (2003). Inclusive leadership: Leadership for inclusion. *International Practitioner Report. National College for School Leadership.* Report downloaded June 25, 2008, from http://www.ncsl.org.uk/media/F7B/53/kugelmass-inclusive-leadership-full.pdf

Lambert, L. (2003). *Leadership capacity for lasting school improvement.* Alexandra, VA: Association of Curriculum Development.

Lambert, L. (2002). A framework for shared leadership. *Educational Leadership, 59*(8), 37–41.

Lindsay, G. (2003). Inclusive education: A critical perspective. *British Journal of Special Education, 30*(1), 3–12.

Lupart, J. L. (2001). Meeting the educational needs of exceptional learners in Alberta. *Exceptionality Education Canada, 11*(2–3), 55–70.

McDougall, J., DeWitt, D. J., Kinga, G., Miller, L. T., & Killip, S. (2004). High school aged youths' attitudes toward their peers with disabilities: The role of schools and student interpersonal factors. *International Journal of Disability, Development and Education, 51*(3), 287–313.

McLeskey, J., & Waldron, N. (2002). Professional development and inclusive schools: Reflections on effective practice. *Teacher Educator, 37*, 159–172.

McPhail, J. C., & Freeman, J. G. (2005). Beyond prejudice: Thinking toward genuine inclusion. *Learning Disabilities Research and Practice, 20*(4), 254–267.

Meijer, C. J. W. (2001). *Inclusive education and effective classroom practices.* Report of the European agency for development in special needs education. European Agency for Development in Special Needs: Odense Denmark.

Murphy, J. (2005). *Connecting teacher leadership and school improvement.* Thousand Oaks, CA: Corwin Press.

Naylor, C. (2004). *How teachers in Coquitlam and Nanaimo view Special Education and ESL services.* Vancouver, BC: Teachers' Federation. Retrieved from http://www.bctf.ca/education/InclusiveEd/ResearchProject/dc/SurveyReport.html

Ontario Ministry of Education. (2005). *Education for All: The report of the expert panel on literacy and numeracy instruction for students with special education needs, kindergarten to grade 6.*

Portin, B. (2004). The roles that principals play. *Educational Leadership, 61*, 14–19.

Riehl, C. J. (2000). The principal's role in creating inclusive schools for diverse students: A critical review of normative, empirical, and critical literature on the practice of educational administration. *Review of Educational Research, 70*, 55–81.

Sailor, W. (2002). *Whole-school success and inclusive education: Building partnerships for learning, achievement, and accountability.* New York: Teachers College Press.

Salend, S. J., & Duhaney, L. G. (1999). The impact of inclusion on students with and without disabilities and their educators. *Remedial and Special Education, 20*(2), 114–127.

Sarama, J., & DiBiase, A. M. (2004). *The professional development challenge in preschool mathematics.* In D. H. Clements, J. Sarama, & A. M. DiBiase (Eds.), *Engaging young children in mathematics: Standards for early childhood mathematics education.* Hillsdale, NJ: Lawrence Erlbaum Associates.

Senge, P., Cambron-McCabe, N., Lucas, T., Kleiner, A., Dutton, J., & Smith, B. (2000). *Schools that learn: A fifth discipline fieldbook for educators, parents, and everyone who cares about education.* New York: Currency.

Shadish, W. R., & Reichardt, C. S. (1987). The intellectual foundations of social program evaluation: The development of evaluation theory. *Evaluation Studies Review Annual, 12*, 13–29.

Sindelar, P. T., Shearer, D. K., Yendol-Hoppey, D., & Liebert, T. W. (2008). The sustainability of inclusive school reform. *Exceptional Children, 72*(3), 317–331.

Slee, R. (2006). Inclusive education: Is this horse a Trojan? *Exceptionality Education Canada, 16*(3), 223–242.

Stanovich, P., & Jordan, A. (2004). Inclusion as professional development. *Exceptionality Education Canada, 14*(2&3), 169–188.

Timmons, V. (2006). Impact of a multipronged approach to inclusion: Having all partners on side. *International Journal of Inclusive Education, 10*, 469–480.

U.S. Department of Education. (2000). *Twenty-second annual report to Congress on the implementation of the Individuals with Disabilities Education Act.* Washington, DC: Author.

Usdan, M., McCloud, B., & Podmostkop, M. (2001). *Leadership for student learning: Redefining the teacher as leader. A report of the task force on teacher leadership.* Washington, DC: Institute for Educational Leadership.

Walther-Thomas, C., Korinek, L., McLaughlin, V. L., & Williams, B. T. (2000). *Collaboration for inclusive education: Developing successful programs.* Prentice Hall.

Winzer, M. (2005). *Children with exceptionalities in Canadian classrooms* (7th ed.). Toronto, ON: Pearson Education Inc.

Winzer, M. A. (1998). Inclusion practices in Canada: Social political and educational influences. In S. J. Vitello & D. E. Mithaug (Eds.), *Inclusive schooling: National and international perspectives* (pp. 139–150). New York: L. Erlbaum Publishers.

Woloshyn, V. E., Bennett, S., & Berrill, D., (2003). Working with students who have learning disabilities teacher candidates speak out: Issues and concerns in preservice education and professional development. *Exceptionality Education Canada, 13*, 7–28.

Zollers, N. J., Ramanathan, A. K., & Yu, M. (1999). The relationship between school culture and inclusion: How an inclusive culture supports inclusive education. *International Journal of Qualitative Studies in Education, 12*, 157–175.

ALAN L. EDMUNDS, ROBERT B. MACMILLAN,
JACQUELINE SPECHT, ELIZABETH A. NOWICKI
AND GAIL A. EDMUNDS

13. PRINCIPALS AND INCLUSIVE SCHOOLS: INSIGHT INTO PRACTICE

INTRODUCTION

One of the primary outcomes of the educational reforms of the 1990s was the merging of regular and special education into inclusive education: "an educational philosophy that considers student diversity to be a reflection of society, thus, it emphasizes that students with exceptionalities be taught in the regular classroom and it reinforces the notion that student differences are accepted and respected" (Edmunds, 1999, p. 27). The fundamental underpinnings of inclusion are educational systems that are dynamic, holistic and collaborative in approach (Lupart & Webber, 1996; O'Brien & O'Brien, 1996; Stainback & Stainback, 1996). Edmunds & Edmunds (2008) more specifically defined inclusion as "an overarching philosophy that advocates for a commitment to considering the regular classroom as the first placement option for the education of students with exceptionalities (p. 24)."

As special education continues to evolve, principals must be dynamic leaders who champion school transformations that result in maximal outcomes for all students. School leaders must have a full understanding of the change process (Fullan, 2001) wherein: a) change is a process; b) change is made by individuals who, in turn, change institutions; and, c) as innovation occurs, considerable personal attention is paid to those who enact innovation. Ryan (2004) summarized educational leadership as the key to inclusion because leaders are in a position to address the many challenges of inclusive education and they are unilaterally able to mobilize support for inclusion, facilitate inclusive practices, and monitor teachers' efforts toward implementation.

There were several reasons for undertaking this study. First, principals are not always aware of all the parameters that affect inclusion (Edmunds, 1999; 2003). Second, administrators' assumptions and attitudes affect their approach to the success of the implementation of the change process (Fullan, 1982; 1991; 2001). Third, being responsibile for all educational policies, principals need the best information available to effectively evaluate and monitor inclusive practices in their schools. Finally, while Prestine & Nelson (2005) describe schools as *professional learning communities* in which teachers are supported by strong leadership in order to "ratchet up the overall quality of teaching and learning (p. 56)", the pragmatic workings to achieve this are elusive.

A. L. Edmunds and R. B. Macmillan (eds.), Leadership for Inclusion: A Practical Guide, 143–159.
© *2010 Sense Publishers. All Rights Reserved.*

> If communities of practice do indeed present promising avenues for improved
> student learning, there is a pressing need to explore the conditions necessary
> to support and sustain them. ... How a school, and especially a leader, goes
> about creating, nurturing, and sustaining learning communities focused on
> instructional improvement is not clear-cut (pp. 56–57).

The objective of this study was to assist principals to conduct a pragmatic
examination of the inclusive practices of their schools. Under the guidance of the
research team, principals reflected on and documented extant inclusive practices
and by comparing these with exemplary models, entertained the possible need for
change. It was hypothesized that not all principals had comprehensive
understandings of inclusive practices and that their participation would help them
uncover the strengths and weaknesses of inclusion in their schools. This research
framework allowed a specific unit of analysis (inclusion) to be examined across
three parameters vital to investigations of the interfaces between leadership and
school practice: the individual (the principal); the interpersonal or group (the
teachers); and the institutional/cultural (the school) (Rogoff, Radziszewska, &
Masiello, 1995).

METHOD

All 56 principals from an Ontario school board were invited to participate.
Twelve agreed to collect data from their respective schools (11 elementary,
1 secondary; 8 females, 4 males). A total of nine principals submitted comprehensive
data sets.

Participants were provided with data collection packages to document the six
fundamental components of inclusive schools (Bunch, Lupart & Brown, 1997;
Edmunds, 1999; 2003): 1) physical resources; 2) philosophy, policies, and
mandates; 3) school environment; 4) school personnel; 5) delivery of special
education; and, 6) classroom teaching practices. The study was interested in
whether there was a predominantly positive or negative indicator of each
component; not to determine different levels, degrees, or qualities of each
component. This approach was implemented because of the highly contextual
nature of practices in schools, the inherent difficulties in developing consistent
evaluation mechanisms across schools (Edmunds, 19999; 2003; King &
Edmunds, 2001), and because a "standardized" evaluation could be viewed as
potentially intrusive/threatening. Nonetheless, some principals spontaneously
provided comments on the quality of some components.

The study involved three workshops: 1) a fall workshop to discuss inclusion and
to demonstrate how to document inclusive schooling; 2) a winter workshop to
discuss progress-to-date and to solve research problems/challenges; and 3) a spring
workshop to share findings and conclusions, strategies for future practices, and
reflections on the research process. Between workshops, participants gathered data
in their respective schools with support from the research team by telephone and
email.

RESULTS

School Demographics

The nine school profiles are presented in Table 1. The percentage of students with individual education plans (IEPs) ranged from 6% to 19%, the number of educational assistants (EAs) ranged from 1 to 5, with five schools identified as urban while four were identified as rural. Four schools primarily served middle to upper class families, two served lower to middle class families, and several were located in multi-cultural communities.

Table 1. School profiles

School	Grade Range	Number of Students	Students with IEPs	Specialized Personnel
#1	JK-8	335	21(6%)	4.5
#2	JK-8	214	33(15%)	5
#3	JK-8	241	25(10%)	4
#4	JK-8	279	22(8%)	4
#5	JK-8	280	16(6%)	2
#6	9-12	378	70(19%)	5
#7	JK-8	267	21(8%)	4
#8	JK-8	243	20–35(8–14%)	2
#9	K-8	257	19(7%)	6

Table 2 details the unique location, programming, staff turnover, family demographics, parent involvement, and/or student academic needs that made certain schools standout.

Table 2. What makes your school unique?

– very high turnover in leadership as well as in the SPST position
– school is part of a complex jointly owned by the Public and Catholic Boards
– designated a French Immersion school
– offer both an English Program and a French Immersion Program
– high ESL population that is not defined "ESL" according to Ministry standards
– multi-ethnic population
– the parents of many of the students also attended this school
– only Catholic school in small rural town
– families are either involved in farming or they have moved from the city to the new subdivisions surrounding the farms
– all students are bussed to school
– no students are bussed to school
– privileged families who value education
– exceptional level of parent involvement
– high number of children with significant academic needs

Fewer than half the principals were able to provide an historical perspective. Those who did gave brief descriptions primarily focused on when their school last provided self-contained classrooms. It was obvious that the historical contexts of special education and inclusion were not part of the principals' knowledge base.

Physical Resources

All nine principals indicated that their schools had both a gymnasium and a library, four included a computer lab and/or science lab as physical resources, and only two mentioned they had learning resource centers. The Table 3 data makes it clear that not all schools were fully accessible and able to accommodate students with physical disabilities. Four principals described accessibility in a highly positive manner, two provided only negative comments, and three gave both positive and negative comments on accessibility. The issue of accessibility appeared to be a touchy subject for most principals. This was primarily due to their lack of control/influence over capital cost funding, although some did acknowledge that some issues were within their budgetary control.

Table 3. Physical accessibility within the school

Positive Aspects
– fully accessible on three floors with elevator and handicap bathroom
– fully accessible – one floor school
– elevator to lower level
– wheelchair access
– special needs bathroom
– accessible stall in each washroom
– chairs have "hush-ups" on the legs to reduce noise

Negative Aspects
– multi-level/not wheelchair accessible
– one level but not fully accessible
– no access to portable classrooms
– no automatic door openers
– washrooms have limitations

Philosophy, Policies, and Mandates

Most principals indicated that the inclusion philosophy, policies, and mandates adhered to were those provided by their Board and/or the Ontario Ministry of Education. The Board's philosophy was:
– all students should have an opportunity to learn to live and to contribute as responsible Catholics;
– every student has an inherent right to a caring, effective, and inclusive education;
– schools today reflect a multitude of diverse needs that influence learning;
– all students have a right to participate fully in opportunities for learning and growth appropriate to their needs and gifts;

- educators have a responsibility to provide these students the opportunity to share the school experience which their brothers, sisters, and friends enjoy;
- an attitude of welcome acceptance, and indeed, celebration of individual differences and unique gifts is to be encouraged and supported; and,
- in the school community, each individual member is valued, diversity is celebrated as the norm, people are of equal worth, relationships are of mutual benefit, and belonging is nurtured.

Other influential policies, mandates, and documents included:
- Education Act;
- Safe School Act;
- Special Education Standards – IEP Standards;
- Catholic Education Graduate Expectations;
- School Improvement Plan;
- Education for All; and,
- Special Education Handbook.

School Environment

All principals expressed the intention to foster schools that provided a welcoming environment for all students. Some indicated, however, that their schools were especially proactive in creating supportive environments for students with special needs. In terms of school environment, the principals identified several positive and negative influences (see Table 4). They most frequently identified a positive/ motivated staff, EA support, and parental involvement as positive factors; conversely, they most frequently indicated a lack of resources and a lack of staff expertise as barriers.

Table 4. Factors affecting school environment

Positive Factors	Principals Making Comment
– positive/motivated staff	(6)
– EA support	(4)
– parental involvement	(3)
– creating a sense of belonging/acceptance	(2)
– effective communication	(2)
– supportive community	(2)
– small school environment	(1)
– Catholic teachings	(1)
– skilled learning services staff	(1)
– including all students in all activities	(1)
– accessible play area	(1)
– up-to-date technology	(1)
– Board support	(1)

Table 4. (continued)

Negative Factors	Principals Making Comment
– lack of resources	(5)
– lack of staff expertise	(3)
– teacher mindset	(1)
– negative attitudes amongst staff	(1)
– philosophy versus practice	(1)
– inadequate classroom space	(1)
– large class size	(1)
– lack of accessibility	(1)
– lack of communication	(1)
– lack of community support	(1)
– lack of Board expertise	(1)
– rural location	(1)
– cultural biases	(1)

School Personnel

Internal personnel. All nine principals indicated that they had special education personnel and this most commonly included a Student Program Support Teacher and educational assistants. These and other staff members received professional development through staff meetings, individual training sessions, school workshops, school board workshops, and conferences. One principal stated that:

> System wide, professional development in special education has been virtually non-existent. The Board does not allocate any funds to this area. The focus for training is subject specific curriculum driven. The Ministry approach to allocating funds for training is hugely flawed. Over the past several years, monies have been provided in a reactive manner. There is no strategic planning regarding its use. It arrives at the eleventh hour and there is a scramble for it to be spent. There are unreasonable time lines and no consideration for what might be going on within the schools. The concept of *if you do not use it, you lose it* drives so many decisions. This is an uninformed, ineffective way to make decisions. It is irresponsible, wasteful and shameful really.

External personnel. The principals also indicated that a number of external persons were available including:
– psycho-educational consultant;
– speech-language pathologist;
– occupational therapist;
– physiotherapist;
– recreational therapist;
– augmentative communication therapist;

- keyboarding therapist;
- autism specialist;
- affiliate liaison teacher;
- behaviour resource teacher;
- blind and low vision teacher;
- deaf and hard of hearing teacher;
- curriculum resource teacher;
- nurse; and,
- social worker.

The only individual to express dissatisfaction with the specialist personnel available was the principal of a French Immersion School.

> We currently have a special education teacher who speaks and understands French. She currently receives on-going professional development. Unfortunately, she does not have access to materials and supports necessary to meet the diverse needs of a wide range of students.

Attitudes of school personnel. The principals indicated that most teachers were supportive of inclusion, however, "implementing the strategies that are required to fully include students is sometimes frustrating and teachers get overwhelmed" was a common theme. Teachers voiced considerable frustration with the lack of support personnel, the lack of time to prepare and implement curricular differences, large class sizes, limited resources, and dealing with ongoing behaviour problems. As one principal explained, "most staff feel they know what an individual child needs to learn, however the class size, limited preparation time, and limited resources prevent this child from receiving what they need." Another principal stated that these frustrations led to an "abdication of responsibility" as teachers pay more attention to the other children and let the SPST and EAs deal with children with special needs. Clearly, teachers were/are challenged by inclusive classrooms and this, in turn, created challenging situations for those in leadership:

> I have witnessed attitudes that I celebrate and attitudes that shame me. Some of the staff members continually search for any way possible to include all children and celebrate their strengths. I have seen others who believe that children with needs should not be in our school. There are those people who think outside of the box and will stop at nothing to help a child feel successful. There are very good teachers who can't seem to let go of their pre-conceived ideas of "what children should know" and have such a hard time finding alternative ways of teaching and of assessing. Where I have witnessed the biggest deficits in special education are the issues that involved contractual issues and attitudes. People who insist on leaving the second their day is done. People who will not participate in professional development when it is offered outside the hours of the regular day. People who refuse to do something extra because it is not in their job description. People who make choices that involve children not because it is in the best interest of the child but because it is more convenient for them.

Teacher Preparedness

When asked how prepared teachers were to teach/manage children with special needs, seven principals reported significant difficulties. One stated that "on a scale of 1 to 10 (1 being extremely poor and 10 being excellent) teachers in my school are hovering around a 4." Another estimated that while approximately 50% of teachers had some special education training, most "feel inadequately prepared to address special needs, particularly behavioural concerns". The principals cited a lack of preservice training, not enough specialized training once teachers are in classrooms, and a lack of initiative by some to upgrade their skills. Several principals noted that some teachers, regardless of background, were just more naturally skilled when it came to meeting the needs of children in inclusive classrooms. As one principal summarized:

> Teachers are not prepared well to teach/manage children with special needs. There are however, teachers who have natural gifts and talents who strive to meet the needs of individual students and do an amazing job on a daily basis. Even teachers who have some background or experience in special education struggle to find a way to reach students and turn on those "light bulbs", those "aha" moments when children truly understand. While we embrace those students who have special needs and welcome them into our schools and our classrooms with open arms, the lack of resources and the multiple demands on educators makes it difficult. Expectations for learning that are determined by an outside group and perhaps are not realistic, get in the way of allowing children to learn at their own pace. Restrictions against valuable programs such as life skills cause grief for those who see the value in gaining such skills. Legal liabilities limit the scope of programs that would see students outside the walls of the school and in the community – exploring, discovering, shopping, baking, etc.

> Large class size and the amount of curriculum expectations often put educators in survive mode. All of their altruistic thoughts of differentiated instruction fly out the window. Class make up is not what it used to be. There are so many situations to deal with, teaching has become even more complicated. While behaviour problems have increased, respect for authority has decreased. Teachers need to graduate with a whole bag of tricks to ensure that they will have good class management skills.

> We know so much more about how kids learn and we have identified so many disorders and syndromes, teachers need to enter the classroom for the first time, prepared for everything. We no longer have the "special ed" classes with the specialist teacher at the front. Every classroom is a special ed classroom. Every teacher needs to be prepared better.

Delivery of Special Education

As one principal noted, schools within the board adhered to the board's special education delivery model.

The first choice is always the classroom to support students. We try to provide early intervention by providing support as soon as it is needed. EAs and the SPST support many students in many classrooms throughout the day. They provide support when it is needed. Our goal is independence for all students.

School based team. All principals stated that the needs of students with exceptionalities were considered by a school based team. The teams comprised, as a minimum, the principal, an SPST, the student's classroom teacher, and the student's EA (if applicable). Some indicated that other personnel were part of their team, including social workers, chaplains, vice-principals, and other teachers. Two principals stated that students with special needs participated as appropriate. The majority of principals provided brief descriptions of how school based teams functioned. For example, as one principal explained,

Together we identify challenges; review and share student data; discuss possible strategies and recommendations; monitor progress; manage resources; and seek affiliate team support. As principal I provide leadership and support to ensure all school team members understand and carry out their roles. I chair IPRC meetings and ensure that IEPs are completed and implemented…The teacher is seen as the curriculum expert. He/She contributes front line knowledge of the student's strengths, needs and interests, maintains communication with all stake holders, develops and reviews modified or alternative expectations and implements teaching and assessment strategies. The SPST coordinates the student's IEP, prepares necessary information for IEP meetings and provides diagnostic assessments. Together we attempt to provide an interdisciplinary team approach to serve programming needs of our students and to provide support to parents.

Assessment. Only one principal described how students were identified/assessed for special learning and/or behavioral needs:

The school based team is the first step in a protocol.
Student concerns are discussed.
Strategies are developed and tried.
May involve some informal testing.
If issues are not resolved, student is referred to Area Team.

The remaining principals simply described how students with special needs were managed by the school based team.

Classroom Teaching Practices

Differentiated curriculum. Few principals provided explicit information about how curricula were differentiated. Two explained that teachers: 1) significantly decreased the amount of student work; 2) changed the grade level of some subjects;

3) reduced the depth and breadth of topics covered; and/or 4) modified projects to reflect student abilities. Another principal noted that teachers did not necessarily differentiate:

> I am not convinced nor have I seen much evidence of a differentiated curriculum by most teachers. I believe that our teachers are aware of needs but are for the most part, muddling through flexible classroom teaching routines...The struggle lies within the importance of "covering" curriculum, rather than the importance of allowing students to become partners in their own success...More professional development to assist teachers to expand their repertoire of instructional strategies is needed.

Accommodations. The principals listed a number of accommodations made for both inside and outside classrooms (see Table 5). The most frequent accommodations within classrooms were the use of assistive technology, preferential seating, extra time for assignments, and testing accommodations. Only "Buddy Programs" and time spent working with learning resource personnel were identified as outside classroom accommodations.

Table 5. Accommodations

Within the Classroom	Principals Making Comment
– assistive technology	(6)
– preferential seating	(4)
– extra time to complete assignments	(3)
– testing accommodations (i.e., oral)	(3)
– a scribe is provided for written work	(2)
– cueing students	(2)
– sound system	(2)
– material is read to student	(1)
– rephrasing questions	(1)
– pre-teaching	(1)
– repetition	(1)
– varied learning materials	(1)
– "chunking" the work assigned to students	(1)
– providing copies of notes	(1)
Within the School	**Principals Making Comment**
– "Buddy" Programs	(3)
– time spent with learning resource personnel	(3)

Evaluation

Few principals addressed the issue of student evaluation in depth. Most simply stated that evaluation followed the criteria outlined in students' IEPs. One principal indicated that evaluation issues were emphasized in her school:

> Teachers are reminded in a number of ways that they must decide how they will assess all students prior to starting units of study. They are also reminded regularly that they must consult the IEPs of students with special needs regarding assessment strategies. Assessments are shared and discussed at the divisional levels. Dialogue about the importance of assessing students fairly and equitably is continuously addressed during staff meetings and early dismissal and in-school in-service sessions.

Behaviour Management

While one principal indicated that there were no behaviour issues in her school and therefore this question was "not applicable"; all others responded with descriptions of how behaviour was managed. Two principals stated their school's philosophies regarding student behaviour:
- All students are given opportunities for ownership of their behaviour.
- Students with behaviour needs are part of the process for developing a plan.
- Focus is on success – break day into small chunks for success.
- Discipline with dignity.
- Firm, fair, consistent expectations and consequences.
- Progressive discipline.
- Intervention is not punitive.
- Our objective is to change behaviour.
- Consistency is key.
- Parent partnerships are essential.

Principals' Reflections

Several principals indicated that their involvement in the project was a positive experience that would affect their future practice. One plans to "assess the inclusivity within the building" and "work with the community to build Professional Learning Communities and a clear School Improvement Plan". She stated that inclusion will be "on the forefront of my mind". Another was made even more aware of the "constant power struggle" exhibited by several EAs, the impact this struggle was having on all personnel, and the need for her to "confront" the situation.

> I already had a handle on the negativity that existed by one group of employees but I am surprised at the impact that this negativity has on the entire school. We have tried many subtle things to turn this around. I have used language that values the work that they do, invested in their learning by

sending them to conferences, focused on positive interactions, etc. We are also involved in an initiative through our board that focuses on Teacher/EA relationships. I had hoped that this would provide an opportunity to produce some positive change. I am afraid that none of these subtle actions have produced the positive change I had hoped for...I have been working with individuals at the board office and we have been discussing the need for a supervision tool that is appropriate to the role of EA.

Another principal was "surprised" to learn that teachers in his school gave lip service to the accommodation and modification process:

> ...the implementation process is far from where we ought to be...This [research] process has given me time to think deeply about where our school is in terms of inclusivity and differentiated instruction. The next steps will be to begin the "what" to determine the "how". Leadership Council will be given direction to begin planning what this might look like in 2006/2007. Together we will begin the process.

Others identified other areas needing improvement. One principal stated that "there is a need for the school to become more involved in Board pilot projects and future studies on inclusion". Another heard that while her staff felt supported in terms of students with special needs, they felt she was not involved enough on a daily basis. For other principals, their involvement in this project was simply an opportunity for them to reaffirm their confidence in the inclusion practices of their schools.

DISCUSSION

The intent of this study was to guide and educate principals as they examined inclusive practices in their schools. It was hypothesized that not all principals had a complete understanding of inclusive practices and that their participation would help them uncover the strengths and weaknesses of inclusion in their schools. Both hypotheses were affirmed for all principals, but to varying degrees. In this discussion, we highlight four key implications that emerged from the findings: 1) inclusive practice; 2) professional development; 3) attitudes; and 4) school environment, and we suggest how each can be realized, with principals leading the way.

Inclusive Practice

In terms of the six major components of inclusion, most principals expressed satisfaction, or neutrality, with regards to the *philosophy, policies, and mandates* contained in Board and/or Ontario Ministry of Education documents. Principals abided by the policy and regulatory structures and was perhaps why only one principal reported on school-designed philosophy statements. Principals also seemed satisfied with their *delivery of special education,* although the information they provided on the school-based team and the student assessment process lacked detail, especially regarding how students are identified and assessed. Similarly, principals provided limited data regarding *classroom teaching practices.* In most cases, they briefly addressed curriculum differentiation and student evaluation with little insight to how these practices were actually carried out. They were more forthcoming regarding in-class accommodations but presented few examples of accommodations made outside the classroom. They also provided positive examples of how behavior was generally managed.

Collectively, the principals indicated that three components of inclusion were in need of attention. More than half considered their *physical resources* to be inadequate. In terms of the *school environment*, principals mostly focused on school culture with their primary goal being to make every student feel welcome. Attaining this goal was primarily facilitated by staff attitude, EA support, and parental involvement. School culture is important because unlike school and class size, it is something over which educators have control (Higgins-D'Allesandro & Sadh, 1997). Solomon, Watson, Battistich, Schaps, and Delucchi (1992) reported that teacher promotion of active student participation and teacher modeling of positive interpersonal behaviours results in a sense of community. DeWit et al.'s (2002) comprehensive analysis found that students who reported favorable ratings of school culture also reported a strong sense of school membership based on classmate and teacher support.

Unfortunately, principals identified a lack of resources and a lack of staff expertise as significant barriers to full inclusion. In fact, there was considerable concern regarding *school personnel* and the roles they play. The principals recognized that while most teachers support inclusion, many were frustrated by a lack of support personnel, limited preparation time, large class sizes, and limited resources. The principals also observed that teachers were not prepared to address special education needs, including behavioural issues.

Several principals indicated that being involved in the study was indeed a learning process. As one principal stated, "…this process has given me time to think deeply about where our school is in terms of inclusivity…". According to these principals, inclusive practices could be improved with clearer delineations of staff roles, enhanced staff relationships, and more attention to specialized classroom practices. Overall, the principals indicated satisfaction with their participation saying it "served as a springboard for conversation" within their schools.

The data clearly revealed that inclusion was valued, however, it was also evident that there were significant challenges to the implementation of effective inclusion. As hypothesized, there were instances where it was apparent that principals were not fully aware of current practices and lacked clear understandings of what these practices entailed. The vital role of principals in the successful implementation of inclusion policies and special education practices cannot be overstated. As administrative and curricular leaders, they have the unique ability to unilaterally set or change the overall direction of a school. It is critical, then, that they have a clear understanding of best practices related to inclusion.

Professional Development

Professional development (PD) is definitely one avenue that could diminish or eliminate some of these barriers. As educational leaders, principals play a significant role in determining the level and type of PD in their schools. There was strong evidence that teachers in the schools in this study required PD that addresses the practical and logistical aspects of inclusion. It behooves principals to assuage these needs. If not, they run the risk that teachers' perceptions of inclusion will shift towards negative as their documented frustrations grow. While prior research confirms that teachers' attitudes towards inclusion can be improved through pre-service and in-service learning (Bender, Vail & Seoa, 1995; Downing, Eichinger, & Williams, 1997), knowledge alone is not enough; teachers and educational assistants require opportunities to put theory into practice (Avramidis, Bayliss & Burden, 2000). Factual knowledge needs to be converted into procedural knowledge, and this occurs through personal motivation, purposeful effort, and practice. Principals need to demand from school boards PD opportunities for their staff, and they must also encourage their staff to become proficient in the inclusive practices that are presented. Another positive outcome of specifically targeted PD would be the clear delineation of teacher and EA roles. This would go a long way towards diffusing the friction evident in this study. Similar concerns about less-than-positive relationships between teachers and support staff operating under inclusive models have been reported elsewhere (e.g., Pudlas, 2003). If one of the key roles of the principalship is to establish harmonious and synchronized interactions, PD related to teacher and EA roles is important.

Professional development, however, should not be only directed towards teachers. If PD is an ongoing commitment to ensure that one's skills and abilities are relevant (Edmunds & Edmunds, 2007), then principals need to turn the spotlight on their own strengths and shortcomings. While this takes courage in light of considerable pressure to be seen as a more-than-capable leader, we contend that principals that willingly seek out and engage in their own PD set the most exemplary example.

Attitudes

It is encouraging that all principals expressed positive opinions about the *philosophy, policies, and mandates* that affected inclusiveness, and also stated that their goal was to make all students feel welcome. However, it is interesting to note the general lack of formal school-wide policies and structured student-based programs that deal specifically with the psychosocial aspects of inclusion.

One of the greatest barriers to successful inclusion is the negative attitudes children have about classmates with special needs. Inclusion has been mandated for several decades, but current research continues to show that children have negative biases towards peers with special needs. These biases stem from misinformed beliefs about disabilities and coincide with less positive feelings and less desire to interact with peers with disabilities. Children with special needs are at greater risk for social rejection, isolation, and bullying and the negative effects of these experiences can last well into adulthood (Nowicki, 2006). On the other hand, successful inclusion encourages positive attitudes and interactions between children with specials needs and classmates. Contact between children with and without special needs is necessary within structured and supportive environments

(Maras & Brown, 1996; Rimmerman, Hozmi & Duvdvany, 2000). High quality programs need to be in place to supplant mere contact situations which do not necessarily foster positive attitude changes. Principals in this study were aware of the importance of working with teachers to ensure that good inclusive practices were in place, but it is critical that they also be tuned into the social dynamics between children. Inclusive schooling must not only provide sound pedagogical practices tailored to meet the needs of all children, but must also provide opportunities for children to learn about, accept, and to interact with peers in positive ways.

School Environment

DeWit et al. (2002) defined school environment as a combination of school climate (e.g., class size, school size) and school culture (e.g., student behavioural norms, quality of relationships between students and staff). Examinations of school environment in relation to student participation have revealed a mixed relationship between school size and participation (De Wit et al., 2002; Lindsay, 1984; Holland & Andre, 1987; Simeonsson et al., 2001). Students with disabilities attending small schools had the lowest participation scores. Participation scores were also found to be low as schools became very large (Simeonsson et al., 2001). De Wit et al. further reported that large schools were significantly less likely than smaller schools to experience disciplinary referrals and incidents of student victimization and that small school size enhances the sense of school community. Clearly, therefore, school climate is a variable that relates to the sense of participation and community and although the exact nature of it may vary, it should be considered when investigating school environment. Positive and sustained school culture attracts and activates its participant members because of the goals of the school and the values that underpin them. Principals enhance school culture by developing and celebrating common beliefs and attitudes amongst teachers and staff. By actively seeking out and implementing appropriate and timely professional development in inclusive practices for all school personnel, educational leaders will improve instructional applications, foster ongoing positive attitudes about inclusion and students with exceptionalities, and cultivate authentic school environments that move inclusion forward.

This chapter is an abridged version of Edmunds, A. L., Macmillan, R. B., Nowicki, E., Specht, J., & Edmunds, G. A. (2009). Principals and inclusive schools: Insight into practice. *The Journal of Educational Administration and Foundations, 20*(1). Published with permission.

REFERENCES

Avramidis, E., Bayliss, P., & Burden, R. (2000). A survey into mainstream teachers' attitudes towards the inclusion of children with special educational needs in the ordinary school in one local education authority. *Educational Psychology, 20*(2).
Bender, W. N., Vail, C. O., & Seoa, K. (1995). Teachers' attitudes to increased mainstreaming: Implementing effective instruction for students with learning disabilities. *Journal of Learning Disabilities, 28*, 87–94.

Bunch, G., Lupart, J., & Brown, M. (1997, April). *Resistance and acceptance: Educator attitudes to inclusion of students with disabilities.* North York: York University.

DeWit, D., Akst, L., Braun, K., Jelley, J., Lefebvre, L., McKee, C., et al. (2002). *Sense of school membership: A mediating mechanism linking student perceptions of school culture with academic and behavioural functioning.* Centre for Addiction and Mental Health.

Downing, J. E., Eichinger, J., & Williams, L. J. (1997). Inclusive education for students with severe disabilities. *Remedial and Special Education, 18*(3), 133–142.

Edmunds, A. L., & Edmunds, G. A. (2007). *Special education in Canada.* Toronto, ON: McGraw-Hill.

Edmunds, A. L. (2003). The inclusive classroom: Can teachers keep up? A comparison of Nova Scotia and Newfoundland & Labrador teachers' perspectives. *Exceptionality Education Canada, 13*(1), 29–48.

Edmunds, A. L. (1999). Classroom teachers are not prepared for the inclusive classroom. *Exceptionality Education Canada, 8*(2), 27–40.

Fullan, M. G. (1982). *The meaning of educational change.* New York: Teachers College Press.

Fullan, M. G., & Stiegelbauer, S. (1991). *The new meaning of educational change* (2nd ed.). New York: Teachers College Press.

Fullan, M. (2001). *The new meaning of educational change* (3rd ed.). New York: Teachers College Press.

Higgins-D'Allesandro, A., & Sadh, D. (1997). The dimensions and measurement of school culture: Understanding school culture as the basis for school reform. *International Journal of Education Research, 27*, 553–569.

Holland, A., & Andre, T. (1987). Participation in extracurricular activities in secondary school: What is known, what needs to be known? *Review of Educational Research, 57*, 437–466.

King, W., & Edmunds, A. L. (2001). Teachers' perceived needs to become more effective practioners: A single school study. *Exceptionality Education Canada, 10*(3), 204–220.

Lindsay, P. (1984). High school size, participation in activities, and young adult social participation: Some enduring effects of schooling. *Educational Evaluation and Policy Analysis, 6*, 73–83.

Lupart, J., & Webber, C. (1996). Schools in transition: Issues and prospects. In J. Lupart, A. McKeough, & C. Yewchuk (Eds.), *Schools in transition: Rethinking regular and special education* (pp. 3–42). Scarborough, Ontario: Nelson Canada.

Maras, P., & Brown, R. (1996). Effects of contact on children's attitudes toward disability: A longitudinal study. *Journal of Applied Social Psychology, 26*, 2113–2134.

Nowicki, E. A. (2006). A cross-sectional multivariate analysis of children's attitudes towards disabilities. *Journal of Intellectual Disability Research, 50*, 335–348.

O'Brien, J., & O'Brien, C. L. (1996). Inclusion as a force for school renewal. In S. Stainback & W. Stainback (Eds.), *Inclusion: A guide for educators* (pp. 29–48). London: Paul H. Brookes.

Prestine, N. A., & Nelson, B. S. (2005). How can educational leaders support and promote teaching and learning? New conceptions of learning and leading in schools. In W. A. Firestone & C. Riehl (Eds.), *A new agenda for research in educational leadership* (pp. 46–60). New York: Teachers College Press.

Pudlas, K. A. (2003). Inclusive educational practice: Perceptions of students and teachers. *Exceptionality Education Canada, 13*(1), 49–64.

Rimmerman, A., Hozmi, B., & Duvdevany, I. (2000). Contact and attitudes toward individuals with disabilities among students tutoring children with developmental disabilities. *Journal of Intellectual & Developmental Disability, 25*(1), 13–18.

Rogoff, B., Radziszewska, B., & Masiello, T. (1995). Analysis of developmental processes in sociocultural activity. In L. W. Martin, K. Nelson, & E. Tobach (Eds.), *Sociocultural psychology: Theory and practice of doing and knowing* (pp. 125–149). New York: Cambridge University Press.

Ryan, J. (2004, May). *Inclusive leadership: A review.* Paper presented at the annual meeting of the Canadian Society for the Study of Education, Winnipeg, Manitoba.

Simeonsson, R. T., Carlson, D., Huntington, G. S., Strutz McMillen, J., & Brent, J. L. (2001). Students with disabilities: A national survey of participation in school activities. *Disability and Rehabilitation, 23*(2), 49–63.

Solomon, D., Watson, M., Battistich, V., Schaps, E., & Delucchi, K. (1992). Creating a caring community: Educational practices that promote children's prosocial development. In F. K. Oser, A. Dick, & J.-L. Patry (Eds.), *Effective and responsible teaching: The new synthesis* (pp. 383–396). San Francisco: Jossey-Bass.

Stainback, S., & Stainback, W. (1996). Concluding remarks: Concerns about Inclusion. In S. Stainback & W. Stainback (Eds.), *Inclusion: A guide for educators* (2nd ed., pp. 383–386). London: Paul H. Brookes. Boston: Pearson Custom Publishing.

CPSIA information can be obtained at www.ICGtesting.com
Printed in the USA
LVOW071730130513

333556LV00004B/146/P